PULSE:

Understanding the
Vital Signs
of Your Business

PULSE:

Understanding the
Vital Signs
of Your Business

Frank Coker

AMBIENT
LIGHT
PUBLISHING

Pulse: Understanding the Vital Signs of Your Business
First Edition Trade Book, 2014

Published by Ambient Light Publishing, Bellevue, WA 98006

To order additional books:
www.amazon.com
www.ambientlightpublishing.com

Or, visit the Corelytics website at www.corelytics.com

E-book also available

ISBN: 978-0-9893086-0-1
Editorial: Arlyn Lawrence, Inspira Literary Solutions, Gig Harbor, WA
Book Design: Brianna Showalter, Ruston, WA
Artwork: Cory Lee, Bothell, WA
Printed in the USA by Bookmasters, Inc., Ashland, OH

DEDICATION

This book is dedicated to my wife, Carol, who has been incredibly support-ive and encouraging in all (well, most) of my many entrepreneurial twists and turns. This journey could not have happened without her. I would also like to make this dedication to my son and daughter, their awesome spouses and our six wonderful grandchildren. They are the inspiration that makes it so important to push for a better world and a more certain future. They are all living proof that dreams can be far exceeded by reality, but not without the struggles that put it all into motion.

An additional special appreciation goes to Kris Fuehr who spent major time and effort over the 12 months it took to put this book to-gether. Essentially every Saturday morning was spent in a coffee shop working on plans and actions that led to this major accomplishment. Her energy, diligence, and fabulous perspective on small business own-ership were key to ensuring that the needs of the entrepreneur were always at the forefront.

PULSE: Understanding the Vital Signs of Your Business

TABLE OF CONTENTS

APPENDIX

PULSE:

Understanding the
Vital Signs
of Your Business

ACKNOWLEDGEMENTS

It takes a village to write a book. It takes experts, sounding boards, cheer-leaders, and lots of midnight oil. The combined chemistry can create very cool results.

I should probably start by thanking the many hundreds of companies, business owners, and managers with whom I have had the good fortune to work over the decades. Also included are all of the consultants, business advisors, coaches, professors, investors, and industry thought leaders I have known along the way. Though there are far too many to list here, they all contributed in many ways and are collectively the author behind the author.

I would like to make a special mention of the University of Washington Information School where I have been privileged to teach in the Masters of Science of Information Management (MSIM) program for the past ten years. I also served on the MSIM Board of Advisors for over 11 years. I watched it grow from a hot new idea under the leadership of Mike Eisenberg, PhD extraordinaire, friend and inspiration, and the visionary that launched the iSchool phenomenon at the UW. He is an integral player in the global iSchool movement. I put a lot of miles on my car driving Mike around to many of the high-profile CIOs around the Puget Sound to get him introduced to our emerald economy when he was still a new transplant recruited from Syracuse University.

I must also include a salute to the formative role that professional associations played in building the background that led to this book. I served as president of the Institute of Management Consultants, PNW Chapter, and of the Society of Information Management, Seattle Chapter. I have more than 20 years with them as officer and board member of both associations. I really appreciate the many doors these relationships have opened. I would like to seize this moment to underscore the importance of being part of a professional association and being a participant at some level. Professional associations can add many dimensions of learning and many opportunities to give back to the community.

In the more recent past, Todd Ostrander, a partner at OneAccord, gave me a nudge to write this book. OneAccord is a consulting firm with a mission to help companies achieve top performance. Todd has been an advisor to my company for almost two years. He recognized the importance of what we are doing and how it could help business owners put their companies on healthy and sustainable tracks. Much appreciation goes to Todd for being a catalyst and a great sounding board.

A highly important piece of this picture is the inner-circle team. This book could not have happened without these key players. First is Arlyn Lawrence, a super editor and voice of practicality. She brings the experience of having put together many books for business and professional audiences. She really knows how this process works.

Huge thanks goes to the team MVP, Kris Fuehr. In addition to her extensive work on the book, and the many Saturday morning coffee shop meetings, she is also a key player at Corelytics. She brings her own sense of vision about how the business world needs the new generation of analytical tools being offered and planned by Corelytics. She is great at explaining how these tools and concepts will play an important role in building high-precision businesses in the coming years. Kris has been an inspiration to many entrepreneurs and early stage business owners. She has shown a real knack for articulating concepts and messages in a way that turns on the light bulbs. Kris brought energy and persistence that was indispensable in making this book a reality.

Finally, a special tribute goes to the 25 world-class professionals that have added their wisdom and perspective to this book. Their ideas and quotes are sprinkled throughout and the full text of their thoughts is compiled in the Appendix. These contributors live and breathe the challenges of the business world every day. All of them have achieved many wins and have overcome some pretty harsh challenges, but they all know the importance of continuing to move forward regardless of the barriers. To them I express much appreciation and I am certain you will feel the same.

Professor (n) \prə-ˈfe-sər\ (1) a faculty member of the highest academic rank at an institution of higher education (2) one that professes, avows, or declares (3) a teacher at a university, college, or sometimes secondary school.

I am not a tenured professor but rather an adjunct faculty member at the University of Washington. I am tagged with the professor label by students and by my company's marketing team. I'm just glad they don't say, "Hey, old dude at the front of the room, I have a question.…" While I am fine with the label, I want to underscore a special level of respect and appreciation for the professors that have made teaching and advancing higher education their life's work. They deserve a special note of gratitude from everyone who benefited from their contribution to the betterment of the planet.

Regards,

"Professor" Frank
July 2014

INTRODUCTION

If I could just gather up all the proposals, business plans, contracts, procedural manuals, and work plans I have written, I could be regarded as a prolific writer. But, sadly, a lot of those writings were read by just a few people and then put up on shelves where they collected dust. One way to rationalize all this is to claim it was a grand rehearsal for this book.

What my decades' long trail of business writing reveals is that I have been up close and personal with lots of companies. I have delved deeply into many businesses large and small, successful and stalled, well-structured and chaotic, intentional and accidental, service centric and product centric, old school and new school, healthy and unhealthy. All these businesses, like people and snowflakes, are unique and come with great potential, but not all businesses achieve their potential. In too many cases the things that lead to poor outcomes could have easily been changed. But for most companies, when the realization dawns that there is a problem, it is too late and the cost of correction is just too high. As you probably know, 50 to 80 percent of all new companies end in failure because they were not sustainable[1]. The cost of these failures is huge for everyone on the planet, directly or indirectly, because these small businesses represent over half of the global economy.

I have had both the pain and pleasure of founding or cofounding six companies, have been in many of the CEO, CIO, CFO, and COO seats within companies, served on boards, worked on due diligence teams for venture capital firms, and know the anatomy of business. But even so, the definition of success is different for every company. The requirements of owners, investors, employees, and customers are unique, and the needs of the market continually morph making it very difficult to find solutions that apply in all cases. Still, there are patterns and evolutionary trends that are constant. There are human factors and developmental stages of business growth that tend to remain the same. This is where we need to look to find solutions to improve the odds of success for new businesses.

As I reflect on all this, there are compelling realizations that make writing this book a must. To begin with, it is important to recycle our learning. Lessons learned need to be plowed back into the next generation of entrepreneurs so the world of business can evolve. But the more dramatic question is: What would our world look like if we could help improve the odds of business survival by just a few percentage points? How many more people would be employed and how many more schools and bridges could we build? How many of the disenfranchised, instead of being a drain on society, could have a meaningful role? Before we get carried away, the goal of this book is much more modest, but it definitely could be an important part of a high-impact solution. This book is all about bringing new ways to understand businesses into the light. Most basically, it is intended to help business owners, entrepreneurs, and managers see more accurately what lies ahead for their businesses. With the right visibility and insight, it becomes easier to make the right decisions and have great outcomes for everyone involved.

To get more specific, this book is laced with concepts involving **predictive analytics**, business intelligence, business trends, and forecasts—all presented in the context of the decisions business owners face every day. It's all about the practical and easy-to-use aspects of a science that can dramatically improve the outcomes of business. The goal is to skim over the science and stay focused on the specific problems needing to be solved. When you use your calculator, you don't need to know about the programming and circuitry that make the math work; you just need to know the answer to the problem. In a similar way, there is much to be said about the mechanics of **predictive analytics** and specific mathematical approaches—some work well and others don't. What is more important, however, is how this technology can be used to achieve better business outcomes. That is the big payoff!

Why now? Why here? To begin with, I have been immersed in this topic for decades and have created many financial models, scenario evaluations, and forecasts. In doing so, I have come to realize that the people who need this information the most don't realize they need it and can't get at it. The big guys do this kind of analysis every day. The entrepreneurs are left to scrounge for the insight that will help grow a business, often substituting hunches for solid information. The problem is compounded by the very nature of most entrepreneurs. They often skirt conventional wisdom and second guess answers provided by others. At some level, most entrepreneurs see business management concepts as an annoyance because the thing they are really passionate about is in their area of expertise, which usually has little to do with the mechanics of business. But, ultimately, it's the mechanics of business that determine the winners and losers.

The question becomes how can we make business insight easier to access and more affordable? At the same time, how can we enable entrepreneurs to make informed choices that put this insight to work in their businesses? Part of the answer is to simplify. We need to bury anything that adds complexity and bring to the surface only the things that are easily understood. In the end, this is the gift of technology.

A large part of the perspective presented in this book is from work accomplished with software tools I designed to support business management and decision-making. For the past 10 years I focused extensively on cloud-based analytical tools (before the term "cloud" was in vogue) and statistical concepts now referred to as "**predictive analytics.**" I designed and built financial models, forecasting tools, and management dashboards for big companies like Cisco and Microsoft and for small businesses in a wide variety of industries.

In parallel with developing software tools, I have had the good fortune of teaching at the University of Washington as an adjunct faculty member in the Masters of Science of Information Management program in the "iSchool" for the past 10 years. iSchool is short for Information School. Of course, I must brag about the fact that the University of Washington is rated number three in the U.S. News rankings of Information Schools. The iSchool phenomenon is one of the fastest growing areas of academic focus on an increasing number of campuses worldwide. Currently there are 55 graduate level iSchool programs globally, up from less than five only ten years ago. The primary mission of these programs is to advance learning and discovery at the intersection of people, technology, and information. Much different than the IT offerings in computer science departments and far different than the MIS programs in business schools, the iSchool views the world from the broad perspective of the people, workforces, markets, and entrepreneurs that use technology and information to build social fabric, business opportunities, and insights into how we understand our world.

Our goal is to support and enhance human engagements with information and technology.

Harry Bruce, Ph.D.,
Dean of the University of Washington Information School
More information: Appendix 120, New Era of Information

The combination of starting new businesses, coaching hundreds of companies and teaching highly motivated students all conspired to create an inescapable light bulb moment for me. The light came on after doing a complex modeling project for the zillionth very small company. I had been using models and concepts I had packaged over the years to make these projects affordable and repeatable. Why not go a step further and make these tools "self-service" so more small companies could have the benefit at an even lower cost?

This dream became a reality in 2009 when we rolled out the Corelytics Financial Dashboard. In the years since, there have been many refinements and discoveries about what it takes to build a self-service financial dashboard. With more than 3,000 companies having experienced the Corelytics offering and more than a 400 accountants, consultants, and business advisors engaging in the Corelytics Advisor Network at various levels, we have added a lot to our understanding about how a complex science can be made easy and compelling for small business owners and leaders.

One important discovery is the often misunderstood difference between graphs and analytics. There are many reporting tools and dashboard solutions in the market that do great things and make big claims, but, contrary to what they say, they are not analytical tools. For the most part they are great ways to see static accounting information in a more colorful and graphic way. Graphics may be helpful but are not the same as analytics. A **predictive analytics** tool must have the ability to produce

trend lines, normalize trajectories, do forecasts based on trends, and understand the difference between leading and lagging indicators. Even some of the most expensive dashboard tools in the market today don't do some of the basics of **predictive analytics**. The Corelytics dashboard makes these **predictive analytics** available to the small business at a very low cost and in a highly automated way.

We are a long way from a final destination—if that even exists. Our road map for the foreseeable future is well laid out but we also have a process for incorporating new learnings that continue to pop up as we build our base of users. Many new discoveries are in the making, but the evidence is clear: The benefit from a standardized and streamlined **predictive analytics** dashboard can be transformative. It can change everything.

> *In rally racing, a popular mantra is, "You go where you look." One of the most important lessons we teach is how to see the road. Most people don't look far enough ahead. They focus on the taillights in front of them, not what's happening down the road. Learning how to avoid such tunnel vision so you can see the bigger picture of what's coming at you is a major part of the learning to drive fast.*

#122 – Lessons from a Race Car Driver – Nate Tennis Sr. Instructor,
DirtFish Rally School
Lessons from a Race Car Driver
Read more: Appendix Contribution #122

When small businesses owners can see the road ahead they can reduce the cost of course correction and pick up speed. But there is a discipline required and that is often the hardest part of building a successful business. We know that entrepreneurs are resistant to discipline. In fact, entrepreneurs do what they do because they are unconventional and are attracted to serious off-roading. They want to bring their expertise to a market in a new and creative new way. Structure gets in the way for them.

But, alas, putting structure in place is the only way an emerging new idea can become a sustainable and healthy business. However, if you

push that message on an entrepreneur too soon it can be a discourage-
ment and the new idea will not germinate. But there are many that have
accumulated just enough scar tissue to know that some structure and
process is needed in order to make their businesses survive and prosper.
At this point, it becomes clear that driving on a paved road is better than
plowing across country through ditches, over boulders, and around fallen
trees.

Today the opportunities for small businesses have never been more
exciting! And yet the realities are more grim. There are exploding new
needs and interests worldwide as the pace of the economy accelerates and
as the global market becomes much more integrated. There are new and
economical ways of reaching markets, building workforces, and getting investment dollars. There are many new ways for entrepreneurs to put their
expertise in high gear and get big results. But at the same time, there is
much less tolerance for error and solutions with a poor fit. Markets will find
good solutions and will not wait around for less than optimal solutions. It
is in this intensified small business world that **predictive analytics** and the
Corelytics dashboard can make a large contribution.

With that said, the purpose of this book is not to sell the Corelytics
dashboard but rather to sell the ideas on which the dashboard is based.
There are multiple ways for entrepreneurs to achieve the goal of getting
a clear vision of the road ahead. Much can be accomplished with any
number of different tools. The most important part is the learnings and
insights that have been derived from the dashboard. These insights can
be transformative with or without a dashboard. I will use the Corelytics
dashboard to illustrate points, but entrepreneurs and consultants will
know there are multiple tools in the market—and, when all else fails,
there are always spreadsheets.

Along the way I will introduce you to a new concept called Business
Management 3.0 and the concept of vital signs. These concepts drive
home the fact that the demands of business are fundamentally changing.
Moreover, the necessary solutions cannot be the ones that worked in the
past. The challenges of today require new solutions more appropriate for
today and tomorrow. Hanging on to solutions of the past will sink many
companies in the months and years ahead. But this has always been true.

All those companies that manufactured buggy whips either transformed or disappeared. Business Management 3.0 teaches recalibration and applies new approaches to new realities. It applies new measurements that provide a more complete story. It's about moving forward faster and with greater clarity and certainty. That is what our new economy wants from us.

So, let's dive into the wonderful and overly complex world of small business and see if we can sort out the new landscape. By helping small businesses retool we can reduce their high mortality rate worldwide.

CHAPTER ONE

The Changing Landscape

He that will not apply new remedies
must expect new evils;
for time is the greatest innovator.

- Francis Bacon, "On Innovation,"
Essays, 1597

Everything is changing! This has always been true but never at the pace and global breadth we are seeing today. The way we communicate, the way we build brands, the way we deliver value, and the way we build equity are all changing. As margins shrink and global connectivity erases boundaries, we have less room for inefficiency and less room for error. Business processes need to be more precise, more measured, more predictable, and more responsive to market dynamics. Some of the old fundamentals of business will persist, but many old approaches are giving way to totally new methods.

So, how do you, the business owner or manager, get on top of this? How do you make these changes work in your favor? How do you turn the threat of change into opportunity and economic value? This chapter will set the stage and put the changing business landscape into perspective. The subsequent chapters are all about embracing the changes that are happening now and coming at us every day. The goal is to put these changes to work for your benefit.

Growing a healthy business is not unlike raising a healthy child. As I joyously experience my grandchildren making their way in this world, I am continuously amazed at the advances in the science of evaluating, measuring, nourishing, and encouraging youngsters on a healthy growth path. While I thought my wife and I did a great job with our kids, the science and knowledge of today equips our kids to raise their families with far more awareness of how food choices, entertainment, toys, feedback, and social experience all play into family health and happiness. The knowledge base they have to work with is way beyond that of their parents, but there is also a lot more misinformation.

I am also seeing new trends in today's knowledge base being used to make businesses healthier, happier, stronger, and more likely to achieve success. Not only are the opportunities greater and the resources more plentiful, there are now support systems available for companies of all sizes to identify and build strength in areas that didn't even exist a few years ago.

But there is a dark side to these advances. In a rapidly evolving business environment, the companies that don't move with the trends become highly disadvantaged. Ultimately they get left on the wayside or sent to the graveyard. That's why companies today must shift gears to become more virtual, agile, flexible, networked, digital, accessible, integrated, and scalable (whew – but that's not all!). If they don't, other companies will—and they will push aside the ones that can't keep up.

The most fundamental element changing everything today is INFORMATION. There is more of it. It is easier to access. It is constantly increasing and permeates everything. Information is increasing in every industry, country, and business large and small. We could easily drown in the rising sea of information, but it also is the very thing that could liberate people, countries, civilization, and businesses. So, our mandate is to put information to work and make it a source of strength. Information can work in our favor or it can simply slosh around us and create confusion and disorder. We can use information to tell us what information is important. Information about information can automatically build on itself so we can see more clearly and understand more precisely where we are headed. The right information can help us know where we need to make changes to improve our journey and maximize outcomes. To put information to work, we must use information engines that consume information and present back to us fully digested and synthesized pictures that are easy to understand and to which we can easily respond. Additionally, this needs to be available anytime, anywhere, and on any device.

Our management processes must be able to apply structured process and continuous feedback in order to produce insight that can lead to informed decisions. Highly effective business organizations will develop cultures centered on continuous measurement, monitoring, predicting, learning, and adapting to change.

Our evolving information management processes need to show the gaps between planned, potential, and actual performance in an immediate and timely way. To be most helpful, we need information that recognizes relative importance. This information needs to point to the biggest and most urgent gaps and to the biggest opportunities for performance improvement. Ultimately our information engines will analyze our performance patterns, provide diagnostic summaries, and then prescribe actions and corrections that will close the gaps and seize opportunities. This takes us to a place we have always known to be important but have never been able to systematically deliver on in the past—proactive management. When a whole organization sees the same picture and is responding to the same information the concept of proactive management goes to a whole new level.

Predictive analytics, trend analysis, and forecasting with benchmarks on how other businesses are doing is an amazing new paradigm. I think all businesses, particularly small businesses, need to get on this track to stay agile and financially viable and compete. They need to pay attention and keep the finger on the pulse of the performance and be able to take corrective action in real time using the new transformational tools that are making possible a the new world of business—Business 3.0—and create a new definition of what it takes to run an agile business. It's now inexpensive to put those tools to work in the business to enable it to thrive."

Len Jessup, Dean of Eller College of Management & Halle Chair in Leadership
Read more: Appendix Contribution #112

Throughout this book we are going to talk about the many ways that "information about information" is the key to building successful organizations and relevance in local and global conditions. Information about information is a topic that all by itself can take many books to fully explore—a very deep topic with a language all its own (e.g., meta data, taxonomy, data curation, relational data, and so on). As a broad topic, information about information also includes many analytical methods that make data comparable, measurable, and meaningful over time. We are not going to dive deeply into these concepts, but it is important to have a general understanding of how these analytical methods can create a clearer picture of "how things are." These methods can also create an easy to understand picture of where things are headed and where they will probably be in the future.

Be prepared to toss around terms like **predictive analytics**, pattern recognition, trends, leading indicators, and rolling time frames. When you combine these concepts with common business terms such as key performance indicators, performance metrics, benchmarks, margins, overheads, contribution, and profitability, you get an awesome cocktail of informational ingredients that can create fabulous precision in understanding, more effective controls, and a much better ability to produce a desired outcome.

All of these concepts apply to for-profit and not-for-profit organizations, small and large. Most large organizations have used many of these methods for decades, but it has been labor intensive and required lots of expertise. The resources and expertise have not been within reach for most small businesses and non-profit organizations until more recently. New tools and more comprehensive data are completely changing this picture. They are changing everything about the way small and medium-sized businesses and non-profit organizations deliver value to their target audience and the way they control the results of their labors.

You May Not Be Doing as Well as You Think

Joe and Teresa Bell of Citrus Networking Group in Florida are a husband and wife team. Teresa would sell, sell, sell while Joe deployed the technology. They had been in business for over six years working feverishly with clients. Teresa was on a roll, sales were great, and they thought they were making great money. They bought a nice car and upgraded their offices. However, when they stopped to analyze their trends and forecasts, they came to the stark realization that their business was *dying*.

The places they thought they were making a good profit were actually from the very customers they would later have to let go. The staff that had been right for them years ago was not going to propel them ahead in their new business model. "I didn't have any idea why things weren't going well. We felt we were going through a real growth spurt," Teresa stated. "Thankfully, we were able to see what was really going on and turn it around."

Two years later they have a restructured team, a slimmed down customer base, and a tightened overhead. Not only did they rescue their business but they established their acumen around forecasting and tracking progress based on where they wanted to be. They are now confident the growth track they are on is truly *healthy growth*.

The things that made businesses successful 10 and 20 years ago are not the same as what will be required in the next 10 years. This is further complicated by the fact that any business wanting to grow and build value must go through its own evolutionary process. The things that made them successful in the past will not work as it becomes larger and more complex.

Whether you plan to grow your company or not, whether you plan to build your company's value in the market or not, one thing is certain: *all markets evolve over time and require more complex solutions.* Your business must be able to navigate a more complex environment if you want to stay in the game and, more importantly, if you want to thrive. This means you will need to add more products and services, more lines of business, more price options, more contractual arrangement, more types of expertise in your company, more marketing messages (one-size-fits-all messages are less effective than multiple targeted messages), more partnerships, and the list goes on. While we all strive for simplicity and focus, it is very rare that this is possible. Markets tend to demand complexity and then, as we figure out how to respond, we become even more complex as a business.

The Natural Progression of
Complexity

The ultimate challenge in all markets and businesses is to find new ways to simplify and get out in front of growing complexity. In virtually all healthy markets we are seeing growing competition from around the globe, which is driving changes in pricing, which drives the way we look at costs. Add to that technology driven changes that shorten delivery and decision cycles. Everything about every business is changing and will continue to do so in the years ahead, just as they have in the past, only faster. Business owners wanting to build a company with growing value, so they can cash out at some point in the future, have an even greater challenge: they need to evolve their business faster than the pace of change in their market or else their business will actually lose value. On top of the dynamics of a changing market, this means individual businesses need to run ahead of the complexity curve for the market in order to build value!

This may all seem daunting and it is. But there are many ways to navigate increasing complexity, maintain sanity, and, at the same time, achieve high aspirations. It begins with understanding business performance in the context of a bigger picture. A more complete picture leads

The Changing Landscape

to more informed decisions and a much higher probability of hitting targets and achieving real success.

> *If your customers, your staff, and members of your relationship ecosystem don't understand what you do or what you're trying to do, then ultimately, it's going to flat line. I would say the majority of the time it's just very easy to get lulled into a sense of false security in thinking you're in a better position than you actually are. CEOs should be running companies and keeping track of the changing forces. They're in charge of strategy and ultimately execution.*

Gareth Wade, Principal, One Accord Partners
Read more: Appendix Contribution #125

In the next few chapters we'll take a close look at the seven secrets to business success in an evolving economic environment, namely:

1. **Predictive analytics** – using tools that let you see what's ahead
2. **Business intelligence** – combining internal and external data to get a more complete picture
3. **Financial goal management** – setting and tracking financial goals; tight and early focus on areas that need tuning
4. **Team participation** – getting the whole team on the same page and pulling in the same direction
5. **External expertise** – using peer groups, business advisors, and industry experts to stay out in front
6. **Financial strength** – balancing assets, debt and equity to build a sustainable and valuable business
7. **Agility** – gaining an ability to embrace and manage change while keeping a steady drum beat

Yes, everything about business is changing. Markets are becoming less local and more global. Companies are becoming increasingly virtual and able to provide products and services anywhere in the world. Don't be surprised if a competitor from the other side of the planet suddenly starts wooing your customers and clients. Even if they don't take your customers and clients away, global competition will create a new set of customer expectations for products, services, and prices.

This is just one of many trends that are reshaping the business world. Here are a few more:

Economic Forces

- Fewer community-based businesses, more businesses with regional and global reach
- Slower GDP growth in developed countries
- Local economies increasingly affected by global events and global market conditions
- Aging workforce, employee payroll and benefit costs moving in erratic directions
- Increasing use of contractors, consultants, and outsourced service providers; more "free agent" and virtual employees
- Increasingly complex business ecosystems—more points of connectivity and interaction
- More regulations with increasing compliance demands

Market Forces

- Accelerating advances in technology
- Broader and deeper adoption of technology by organizations and individuals
- Falling prices and shrinking margins for technology and information
- Shorter time-to-market requirements for new innovations

Implications

- Greater need for high-precision management and tighter decision-making processes
- More metrics-driven business processes; information-driven management is key
- Organizations becoming more dynamic; change is the new norm
- Greater reward for leaders that understand agile business processes

No matter how you look at these conditions, they are going to affect all businesses. Even if you think your business is immune to these changes, your customers and clients are not. There is a fundamentally new way of doing business where making intentional, informed choices requires information and business acumen.

Unfortunately, historical survival rates for small business have largely been driven by chance—or luck. The business survival rate for new businesses is only 50/50 over five years.[2] In other words, business survival rates are exactly the same as getting heads with the flip of a coin.

If you ask a venture capitalist, he (or she) will tell you he considers himself successful if one out of ten of the companies in which he invests becomes a big success. And that is after he has screened hundreds of companies to find the ten in which to invest! What if we did just a little bit to improve the odds of positive outcome? What would that do for the U.S. economy? What would that do for employment? What would that do for investors looking for places with a reasonable likelihood of success?

Just think, if we could make small businesses even a little more likely to succeed, it would be easier for investors to invest, people would feel more safe starting a business or going to work for small companies, fewer people would experience termination notices, and the list goes on. Just a few percentage points of improvement on each of these items would result in a huge impact on our economy.

Small Businesses Drive the Global Economy

Small businesses generate more than 50 percent of the GDP[3] and employ about 70 percent of the workforce.[4] Since the U.S. GDP is about $14.5 trillion and the number two global economy is China at $5.9 trillion[5], you can see that the small business engine in the U.S. is bigger than the entire GDP of China. Small business, too, is an even larger percentage of the global economy outside of the U.S. So, while the media spotlight is generally on big business, it is small businesses that are doing the heavy lifting.

The challenges for small businesses are increasing at a pace faster than ever before. Not only is the global economic squeeze making it harder for small businesses to thrive, new pressures from technology and global communications are changing the way the world does business. The simple fact is, small businesses cannot stand still and expect to thrive.

Thankfully, small businesses have the opportunity to play all the new global pressures to their advantage. By adopting affordable new technologies, they can do transactions faster than ever before. They can reach larger markets and find out what is important to their customers in ways never before possible.

To evolve, small businesses must really get to know their numbers and manage their performance with precision. It used to be okay to count up the money at the end of the month, decide which bills to pay, and call it good. In the past two decades most small businesses have put smart accounting software to work to better manage their business. This can give them a much better understanding of accounts receivable, accounts payable, and cash requirements forecasting. But that is no longer enough. It's time for the next generation of business metrics management.

The new reality is that we can no longer look at business as a two-dimensional exercise. It is not good enough to ask how we are doing at a specific point in time. The bigger question is: How am I doing over a period of time and where will that take me in the future? Rather than the static numbers found in an income statement (a.k.a., profit and loss statement) and a balance sheet, businesses need to look at dynamic numbers that show **trend lines** and forecasts indicating where a company is headed. The two-dimensional picture describes *where the company is now*; the three-dimensional picture describes *where the company is going*.

Introducing Business Management 3.0

The roadway for most small businesses has always meandered with occasional bends and plenty of bumps in the road. In the past 20 years the roadway has become a speedway with many more rapid twists and turns. The old school approach of waiting until you get into a turn and then starting to think about how to make the turn doesn't work anymore. If you can't anticipate the turn, there is a good chance you will be off the road and in a ditch before you know what hit you. It is painfully clear that old school static reporting is part of the problem. Reports telling you where you have been simply cannot deal with the new dynamics in the road ahead.

The new Business Management 3.0 approach to financial reporting requires a view of the entire road map including internal data combined with external market intelligence. Just as we have come to view a GPS as a navigation necessity in our cars, it is just as beneficial to have a graphical financial dashboard for your business that shows you where you are and where you are headed. Today, dashboards are viewed as a competitive advantage for making high-precision decisions. Using a dashboard to constantly monitor how results line up with plans and goals is the key to proactive decision-making. We are approaching a time when navigational expertise will be considered a basic necessity for business success and survival.

> *The Corelytics Financial Dashboard is an elegant example, bringing complex business analytics to small-business owners who are not mathematicians or financial experts and giving them an easy-to-understand view of what is happening in their business—and they can get this information anytime and anywhere. So, the analytics that once required many experts and were therefore only found in large enterprises, are now available to even the smallest businesses and are adaptable to fit the needs of the individual user, as well.*

Harry Bruce, Ph.D.,
Dean of the University of Washington Information School
Read more: Appendix Contribution #120

We are in a perfect storm of global economics, new technologies, and new management methods that make it clear we cannot manage business the way we did in the past. Small business is where the new changes are needed the most. Almost as many small businesses are started as are lost each year. This is a tragic loss of economic potential, most of which is preventable but not well understood by the entrepreneurs that place their life's resources on the line to build a dream. Our national and global economies would benefit dramatically if small businesses could see the roadway more clearly and seize control of their destiny.

We now have the data to know that a few well-placed adjustments to the way businesses are managed can have a very large impact on the success and "thriveability" of a company. In simple terms, we know companies that make important small course corrections just a little bit sooner do so at a much smaller cost, have significantly improved performance, and in the long-run have a much more valuable company.

The three core principles for a positive outcome are:
1. Prediction: Seeing what's ahead
2. Performance: Tracking performance in comparison to internal goals and industry trends
3. People: Sharing information with team members and stakeholders who "make the rubber meet the road."

We'll cover the processes you can easily put in place in the following chapters. But first, let's take a look at where we need to shift the way we view and understand business performance.

Learning to read and interpret financial data is imperative to understanding a small business, but not just reciting the sums at the bottom of a balance sheet or presuming the net profit or loss amount at the bottom of a balance sheet is an accurate reflection of the "bottom line." This means fully understanding what these elements actually mean, what they are based on, and what they predict about the future.

Making the Jump into Small Business Ownership, 2013 –
David Nilssen & Jeff Levy
www.makingthejumpbook.com

Changing the Picture
We as a society have become increasingly accustomed to gathering more information quickly through visuals. Following are some examples of what these can look like. Any time you can put something in visual format, do it. It is a key to effective communication.

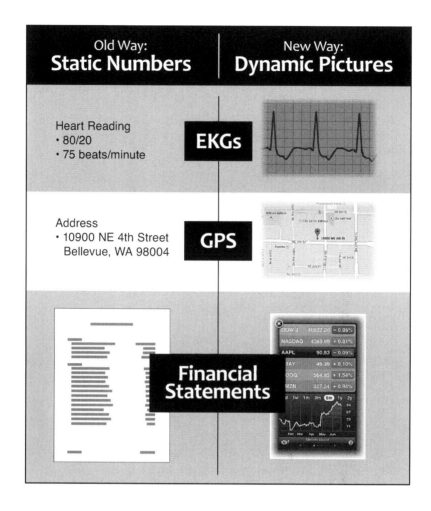

Old Way: **Static Numbers**	New Way: **Dynamic Pictures**

Heart Reading
• 80/20
• 75 beats/minute

EKGs

Address
• 10900 NE 4th Street
  Bellevue, WA 98004

GPS

Financial Statements

BI (business intelligence) has been an important new way to look at a broad collection of information that, combined, provides a better understanding of how a company is performing in the context of the market it serves. But bringing data together from multiple sources to obtain a more comprehensive picture is merely a great first step. Applying **predictive analytics** as the next step can make the data come alive. More than just graphs or color representations, **predictive analytics** can show where the integrated BI picture is heading and where it is likely to be in the future. For the entrepreneur this means using internal plus external data in the form of **trend lines** to determine where things are headed and where outcomes can be shaped, not reacted to, in order to achieve a desired outcome.

Sales

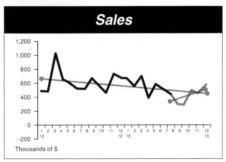

24-Month Growth Trend: **-14.1%**
6-Month Growth Trend: **+18.4%**

With **predictive analytics** you combine long-term and short-term trends (lagging and leading indicators) to show where the curve is bending and where you can expect to see performance go in the months ahead. If you extend the long-term and short-term **trend lines** into the future, it is highly probable that future performance will be somewhere between the two lines.

Global Perspectives: China

> *China's businesses had had ups and downs mainly influenced by the industry situations and China's special regulatory conditions. But, as markets mature and standardize in China, more small business owners realize the benefits of using information and technology. The pressure to keep up with peers, the requirement of participating in the global market, and benefits of gaining knowledge from information to support decision-making, are the key drivers behind the rapidly increasing utilization of technology and information. New tools based on predictive analytics will catch on and be a breakthrough for those who put it to use. In the near future, everyone will wonder how they ever got by without these indispensable analytical tools!*

The Changing Landscape

Yan Ren, Consultant, Sila Solutions Group, Data Management
Read more about Small Business in China: Appendix Contribution #133

Global Perspectives: India

Decision-making is still, to a large extent, based on tribal knowledge and intuition. As awareness about new technologies like Corelytics spreads, businesses will realize the value proposition of predictive analytics for decision-making. In the absence of insights, businesses in India depend on their leaders to make decisions based on experience. With tools like Corelytics filling those gaps, businesses can rely on facts to secure their future.

Anikate Singh, Student, University of Washington, Data Analytics
Read more about Small Business in India: Appendix Contribution #134

Practical Business Intelligence

Scott Smeltzer, President and CEO of On-Site Tech Support, was in the midst of an important acquisition in San Diego. In 2009, On-Site Tech Support moved its business to managed services and found a company in Del Mar it wanted to acquire. In the early stages of trying to figure out if there was a potential for an acceptable deal, the Del Mar company's attorney did not want to give Scott's team access to the company's accounting system. They were happy to share financial statements, but Scott knew the most important information would not be visible in the traditional reports. He knew the more important business intelligence that was buried in the accounting system was key to finding an acceptable purchase price.

So, Scott persuaded them to connect their accounting files to a Corelytics dashboard to create basic visual charts with graphs with trends, without giving access to customer names, bank IDs, and credit card numbers. Scott was then able to split the data into lines of business so he could see how much revenue/expense was attributed to their break-fixed business vs. how much was coming from their remote managed services business. When they applied these visuals, trends, and forecasts, they were actually able to see how the business was growing and which areas needed improvement. "Know what your numbers are doing," Scott advises, "not just what they are. This is key to understanding a business and its market value." From here, both parties were able to have a much more fact-based discussion and were able to put together a deal that made sense to both.

Market BI

There are many data sources for business intelligence, but many of them fall short in helping owners make decisions. That's because they tend to be:

- Survey based – not accurate
- Out of date – data gathered for past year
- Unable to integrate financial and operating data
- Not granular – can't drill down by business characteristics
- Not dynamic – usually not available monthly or quarterly

Data tells you the right path to take. If you adapt as changes occur, and continually measure the impact of changes to the business, you can make consistent progress. But if you don't have the full picture, your success will be based on pure luck (50/50 by market stats).

I believe strongly that when properly trained in how to measure and monitor both real-time and predictive business intelligence, business owners can respond to the rapidly changing landscape in a way that will dramatically improve their odds of success.

> *"Using historical measures to gauge business and process performance is a thing of the past," says Samantha Searle, research analyst at Gartner. "To prevail in challenging market conditions, businesses need predictive metrics – also known as leading indicators – rather than just historical metrics (aka, lagging indicators). Predictive risk metrics are particularly important for mitigating and even preventing the impact of disruptive events on profitability."[6]*

With **predictive analytics,** you can anticipate what is coming and make small adjustments early that make a big difference later. It's the difference between using a roadmap to see where you're headed versus groping your way there. When you're groping, you will never know if you are getting closer to a desired destination. A map lets you anticipate getting to your destination and do things to make your arrival more orderly and more certain.

In later chapters we will discuss how **predictive analytics** work and how they are applied to everyday decision-making and to everyday communications with the whole team in order to get everyone on the same page.

Why a Financial Dashboard?
Each stage of business development has its typical barriers and challenges, but all stages benefit from frequent performance analysis and a clear picture of performance. We have new technologies to help track and interpret data, but there are many solutions that require a lot of time and expertise to get meaningful answers. We refer to this as the "roll your own" solutions.

Thankfully, we can identify four fundamental financial pillars—or "levers," as they could aptly be called—necessary for a solid and balanced business footing. Getting these right will not guarantee success, but getting one of these wrong will almost certainly bring a business to a grinding halt.

The four basic financial levers are:
1. Revenue
2. Operating Costs
3. Financing
4. Investment/divestment

When you drill into these topics, there are endless theories, analytical processes, and management techniques to consider. The real challenge for business owners is to make sure all four are getting the right amount of attention and that they work together to support a successful business—not to pull the business apart.

For example, I constantly see businesses use debt financing to keep their business going when the real issue is that their cost structure is simply too high. They are pulling the wrong lever and will not get onto a solid footing until they address costs. Another common situation is incorrect pricing of products and services. On the surface, if margins are fine, it must be a good time to increase volume. But the sinister truth is that if the margin **trend line** is headed in the wrong direction, all new sales are contributing less to gross profit. This problem is highly invisible when companies do not include all their direct costs in the gross profit calculation. As a result, their growth is actually damaging the business. For them every sale is draining cash causing them to go heavily into debt and depleting the equity value of their company.

There are countless variations on these themes but, in the end, the four levers must be on the right setting or the business engine will burn out. That's where a financial dashboard comes in.

Still, pillars, dashboards, and levers do not exist in a vacuum. They are part of a bigger picture that is produced by company leadership and includes vision, mission, philosophy, culture, priorities, markets, and teamwork. But, here again, if the financial levers are not being managed correctly, the picture will fall apart or just simply go nowhere no matter how cool, important, or valuable it might be. Business owners must keep an eye on the big picture and at the same time constantly assess and manage the financial health of their business as they adapt to and navigate the ever changing landscape.

CHAPTER ONE CHECK-UP

1. In the market with which you are most familiar, what specific examples do you see of the changing landscape as described in this chapter? Are these changes happening slowly or are they accelerating?

2. In what ways are a retrospective accounting view and a forward looking financial management view different and yet important to a business?

3. What would you like your business to attain? Where would you like to take your business? This is a matter of personal preference but each choice has many implications. What are the implications for your preference?
   - Lifestyle – in the business for passion/hobby; not necessarily looking to grow
   - Modest small business – proven revenue-generator but keep it small with minimum complexity
   - Scalable business – built with asset value in mind; worthy of being sold or able to attract investment

4. What do you think the management team needs in a small business to be most successful?

5. What are the advantages and disadvantages of the emerging Business Management 3.0 to a small business owner?

CHAPTER TWO

How a Business Grows

So many dreams at first seem impossible. And then they seem improbable. And then, when we summon the will, they soon become inevitable.

\- Christopher Reeve

Companies are like organisms. They have a life cycle. They are born, they grow, and all too often they die too young. Some get "gobbled up" by other organisms higher in the food chain and become nourishment for their new host. Some experience a stunted growth pattern; some grow exponentially. Some thrive; some starve.

Consider the growth stages of companies. These can be equated to the stages a person goes through from infancy to childhood to adulthood. There is an evolutionary process that businesses follow with very distinct stages of development much like people, communities, civilizations, and the planet as a whole. Many parts within parts all moving forward, all adapting, all evolving. In the same way, individual businesses evolve along with the markets and economies of which they are part.

As we grow from child to adult, we need to leave a great deal behind and pick up new tools, techniques, and disciplines in order to be successful in the new stage of life. In fact, the mindset most likely to retard the developmental process is the tendency to cling to the things that worked in the past. It's a real dilemma. Once we finally figure out an important answer to one of life's riddles, it is time to set it aside and move on to the next. At the same time, there are important lessons we need to bring forward or we will end up repeating unlearned lessons.

All of this serves as a backdrop to understanding what is happening in business today and why the message in this book is relevant. Much conventional business wisdom is rapidly becoming irrelevant and a whole new set of realities is emerging. It's no longer enough to simply offer a product at an attractive price. If you don't have support services, a user community, a knowledge base, and online access you will probably become irrelevant to the market.

The new era of business management is going to bring great change in five areas and will distinguish new generation companies from companies of the past. This new era will require significant modifications to the way business is measured, managed, communicated, and integrated. The five areas are:

1. Measurements – Rethinking key performance indicators (KPIs). It's less about the number and more the *direction* of your KPIs that matter most, especially when **trend lines** in multiple areas are on a collision course.

2. Feedback – Getting the team on the same page and heading where you want to go. It's the dialogue that helps refine goals and direction.

3. Shared vision and understanding – Don't confuse vision with goals (vision is a more qualitative aspiration, whereas goals are more metric driven components).

4. Integration – Tying systems and processes together including sales and marketing, product development, operations, and customer support. Your statistics and metrics cut across lines of responsibility. If metrics are confined to departments, they will perform in silos and parts will not play together.

5. Information – These are the bricks of the building—timely and wide reaching, drawing context from the markets and economies.

The goal of any entrepreneurial endeavor is to bring an idea to life, grow it, and make it thrive as a productive part of a broader market. The best way to accomplish this is to move away from the historically static ways of looking at a business and toward a much more dynamic and "real-time" view. P&Ls and Balance Sheets only tell a small part of the business story. **Predictive analytics**, metrics, and KPIs are the far more meaningful way to understand a business and how it grows.

In the chapters ahead we will explore how new analytical techniques become lenses that show what is really happening in the life of a business and how this information can help you with an in-depth understanding of business "vital signs." We will demonstrate how business intelligence (BI) brings together internal and external data to create a picture with context and meaning. When business owners know which adjustments to make and which dials to turn, their business can be healthy, strong and vibrant.

Understanding Your Organization

Is your company a what or a who?

You are probably familiar with the concept of companies being individual entities with many of the same rights and obligations of an individual person:

> *Despite not being human beings, corporations, as far as the law is concerned, are legal persons, and have many of the same rights and responsibilities as natural people do. Corporations can exercise human rights against real individuals and the state, and they can themselves be responsible for human rights violations. Corporations can be "dissolved" either by statutory operation, order of court, or voluntary action on the part of shareholders… Corporations can even be convicted of criminal offenses, such as fraud and manslaughter. However corporations are not considered living entities in the way that humans are.*

Incorporated entities have legal rights and liabilities that are distinct from their employees and shareholders, and may conduct business as either a profit-seeking business or not for profit business. In addition to legal personality, registered corporations tend to have limited liability, be owned by shareholders who can transfer their shares to others, and controlled by a board of directors who are normally elected or appointed by the shareholders.[7]

Wikipedia, June 4, 2014

There are many interesting parallels between a person and a business entity. Not only do corporations have many of the same legal rights as a person, but people and businesses also go through parallel developmental stages. Structures and processes change as a business moves through stages of growth. Some businesses skip stages. Some stop progressing and remain at a certain stage—sometimes because they get stuck and other times because the aspirations of the owners are being met at a certain stage. To understand how stages work and what the typical options are for moving to a next stage, let's start by understanding the various types of business structure.

Not all businesses are corporations. Sole proprietorships and partnerships are not corporations and have very different legal rights. A sole proprietorship is legally an extension of the owner. The income of the business is treated as the owner's personal income and all legal obligations of the company are actually the personal obligations of the owner. A partnership is much the same but there is generally some contractual provision for splitting income and legal obligations; it does not exist separately and apart from its owners.

A Limited Liability Company (LLC) is a hybrid business entity having some characteristics of both a corporation and a partnership or sole proprietorship. An LLC is a business entity—an unincorporated association, actually, and not a corporation. The primary characteristic an LLC shares with a corporation is limited liability, and the primary characteristic it shares with a partnership is that income and expenses are viewed as belonging to the owners much the same way as a partnership.

A corporation is very different from these. A corporation is a legal entity with its own income, expenses, tax obligations, and its own legal obligations, rights, and privileges. A corporation can have a single owner who owns all of the stock or it can have multiple owners who own shares of stock. All corporations have shares of stock owned by individuals. The shareholders of small corporations are generally few in number and generally have a close relationship with the company. Ultimately, a corporation that becomes large can be listed on a public stock exchange and then owned by anyone who wants to purchase the stock.

It's fairly common for a business to start as a sole proprietorship and evolve into a corporation and eventually into a publically traded enterprise. This is just one way to understand the stages through which a company can evolve. When you think about a business evolution in this way it's easy to see why the management structure and management processes would grow from simple to complex as part of this progression.

Parallel to evolving legal entities are the evolving phases of business maturity. Many books describe different versions of the business evolution process, but following is a version based on a personal history of business coaching and start-up development. Companies rarely follow these phases exactly as defined below but these are generally the steps most often seen as companies evolve. It should also be noted that many companies get stuck at one of the phases below and may spend a long time on a plateau—not progressing further until there is a change in ownership or a major catastrophe. And, of course, companies may be purchased by other companies, which usually (radically) changes everything.

Stages of Business Maturity

There are many variations on the stages of growth outlined in business books. The following is a blend of many but highlights the areas where key changes need to occur to enable transition to a new level of performance.

1. Entrepreneur
   a. Start-up
   b. Experimentation
   c. Establish identity and value proposition
   d. One or two experts central to the business

e. Financing from personal funds, friends, and family
f. Owner compensation based on cash remaining after bills are paid
g. Management information: internally generated by owners; ad hoc estimates of future potential

2. Early-stage
   a. Staff added to extend the capabilities of the key experts
   b. Exploration of new opportunities based on intuition and gut feel
   c. Decisions based on instinct and intent
   d. Formalized Board of Advisors
   e. Trial-and-error business development; building on what works, dropping things that don't
   f. Financing from angel investors and alternative lending sources
   g. Owner compensation driven by tax reduction
   h. Management information: combination of internal operating data, owner-generated data, and easily accessible market data

3. Standardized
   a. Organization units built around repeatable, scalable processes
   b. Formalized measurements of production and services
   c. Formalized Board of Directors
   d. Mid-level managers drive operations; executive management more focused on plans, strategies, and corporate initiatives
   e. Formalized product and service branding and structured messaging
   f. Financing from small investor groups and banks
   g. Management incentive compensation based on goal attainment; earnings retained to build financial strength; incentive plans often feature stock options rather than cash
   h. Management information: combination of internal operating data, market research, industry benchmarks, **predictive analytics** and external expertise; periodically monitored and updated

4. Replicated
   a. Expansion of existing proven processes; additions to existing offerings
   b. Decisions based on market research and validation
   c. Senior management focused on planning, organizational performance, and partnerships
   d. Growth through acquisition
   e. Comprehensive brand strategies and market positioning
   f. Financing from institutional investors, public stock offerings
   g. Management incentive compensation based on goal attainment; earnings retained to build financial strength; incentive plans often feature cash rather than stock options
   h. Management information: combination of internal operating data, market research, industry benchmarks, **predictive analytics**, market analysts and external expertise; frequently monitored and updated

Each stage is generally a step up in company size, revenue, business complexity, and company value. It's like moving from grade school to middle school to high school, etc. Each stage includes bringing some things from the previous stage into the new one, but it also means getting rid of some of things no longer needed that will actually keep you from progressing to the next stage. This last part is the hardest. Letting go of something you are successful with and taking on something new that you may or may not be successful with is tough. And, the longer you have been doing the thing you need to let go of, the harder it is to make the change. It is all about doing something that has ample reasoning and substantial thought but is counter to one's emotional comfort zone.

Let me take this a step further. Think about what it means to be a successful entrepreneur. An entrepreneur is a risk-taker—someone who is willing to try a business idea that may or may not succeed. Entrepreneurs generally don't subscribe to conventional wisdom. They have the ability to do their own thinking, define their own course, and do things the people around them would generally think of as gutsy. They make moves that most people would not.

On top of that, most entrepreneurs are opportunists. They tend to see possibilities most other people don't see. And if other people do see the potential business opportunity, they wouldn't know what to do and therefore wouldn't see it as something worth pursuing. The entrepreneur can see the possibility and potential, and can envision himself or herself being the one to make it happen. Another way of saying this is: Entrepreneurs tend to be people who can imagine something that is not there today being real at some point in the future and see themselves as the key to making the idea become a reality.

Of course, all progress begins with someone imagining a future possibility and then taking steps to make the imagined concept become real. It is the creative process within everyone. It is just that some people are more driven to take bigger steps and bigger risks.

Entrepreneurs tend to be people who can imagine
something that is not there today being real at some
point in the future, and see themselves as
the key to making the idea become a reality.

The Risk of Changing (or Not): Grow or Perish

The real challenge is to understand risks and do enough situation analysis to make smart decisions. As the process moves forward, no new idea can become reality without the participation of more people. It simply requires more individuals to accept the idea and support it or it will never become a reality. Even if the entrepreneur is able to do everything to get the idea off the ground, if there are no buyers or no customers there will be no adoption. Without adoption, a great idea is simply nothing more than a great idea and not a business reality. There is an incredible mountain of ideas that have never become reality.

You can look at the success rate of patents to get a feel for just how difficult it is to take a new idea and create a business success. Only two to three percent of patent applications actually generate financial results. And, I'm sure you know that only a small percent of ideas actually make their way to the patent office because of the cost and time requirement.

In a very similar way, most business ideas get discarded along the way. So, when an entrepreneur actually gets traction, he or she is defying the odds and doing something conventional wisdom would say is impossible.

This is the scenario I'm talking about when I say it's hard to give up the things that once made you successful. The entrepreneur has gained traction by not listening to all the voices around him (or her); now we are telling him he must put some of his entrepreneurial instinct on hold and discard some of the things that helped him successfully defy common logic to get the current results. As you can see, this is a really hard thing to do. Resistance to transformation is going to be huge, which is exactly why so many small businesses stay small. It is exactly why so many small businesses flash into existence and then flash out just as quickly.

Consider the popular concept, "grow or perish." This simply means that if you aren't growing and thriving, you are deteriorating and dying. A company may be able to hold on to status quo for a while but it's a ticking time bomb. It is very unlikely that a company can just keep doing the same thing and continue to be healthy. This is especially true if the rest of the economy is undergoing change and constantly redefining "normal." Add in the fact that the rate of change in the economy is accelerating, and you can be certain that the idea of status quo is out the window. More than ever, "grow or perish' is the mandate.

If you are thinking this is all grim news, let me urge you to reconsider. To paraphrase the famous entrepreneur and author Joseph Sugarman, "In every problem there is an equal or greater opportunity." This translates into: When market turbulence increases, opportunities are being created at an accelerated pace. The opportunities, tools, and resources for building a successful and valuable company are greater than at any time in recent history. So, while human nature is not likely to undergo major changes (we are all likely going to continue to be resistant to change), the resources are there to help make transition to new stages of evolution easier and more likely to produce positive results.

Barriers to Progress

As companies progress from one stage to the next, there are some typical barriers that can completely halt or inhibit progress. Some of these include:

- Owners reluctant to delegate responsibility and control
- Company identity being too dependent on the founder or central expert
- Managers clinging to "this is the way we have always done it"
- Resistance to tracking critical operational data
- Resistance to accountability
- The owner's desire to see the company as a means to a paycheck and not as an asset that will increase in value as the result of smart investment
- Excessive taxes due to lack of planning

Any one of these can stop growth. In many cases, the owner will realize he or she has hit a barrier but won't really understand the cause. Generally it will be impossible for the owner to actually see the problem without getting the help of an outside expert.

Another common barrier is the personal goals of the founder. If the founder started the business because he or she didn't want to work for someone else, he/she may just lock into a certain developmental stage and get comfortable. Sometimes the founder will put a high priority on free time and will not make the effort to move the company to the next level. And there are times when fear of the unknown will cause the founder to stay at a level that matches his or her comfort zone.

There are other similar motivations that stop growth, but they all are subject to change when a new life event occurs. Any business owner that has settled into a comfortable niche will eventually encounter some change that forces them to rethink their business. One obvious and fairly common scenario is a health crisis. This can cause a business owner to rethink priorities and to recognize the importance of building a team capable of running the business for an extended period of time without his or her involvement. This realization can be the catalyst to building a self-sustaining company that can generate income during the owner's absence. Once this doorway is cracked open it becomes easier to think of the business as a self-managing and self-generating engine. And, once that realization occurs, it becomes easy to contemplate creation of multiple such engines.

Life events might also cause a business owner to think about selling a company. For most businesses this thought process starts way too late. It can be shocking to find out your life's work is worth little or nothing in the market. Unfortunately, there are unscrupulous brokers that will encourage business owners to put the company up for sale with the promise of helping them cash in on the company they worked so hard to build, knowing the probability of a sale is just about zero. Once the contract is signed and fees have been paid, the obvious truth is shared with the owner.

A much better outcome can be achieved when the owner plans ahead and commits to a one- to three-year effort to maximize the variables that lead to high valuations. An even better plan is to start out with the idea of building a company with maximum market value. Starting out with the end in mind is the best course for building wealth, and, if done very deliberately, can be accomplished in a three- to ten-year window. But since most business owners don't start with the end in mind, it may require a serious mind shift to start thinking about the end game.

Here is a list of conditions that tend to push valuations down:

1. Earnings are erratic and not showing a consistent growth pattern.
2. Direct costs are too high and therefore margins are low.
3. Margins are growing slower than revenue, indicating that the company is becoming less profitable with growth (this is a major deal killer).
4. Equity has been depleted through owner distributions.
5. Working capital has been drained or the business is not capable of generating the working capital it needs to grow and sustain operations.
6. Overheads are too high for the revenue being generated.
7. One or more lines of business are dragging the company down.
8. No certainty of revenue—there are no long-term customer contracts or, if there are, they are a small part of total revenue.
9. No structure—there is little or no documentation of processes and procedures.
10. No management process—there is no process for routinely measuring, reporting, reviewing, and correcting routine business performance.

How Valuable Is Your Company, Really?

It is important to know there is a type of business buyer that tends to look for businesses experiencing the above problems and are desperate to sell. These are the yard sale shoppers that looking for deals they can fix up and either resell or turn into money makers by applying management expertise. In these deals, if you are the seller, you are at a significant disadvantage. Generally the seller in this situation gets a small fraction of the potential value of the business.

I have seen many business owners who thought their company had value. But when a situation occurred where they actually needed to put their business up for sale they had a rude awakening. I have known business owners who had a sudden health problem and had to pull back from day-to-day involvement in their businesses. That's when it became apparent their businesses were not ready to sell and that all the potential value could not be translated into real value for which a buyer would be willing to pay. These are often very sad circumstances—often bad news piled upon bad news. And yet, more often than not, the business owner had done a lot of things right and was actually close to having a valuable asset. It's the last few steps that make all the difference.

On the flip side, I have seen business owners take their company from a position of very modest income and modest track record to a position of high value to prospective buyers. With concentrated and planned effort, these owners have taken their companies from a position of no value to a position of two to ten times annual revenue. This isn't magic. It is all about making a concentrated effort. It requires goal setting and a clear road map for getting to the desired destination. And, it usually requires a team. More importantly, it requires time. There is no way to transform a business in a matter of weeks or even months. It usually takes two to three years of consistent effort to polish a business and get it to a point where it has value in the market.

If you have never done this before, it is highly unlikely you will just figure this out as you go. Of course, some business owners do and get it right the first time, but that is probably less than five percent of all first-time business owners. For this reason, most business owners will bring in an advisor who will become part of their planning and general business management process. Even highly experienced business experts include advisors as part of their team. Just having a sounding board to think through key decisions is a big part of building a complete picture and getting to a position of maximum business value.

No one valuation method is the solution for any business; you or your professional valuator may use a variety of business valuation methods. Using several will give you a more accurate idea of just what your business is worth and a range of prices that you can use as parameters for your negotiations. Here are just a few business valuation approaches: Earning Value Approach; Capitalized Past Earnings; Buyer's Test Approach; Market Valuation Approach; and Comparable Transactions Approach and others.

Norman L. Harshaw, Murphy Business & Financial Corp
Read more about each valuation approach in Appendix Contribution #121

Determining the approach and method to use in determining sales price value for a particular company is usually a matter of experience and judgment but it's nonetheless important to improve the financial and non-financial factors that will make a business more valuable and attractive before the sale—based on what is important to buyers. Some clients may not even plan to sell their businesses, but they realize that owning a sellable business increases its value— often their largest asset— and gives them more freedom to scale it, sell it, or pass it to their heirs.

Bob Dale, Partner, Austin Dale Group
Read more about valuation in Appendix Contribution #124

We will discuss these points in more detail in later chapters, but at this point the key messages are:

1. Build your company with the end in mind.
2. Build a team that includes solid outside expertise.
3. Set up a routine process for measuring, reporting and adjusting business performance.

Even though it is likely you will change your mind about the "end game" for your company, it is probable your company will simply drift if you don't constantly work toward a destination. Just the act of establishing a destination will give you and your team a sense of direction and an ability to move forward.

At the risk of being a bit repetitive, let me emphasize this last point. A company without defined goals and direction is likely to be tossed around by daily situations and likely to jump at shiny new opportunities. Companies that continually lunge for opportunities without a structured process are just abstract works of art usually with little or no value. It is the rigor of planning, encountering resistance (like weight lifting), and repeating the process with a defined frequency that begins to build business muscle. Without this structured routine workout, it is very unlikely a business will build value.

Alternative Routes

I should point out that just because a business is not growing does not indicate it is failing. It may be failing to build value as a company that could be sold but it may be accomplishing the goals of the owner. In fact, many companies start out as hobbies and then become full-time employment for the owner and that is where they stay. But it is not unusual for some jarring event to occur, which motivates the owner to rethink his or her goals for the business and then redefine expectations and transform it into a growing and valuable entity. The important thing is that the owner understands his or her choices and the impact of decisions. The only tragedy occurs when an owner misunderstands the implications of decisions and has the wrong expectations for future results.

To understand these choices a little better, let's take a closer look at how businesses evolve and how the owner's goals determine future outcomes.

The Transition from Hobby to Business

The hobby business often starts out as a side income or a series of moonlight projects. When the resourceful person realizes the hobby could actually become a primary source of income, things change. All of a sudden it becomes important to track revenues and expenses, pay taxes, name the business, and set up a bank account, and soon the hobby becomes a real business. Now the resourceful person has just crossed the line into entrepreneurship. This transition typically results in creating a combination of feelings that really don't belong together. The entrepreneur is likely to feel euphoria, fear, optimism and desperation, exhilaration and panic. It's likely that all these opposing feelings will occur at the same time or in close proximity. On top of that it is likely the entrepreneur has rejected lots of advice from friends and family. In fact, it is probable that most of the entrepreneur's friends and family are seriously questioning his or her sanity and wondering if they should seek "professional" help. The entrepreneur knows he or she is surrounded by skeptics and, hopefully, a few cheerleaders. However, there are few people who really understand why this choice is so important.

Of course, once the business starts showing signs of stability and all the skeptics become convinced this is actually going to work, the pressure subsides, the skeptics and even the cheerleaders focus their attentions elsewhere, and the entrepreneur soon leaves the crowd of worried onlookers behind. It is always interesting to see how this becomes a new form of feeling disconnected. It is hard to discuss business problems with most friends and family mostly because they don't understand the issues and partly because there are topics that just shouldn't be disclosed in public such as personal problems faced by clients or by employees. All of this can add up to the entrepreneur feeling a bit of isolation. This often becomes the reason why entrepreneurs decide to end their businesses and return to jobs where they feel like they are part of a team and where they don't need to worry about topics in which they have no interest such as finance and accounting. And, of course, the regular job has regular hours and working 24/7 is usually not required.

This thought process can be a big tug-o-war. In the end, most successful entrepreneurs realize that big rewards, and both financial and personal satisfaction, come with risk and stretching and often with some level of pain.

Early Stage or Lifestyle Business

So, now the entrepreneur has a business, an income, and new choices to make. When he or she begins to achieve a stable and rewarding business, he/she will at some point have to decide: Do I put the gains back into the business and grow it further or do I simply take the gains out for personal use? Do I invest or do I consume? Most small business owners decide to take the money for personal use. Therefore, most small businesses stop growing when the owner is generating sufficient personal income.

But there is another reason why a lot of small businesses stay small. When the owner is good at his or her area of expertise, and has figured out how to build a financially rewarding business around his/her expertise, he/she will find some point of equilibrium between effort expended, income generated, and the psychosocial rewards and recognition related to expertise. That becomes the comfort zone where things can stay for a long time. In fact, if the market stays fairly stable, if he/she doesn't need to worry about competition, and if the demand for his or her expertise remains strong enough, it is easy to see why a person would stay put in this idyllic mix.

Unfortunately, very few markets are this stable, and products and services in most areas of expertise tend to change at an increasing pace. The ideal of a stable and unchanging environment is just not likely. So, usually a person can get started in a business, develop an expertise, and then play it out for a while as a "life-style business." But sooner or later he or she will probably need to make a radical shift or become irrelevant to the market.

Transition to a Standardized Business

In case you think the transition from hobbyist to business owner is hard, it is actually much less difficult than the transition to a structured and standardized business. Those who are natural leaders don't generally find this to be a struggle. Since "natural leaders" are usually not entrepreneurs, they are rarely the ones to start a business from scratch. Most entrepreneurs are experts, not natural leaders, and they tend to find this standardization step very difficult.

One way to solve this problem is to bring in a partner or a senior level employee that has the needed leadership skills. However, since

How a Business Grows

most entrepreneurs are not good at organizational development, they often make the mistake of bringing in people with the same skills and perspectives they have. As a result, it creates an even bigger leadership vacuum. Then the owner wonders why the business seems to be stuck. The answer almost always turns out to be that they are standing in their own way!

For some businesses, this stage is as far as they are going to go. The owner has specific ideas about what the business needs and what he or she wants from the business. Even if these ideas are in conflict, the owner will lock in and the business will not evolve.

This state of internal stalemate can last for a long time. But it is also common for some market condition to change and force a rethinking of the business. It can be a loss of customers, the introduction of a new competitor, a change in costs and ability to generate profit, a loss of key employees, or even a natural disaster that changes the game to the point where the owner stops and takes a new look at the realities of the business. In some cases, this results in shutting down the business. In other cases, it is exactly what is needed to increase the resolve of the owner to take the business to the next level.

Sometimes, though rarely, a business owner will reach out to a business expert and seek assistance. This is often viewed as a defeat but, in reality, it is often the first act of leadership that involves building a team with greater expertise. This can become the first step in the next transition. The goal of this transition is to build a capability within the business for it to run itself without the owner being present ("Look Ma, no hands!"). If done well, it puts the business on a whole new course on which the owner can step back and start thinking about how to create additional self-operating teams. He or she can begin stamping out multiple teams and replicating the assembly of successful teams and building a large and scalable company.

Of course, it's never quite that simple. There are always employees that don't work out, market changes that weren't anticipated, and the ongoing pressure to improve performance in order to keep the business viable. But, while certainly not easy, the path of bringing in outside leadership can be a doorway to a whole new way to run a business.

Michael Gerber's book, *The E-Myth,* puts this transition in perspective. It's a paradigm shift for the owner but, when he or she works "on the business" rather than "in the business," new things start to happen. This makes it possible for the owner to become the driver of a business that can grow and build real value.

When the owner moves away from being the expert and builds structure and process that can be delegated, he or she now has a sellable business that can be sold and left without risk of collapse. In other words, in a business that is highly dependent on the owner or is "all about the owner," there really isn't anything to buy apart from the owner. It means the owner needs to sell himself or herself or there is nothing of value to the buyer. Obviously this is not a good thing for anyone.

There are buyers for these kinds of companies. However, such transactions are generally for low value and often include a commitment to work for the buyer for some specified period of time. Sometimes there is a requirement to produce a certain level of results in order to get paid for the company. This usually does not work out very well for either party. Usually the real motivation of the buyer is to get the customers and possibly the employees of the company they are buying, but rarely does this have significant value.

As we will discuss later, the value of a company that has actually transitioned to a standardized business can be many times greater than one that is owned by the company expert. The payback for this transition can be very large and is well worth the effort.

Transition to Replicated Business

The transitions discussed above tie back to the first two stages of business evolution outlined at the beginning of this chapter. This transition very specifically connects to the third stage, which is all about expansion.

In order for the leader to actually build a replicable and scalable business, he or she needs to have multiple parts of the business function in a very predictable and reliable way. It is impossible to build a business if the parts behave in unpredictable and erratic ways. There are many companies with informal procedures that rely on the expertise of specific people within the organization. But, in the end, these businesses hit their own limits and stop growing until they can standardize and fine-tune their processes.

How a Business Grows

When the latter occurs, the business can be more efficient, more profitable, and have more resources to spend on expansion, and the whole engine begins to produce more and better results.

If a company has replicable business units, it is ready to multiply. This is when geographic expansion occurs, new offices are opened, other businesses are acquired, and rapid growth takes place. The company will use its standardized processes as a template and constantly work to have all its business units replicate the same business standards.

At this point corporate management needs the ability to monitor business performance at the individual business unit level and at the consolidated level. The focus of management becomes compliance with process and getting the right people. Company-wide performance standards often take the place of industry benchmarks as these companies work to move all business units up to their internal standard.

Of course, business evolution and growth rarely occur in a straight line. There are usually a few twists and turns. But if the company has learned about the value of having standardized processes, the twists and turns become clues to where more structure and standardization are needed.

Peaks and Valleys

When I was at Price Waterhouse (before Cooper was added) I observed that even the most experienced and sophisticated companies continue to learn and refine their processes. I was hired because of the experience I had gained at IBM selling large systems and projects to companies needing technology-centric business solutions. I had experience in selling, planning, and delivering large projects, so this was a great fit. But I was totally surprised by how the business cycle worked with large projects in a consulting firm. After selling such a large project, I would focus my team's efforts on delivering planned results to the clients. Once we finished the project we were then ready to go sell another project. But that is where the surprise occurred. We went from big revenue to no revenue as we jumped from delivery mode back into selling mode.

As you might guess, a couple of cycles with this experience is all it took. I realized we needed to continue our selling process *while* we were delivering projects so that when we ended one project there would be another project waiting in the queue. When we figured this out and identified how to conduct a continuous marketing and selling process, we discovered we could generate a pretty constant flow of business and much more consistent revenue. Once we had this part down, we realized we could put more teams to work to deliver the projects we could sell because we now had a steady flow. As we expanded our delivery capability, we looked for ways to generate more business flow, which led to improvements in marketing and sales processes. As we built processes we also built metrics we could monitor to see what was working and where bottlenecks were occurring. Ultimately we developed a process for continually improving our processes.

This may sound like a crazy spiral, but the results were dramatic and the company culture evolved to make this work very well. Of course, I'm leaving out plenty of bumps in the road, of which there were plenty.

What It All Means

As we move into the next several chapters we will examine the many ways that measuring and responding to the needs of the business can lead to fine-tuning and improvements as a company grows. This in turn can create an environment of continuous improvement. Continuous improvement can be the foundation for continuous growth and for building value.

This is yet another opportunity to introduce an important concept tying value to trajectory. A big part of the value of a company is the combination of its ability to generate profit today and its ability to generate increasing profits in the future. So, if you have a company that knows how to measure, refine, improve, and then continue that cycle on an ongoing basis, you have a company that is a growth engine. That kind of company can be multiple times more valuable than a company with the same level of profitability today but no demonstrated capability of ongoing refinement and growth in the future.

So, as we consider the topics in the coming chapters, you will see a recurring theme: measure, analyze, forecast, refine, improve, and repeat. This process creates improved processes throughout a company. Once this becomes part of a company's culture, it creates successes that generate more successes.

This is the same dynamic that created Microsoft, General Electric, IBM, and all of the other major blue chip companies that are big engines in the global economy. The press tends to look at the products of the big companies and gives no attention to the many routine processes required for such companies to deliver results. Rarely does the press notice how processes within the big companies are constantly being measured, monitored, tuned, and improved. Of course, major failures in these processes do come to light and can often be newsworthy. But when that happens, the big companies figure out how to build another process to keep the embarrassment from happening again.

As you read the next chapter, think about how these various parts fit into an overall measurement and monitoring process, which then feeds other continuously improving processes, all of which creates performance, trajectory (direction of change), and value.

 **CHAPTER TWO CHECK-UP**

1. When is it most important to introduce standardized processes in a company? When would it not be appropriate?
2. In what way does company evolution need to tie to market evolution? What specific examples would you use?
3. What would prevent a business owner who is an expert from taking steps to become a business leader?
4. What qualities and practices would you expect to see in a business that is positioning for growth and value in the market?
5. What barriers would you expect a company to experience when it moves from an early-stage growth company to a standardized and structured company? What are the benefits of overcoming these barriers?

CHAPTER THREE

Vital Sign Fundamentals

In God we trust, all others bring data.

- W. Edwards Deming

In healthcare, ascertaining the health of a patient includes reading the vital signs including heartbeat, breathing rate, temperature, and blood pressure. After that, physicians move on to a series of tests, many of which may be performed by a lab. But if there is a critical problem with a vital system—such as extraordinarily high blood pressure—the patient might find himself or herself in the emergency room before going any further with a routine exam!

Similarly in business, the first line of examination is *financial performance.* There are a host of areas within a business that should be monitored and managed. These include operating metrics, staffing metrics, quality controls, customer satisfaction, competitive comparisons, and other such items. But if there are financial performance problems, and especially if they are serious, it will be important to identify and focus on the critical issues before going any further.

These are the vital sign categories to monitor in a business:

1. Cash
2. Revenue
3. Expense
4. Profit
5. Working capital
6. Long-term capital
7. Equity leverage
8. LOB performance

We will drill into these in more depth, but first we need to build a bit more context. Vital signs are the topic areas where monitoring should begin, but "signs" are not the destination, they are the pointers. When a vital sign is off track, as in healthcare, you are seeing the symptom— the sign, not the problem. There is always something going on at a more fundamental level that is the actual problem. Using vital signs to detect a problem is of little value if the next step is not taken to find and resolve the underlying problem. But, as any physician will tell you, if you don't monitor symptoms before and after a corrective action is taken, you will not know if you actually treated the right problem or if you used the right treatment for the problem. The vital signs can alert you to a problem. Then they are the evidence that the right corrective action was taken.

To continue the healthcare analogy, it is important to know if a vital sign is static or if it is changing. An elevated temperature that is staying level may require nothing more than making the patient comfortable, where a rapidly increasing temperature may call for emergency actions. The elevated temperature reading may be the same for both cases, but knowing what is happening over time can completely change the picture. In the same way it is important to know the direction of key business vital signs. As in healthcare, early detection can play an important role in minimizing cost and improving outcomes. Much like elevated cholesterol or blood pressure, symptoms can seem relatively harmless in the early stages but can have huge implications down the road. In the same way, vital signs in a business can reveal mission-critical problems early on and can make a huge difference in costs and damage control down the road.

Most business owners use a combination of traditional financial statements (income statements and balance sheets) and spreadsheets to monitor performance and progress. Unfortunately, traditional financial statements can only tell you where you have been and where you are now. They cannot tell you where you are headed and how fast you are going, which are critical pieces of information for making business adjustments.

Most, if not all, large companies also do extensive trend and direction analysis and have done so for many decades. This requires expertise in statistics and analytical processes. But since it can be time consuming and expensive, many smaller businesses skip it or do a much abbreviated version. They generally don't hire staff with sufficient analytical skills, and most entrepreneurs don't know what kind of skills they should be looking for. As a result, monitoring and management of financial performance is generally neglected in smaller businesses.

Unfortunately (but not surprisingly), it's the "gut feel" companies that run into the most surprises and tend to fail. Gut feel is not good for monitoring financial performance and getting maximum financial results. As companies grow there is less room for instinct and analysis, while monitoring becomes the pathway to success.

Generally when a company has more than five employees, or is generating more than $500,000 in annual revenue, it becomes imperative to use metrics to monitor and manage operations. The stages and transitions we discussed in Chapter 2 showed how the various levels of measurement and monitoring are critical to transitioning from one stage to the next. But regardless of business size, the important point is that profitable growth almost always requires a discipline of analysis of the numbers and continuous course correction. Business growth also requires a clear understanding of how financial metrics drive management processes that lead to profitability.

Utilizing Modern Decision-Making Tools

In spite of the many reasons (excuses?) for not analyzing and monitoring financial performance, it is actually the small business that needs analysis as much as, if not *more* than, larger businesses. This is where new low-cost technologies come to the rescue. New analytical tools readily available in the market can now provide easily understandable and fully-digested, synthesized pictures that foster analysis and judgment at very affordable costs. Tools like financial dashboards can provide on-demand access to "information about information" when and where it is most needed. Dashboards can show gaps between planned, potential, and actual performance. Then, with the big picture made visible, management can spend its time on the more important question: *Where do we want to go and what are we going to do?*

Financial dashboards typically provide the instruments and gauges to help answer key business questions in a highly condensed view. Ideally, a financial dashboard will show multiple gauges of performance in a single view so business owners and managers can quickly get a comprehensive picture of what is happening in their business.

Here's what to watch out for: Most dashboards are a collection of customizable tools for assembling and defining certain performance indicators. While this sounds like an ideal approach, flexibility comes with a high cost. Generally the tools are more expensive, take more time to customize, and often lead the entrepreneur to information that is not telling the right story. A more structured and standardized dashboard can be quicker to implement and much more likely to show the needed picture of performance.

In almost all cases, dashboards provide a much better view of performance than do lists of numbers on financial reports. The best dashboards go further with detailed graphs and charts, built-in **predictive analytics**, and, perhaps more importantly, a structured framework that allows your data to be compared to other companies like yours.

We will discuss the topic of comparability to peers in more detail when we zoom in on industry-specific data and benchmarks later in this chapter. But first, let's take a closer look at the data sources used by dashboards for management reporting.

Financial Analysis – Interpreting Metrics for the Big Picture

It is important that the dashboard pull data directly from your company's accounting system and not from a manual input process. One of the biggest problems growing companies run into is "data disconnects." When reports use data from different input sources, there is a risk the data will be out of sync and show conflicting answers. For example, you may have some data recorded as monthly totals and other data recorded as weekly totals. It takes careful analysis and data conversion to make this data work together. The solution might be to find data sources where all the data exists in the form of daily totals so you can establish a common denominator. When companies try to solve this by simply producing separate, non-integrated reports, they will inevitably run into conflicts, which create confusion and user skepticism. The more you use single systems to serve as the data source for multiple purposes, the better.

The major source of vital signs data comes from the company's financial system and is typically found in the P&L and the Balance Sheet. Let's take a dive into these two sources and get a better feel for how this data can be used to monitor the health of a company.

How the P&L Works

The P&L (Profit and Loss Report or Income Statement) is the report of revenues and expenses for a specific period of time. You will typically see P&Ls that cover a month, a quarter, or a year. The P&L starts off at zero at the beginning of the reporting period and summarizes the revenue and expense activity that occurred during the period.

Most business owners start at the top of the report, the "top line," to see how much money they brought in, and then jump right to the bottom to see how much was left over after expenses—the "bottom line" or Net Income or Profit (synonyms). The top line and the bottom line are critically important to understanding performance, but the most important management decisions are based on the detail in the middle of the report.

What the P&L does *not* give you is a cumulative score. If you look at the score for last night's baseball game, you can get a good understanding of how well your team played last night but that won't tell you how it is doing for the season. A P&L gives the score for the current game. But if you want to see the team's win-loss record for its entire history, you need to go to the Balance Sheet for that information.

There are many rules in accounting, many of which are not very well followed by small businesses. But as businesses evolve, these rules become increasingly important and have a big impact on how a company is valued. For example, the following table explains the generally accepted rule for recognizing revenue and expenses. Where most small businesses will just book the revenue or expense when a receipt or payment occurs, the right way to do this is more complicated.

Key Principles of Accounting for the P&L
Based on GAAP Generally Accepted Accounting Principles)

Revenue Recognition	Expense Recognition
Revenue reported on the P&L should be reported in the month in which it was earned. So if a customer prepays for a three-month project, the revenue should be divided across the three months of the project. For tax reporting purposes, small businesses can ignore this principle and just pay taxes based on when the cash is received. So for prepayment, the receipts should be posted to a pre-payment account on the balance sheet and then move to the P&L in the month in which the revenue is earned. Conversely, if the payment is made at the end of the three-month project, the revenues should be billed and recognized each month.	Expenses reported on the P&L should be reported in the month they are incurred. The most common example is depreciation on major assets. Ideally, depreciation should be recorded in each month so that you don't have a big depreciation spike in one month. This concept should also apply to such things as marketing and other expenses that are paid in advance or after the month in which they are incurred.

The P&L tells you how much resource you consumed and how much revenue you produced during the reporting period. The difference between revenues and resources used is the "bottom line" or gain achieved by your company.

Vital Sign Fundamentals

The information you won't find on the P&L is trend data. Trend data tells you whether certain line items on the P&L are trending up or down and how fast they are moving. The numbers on the report may look perfectly fine, but with closer analysis you might see that the data is trending in the wrong direction and needs immediate attention. That's why it is important to use trend data every month in conjunction with your P&L to see short-term and long-term trends for each category of performance.

Example P&L

Jerry's Tech Company
Income Statement (P&L)
For Quarter Ending June 30, 2013

Income		% of Rev		% of Rev
Sales			870,000	
Less: Discounts	4,000			
Returns	800		4,800	
Net Sales			865,200	
Costs of Goods and Services Sold				
Product Costs	180,000	21%		
Technical Staff	240,000	28%		
Technical Contractors	120,000	14%		
Commissions Paid	45,000	5.2%	585,000	
Gross Profit			280,200	32%
Expenses				
Marketing	25,000	2.9%		
Infrastructure	12,000	1.4%		
Depreciation & Amortization	6,000	0.7%		
Salaries	28,000	3.2%		
Utilities	900	0.1%		
Rent	5,000	0.6%		
Interest	800	0.1%		
Taxes	80,000	9.2%	157,700	
Net Income - From Operations			122,500	
Other Income	15,000			
Other Expenses	2,500		17,500	
Net Income			105,000	
EBITDA (earnings before interest, taxes, depreciation, and amortization)			191,800	22%

Reading Your P&L Statement

At the top of the P&L are the revenues. In the middle are the costs of goods sold (COGS) followed by expenses (often referred to as SG&A – sales, general and administrative expenses) with Net Income at the bottom. Any revenues or expenses that are not part of your normal business operations (such as the receipts from the sale of a company car) are called "Other Income and Expenses" and show up below SG&A expenses.

There are many variations on line item titles and groupings in a P&L, but the above format is a fairly common structure. The following guidelines are based on the above example.

- Income, revenue, and sales generally mean the same thing and are used interchangeably.
- Discounts and returns are treated as deductions to sales; all percentage calculations are based on net sales.
- COGS (cost of goods sold) are all costs directly attributed to generating revenue.
- Product costs are the amounts paid to vendors for equipment and software resold to customers. This number should include shipping charges and taxes. Technical staff pay within COGS should include 100 percent of the salary, benefits, and taxes paid to billable staff (staff that generate revenue by the service they perform). In addition, if the owner or other managers allocate a portion of their time to billable work, that portion of their compensation should also be included in COGS and not in company overheads. The amount put in COGS for part-time billable staff should be a defined percent of the person's salary and not based on the number of hours billed. For example, if the owner allocates 60 percent of his or her time to administrative work and 40 percent to billable customer services, then 40 percent of his/her compensation should be listed as COGS. For accounting purposes, payroll should be one line item on the chart of accounts. Then a contra account should be used to show the deduction to the company payroll under SG&A. Another adjusting account in COGS would receive the adjustment for the portion of payroll to be allocated to COGS.

- Contractor COGS should be the hourly fees paid to contractors brought in to provide specialized services for customers.
- COGS Commissions are paid to internal sales staff and any external third party to provide direct sales services.
- Gross profit is a key indicator of business performance. Gross profit is equal to sales minus COGS. Gross profit is sometimes referred to as gross margin dollars. Gross margin percent is equal to gross profit divided by net sales.
- Depreciation and amortization are examples of accounts commonly used to take a large expenditure and spread it over a series of years. For example, if you spend $12,000 on equipment, you might depreciate it over three years. So, each year you post $4,000 to expenses, and decrease the asset value on the balance sheet by the same amount. The number of years should be equal to the expected life of the asset. The IRS has guidelines on normal life spans for common business assets. Amortization is similar to depreciation; for example, a large legal fee or the purchase of intellectual property might be recorded as an asset and then amortized over a multi-year period.
- Salaries in the SG&A section (overhead expenses) should include salaries and hourly wages for all administrative, executive, and operations support staff and should not include salaries for billable staff. Billable staff should be shown in COGS payroll.
- Net Income from Operations is also called profit. It does not include "other expenses" and "other income," which are not generated by operations.
- Other Income, sometimes called "extraordinary income," is any revenue not from normal operations. For example, you may sell old desks and chairs when you remodel your office. You must record this as income, but you don't want to let it get mixed in with normal operating income or you will distort your trend analysis.
- Other Expenses are any expenses not part of normal operations or normal overheads. It is less important to segregate these expenses but technically it is the correct thing to do. These are usually expenses directly tied to any Other Income items, such as the cost of refurbishing the office furniture before you sell it.

- Net Profit is the bottom line after all income and expenses have been taken into account.
- EBITDA (earnings before interest, taxes, depreciation, and amortization) is a way to look at profitability from the perspective of "how much spendable revenue did this company create." By excluding interest, taxes, depreciation, and amortization, you are eliminating the non-cash expenses and overheads that generally are not the result of operations. EBITDA is a more comparable number between similar companies and is also used by banks, lenders, and financial institutions to evaluate profitability.

Balance Sheet Insight

It often comes as a surprise to small business owners that the balance sheet really does matter. The realization generally hits the first time a company tries to get a loan from a bank. Even when the company doesn't have a strong enough balance sheet to meet lending criteria, the owner can always sign for a loan personally and use his/her house or other personal assets as collateral. However, that means there is not enough value in the business to do the heavy lifting and you are taking on all the risk personally. All owners should want their business to stand on its own two feet and carry its own debt—but it takes significant planning to make that happen. Ultimately a business cannot grow if it is unable to carry its own debt.

Even if the P&L is strong, an upside down balance sheet can drain the value of a company. It's very difficult to grow a company that has no strength in its balance sheet. Even worse, a company can be nearly impossible to sell if it has a weak balance sheet. Many owners discover this when an emergency happens (like a health problem or a divorce) and they have to sell their business—and discover the company has no value in the market. This can be particularly sad when you know the same company could have sold for a lot of money if there had been a bit of planning ahead of time. The difference can be huge!

Many accountants advise clients to take all the cash out of their company in order to minimize taxes. That's a fine short-term strategy, but one that can have dire consequences in the long-term. This is just one of many mistakes owners make when they don't see the bigger picture.

Let's take a closer look at what it means to have a strong balance sheet. First, here are a few basics:

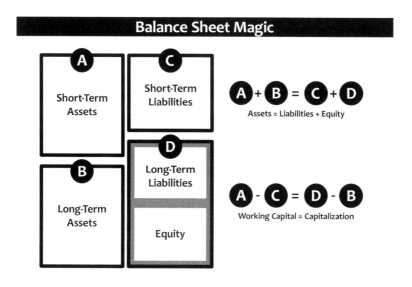

Start by looking at your working capital (short-term assets minus short-term liabilities). Ideally, your short-term assets should be about 1.5 times your short-term liabilities which means working capital should be equal to about half of your short-term liabilities. Anything you do to strengthen your working capital also strengthens your long-term capital (shown as D – B above). The converse is also true. Any time you strengthen your long-term capital, you are automatically building your working capital by the same amount. For example, any time you retain earnings in the company, you are building equity. At the same time, you are keeping cash or other short-term assets in the company. This builds working capital and your company's financial strength.

There is a lot more that can be said about building financial strength, but understanding this picture is important for understanding overall financial performance.

An ideal working capital position for most companies is when current assets are equal to one and one-half to two times short-term liabilities.

That means, short term assets need to be 1.5 to two times the total of short-term liabilities. The next question is, 'Where is the working capital trend line heading'? If capital is heading down while revenues are increasing, there is a danger that the company has fundamental problems where growth is damaging to the company. If working capital is growing as revenue increases there is a high probability that the company is healthy and will strengthen with growth.

Ed Patton, Patton & Associates
Read more: Appendix Contribution #123

Working Capital - Key to Financial Strength

Where the P&L tells you how well you are doing during a certain time period, the balance sheet shows how well you have done for the life of your company. The P&L gives you the score for one game. The Balance Sheet gives you a cumulative score for the whole series of games plus a whole lot more.

Most business owners see their Balance Sheet as a way to track what they own and what they owe (assets and liabilities). But breaking down the parts and understanding the ratios and trends tells a completely different story.

Working Capital is the key to understanding the financial strength of a company. Working Capital is simply short-term assets minus short-term liabilities. It tells you what kind of asset coverage you have for your current debts. Generally, if you have less short-term assets than short-term debt, you are considered to be insolvent and would probably be unable to get bank or other external financing. With short-term assets at 1.5 times current debt, you are generally considered to be in good shape (and higher is better).

However, it is more important to know where your working capital is headed than it is to know your current status. That's where **trend lines** come in. In particular, the working capital **trend line** can tell you a lot about the health of your business. Most importantly, it tells you whether a company is building or losing financial strength.

For the purpose of the illustrations below, assume that the target minimum line is set at 1.5 times the company's short-term liabilities. Healthy working capital **trend lines** show working capital above the target minimum or on its way to being above. Even a falling working capital **trend line** that is above the target minimum is healthy and indicates that available resources are being used to build for the future.

Unhealthy Working Capital **trend lines** generally show Working Capital below the Target Minimum, or recently dropping below. This simply indicates that a company lacks the resources to pay its bills. If the Working Capital is going down, it shows the condition is going to get worse unless something changes.

Companies that don't understand their **trend lines** are often surprised when they find out they are in deep financial trouble. It's just not enough to know that the numbers on your financial reports are fine. Good numbers headed in the wrong direction are not good!

Assessing the Impact of Investments

Making investments is an important part of building a business. Whether investments are in people, equipment, training, or marketing, it is essential to spend money in order to make money. However, for many owners, there is no clear relationship between investment and results. Without data on results, investing becomes guessing. If there is no evidence of a beneficial outcome it would be reasonable to ask, "Why should I make the investment?"

There are a number of ways to collect data to show the impact of investments. For example, you can track the new sales brought in by a new salesperson to see if they are generating enough revenue to justify their salary and bonuses. It's a little harder to assess the benefit of adding a new technician or a new administrative assistant who does not generate revenue. Perhaps bringing on a new administrator is going to free up time for sales staff and this impact can be measured.

Remember that there is a big difference between calculating a desired outcome from an investment and actually achieving the desired outcome. Tracking results of an investment may not tell you the whole story either. It's very possible that the new salesperson is bringing in a bunch of new business, just as planned, but is doing so by reducing prices and hurting your profits. Or, perhaps the new salesperson is bringing in new business by taking sales that would have been brought in by other sales staff. Judging the impact of a new administrative person can be even more difficult. Clearly multiple forms of analysis need to be conducted on a regular basis in order to catch subtle issues.

Then there is the issue of timing. When are you going to see the financial benefit of an investment? It's highly unlikely it will be seen immediately. Most likely it will be two to six months and sometimes a year before benefits begin to show up when you invest in a new sales person.

One interesting way to test the overall impact of new investments is to use trend analysis. Here is how that could work: Let's say you hired a new sales person eight months ago and want to see what kind of overall impact the new person contributed. Rather than looking at the performance of the individual, trend analysis can let you see overall impact on sales. The **trend lines** should let you see the before and after impact of hiring the new person.

The first step would be to see what your growth trend looked like just before you hired the new person and what your growth trend looks like for the latest month. This should include the growth trend in gross revenue, gross profit, and net profit. If you don't see a noticeable improvement after eight months, it is pretty likely the new person has not made a measurable difference. Of course, if there is a trend improvement you still can't be sure the new person made it happen. But, if there is no improvement you can be pretty sure that adding the new person did not result in improved performance.

The reason we would use trend numbers for this analysis is because just looking at monthly data right off the P&L is not likely to give you meaningful data. Monthly numbers tend to swing widely and don't show a pattern. By using trend numbers, you are smoothing out the data and getting a much clearer picture of fundamental changes in your business. Plus, trend data made up of either 12 or 24 months of actual performance data will smooth out the impact of seasonality and any major year-end transactions. Comparing 12-month growth rate trends from one month to another month is a much better way to understand what changes are actually occurring in your business.

For most businesses, there are usually multiple investments that need to be evaluated at the same time. When multiple investments occur simultaneously there is no practical way to single out the impact of one particular investment. This makes it all the more important that the business be monitored from a trend perspective. Over time, if multiple investments do not result in growth and improved profitability, then you must conclude you are either making the wrong investments or that some other factor is keeping your investments from producing the expected improvements. If the answers are not obvious, it may be time to bring in an expert to help analyze why investments are not achieving desired results.

Vital Signs Drill Down

Not only is it important to be sure that revenue and profits are moving up together, it is equally important to make sure all vital signs are in sync. Each vital sign can be viewed from multiple angles:

a. Long-term growth – 24-month growth percentage
b. Short-term growth – six-month growth percentage

c. Growth with a turn – 24-month growth combined with a short-term trend (six-month) showing a potential new direction
d. Benchmark comparison – growth relative to market growth in a specific market segment
e. Relative long-term growth – comparing all other **trend lines** in the company to long-term revenue growth. This is fundamental to finding areas of the business that are underperforming.
f. Relative short-term growth – comparing short-term trends in all areas of the company to short-term revenue growth. This can uncover early warnings for areas that may have been fine in the past but are moving away from alignment with revenue in the short-term.

Understanding Performance through Ratios

After reviewing growth and relative growth, the next step is to look at ratios. Just like basic trend analysis for financial data, there should also be a trend analysis for ratios. As we have discussed, it is all too easy to think financial performance is just fine when you look at a financial statement and observe the numbers are in an acceptable range. But when you look at *trends*, you can immediately see if an acceptable number is actually on its way to disaster. The same principle applies to ratios, which can look great until you zoom in on trend data. A perfectly acceptable accounts receivable ratio may reveal an emerging trend that will change AR from acceptable to unacceptable if you allow the trend to continue. Here is a list of ratios that should be reviewed every month:

- **Gross margin percentage** - gross profit divided by net sales (total sales after returns and discounts)
  Meaning: percent of revenue left after subtracting direct costs
- **EBITDA percentage** - Earnings before interest, taxes, depreciation, and amortization - EBITDA divided by net sales
  Meaning: ability to generate cash from profits
- **Net profit percentage** - Net profit divided by net sales
  Meaning: the percent that bottom line profits are of total sales
- **LOB percentage of revenue** – LOB (line of business) net sales divided by total net sales for the company

Meaning: percentage of the company's revenue coming from a specific LOB

- **LOB percentage of gross margin** – LOB gross profit divided by total gross profit for the company
  Meaning: percentage of the company's gross profit from a specific LOB
- **LOB contribution** – LOB net income divided by total net income for the company
  Meaning: LOB bottom line contribution to company profits
- **Quick Ratio** – Short-term assets (excluding inventory) divided by short-term liabilities. These should be above one or the company is considered to be potentially unable to pay off its current liabilities with existing liquid resources
  Meaning: ability of the company to pay off short-term liabilities
- **AR Days** – Accounts receivable divided by average revenue per day; the ideal number varies by industry, but more companies are pushing to less than 30 days of AR by insisting on credit card and ACH payments and moving away from conventional billing cycles; conventional AR should be less than 45 days
  Meaning: how many days' worth of revenue is owned by customers
- **Assets to liabilities** – Total assets divided by total liabilities. This should be greater than one to one or the company has a negative net worth or negative book value
  Meaning: how able is a company to pay all liabilities using company assets at book value
- **Profitability** – EBITDA as a percent of total revenue for the past 12 months. This number should exclude owner incentive compensation. If it is less than five percent, the company would be considered marginal. Between five and ten percent would be considered solid; above 10 percent it would be considered a front-runner.
  Meaning: ability to generate cash from profits
- **Working Capital** – working capital is computed by subtracting current liabilities from current assets. Ideally, total current assets should be 1.5 times total current liabilities so that working capital would be approximately equal to half of current liabilities.

Meaning: ability to pay bills and cover the cost of operations

- **Leverage Ratio** – Total liabilities (short-term and long-term) divided by equity. This ratio could be as high as two to one. However, at this level it will be harder to borrow because the cost of loan repayment is likely to be too high.

  Meaning: the amount of debt being put to work relative to investor equity [Special caution: A low leverage ratio can be as bad as a high ratio from the perspective of an investor. At the low end it means that all the growth is being supported by equity investment, which can be highly dilutive. At the high end, the ratio indicates that the company is getting buried in debt. Generally an experienced banker can help pin point the ideal ratio for a specific industry.]

- **Cash to Sales Ratio** – total average month-end cash divided by average monthly sales. Ideally, companies should have one to two times their monthly sales in cash plus the unused line of credit; companies are considered a high risk if they don't have sufficient cash reserves to weather severe storms.

  Meaning: ability of the company to survive a dip in sales

Each ratio **trend line** should be reviewed to see if it is growing faster or slower than long-term revenue growth. You want to see your quick ratio, assets to liabilities, profitability, working capital, and cash to sales ratios growing as fast as, or faster than, revenue growth. If they are growing more slowly, it is an indication the company is losing ground as it grows. The flip side is that AR days and the leverage ratio should grow slower than revenue growth. If they are growing faster than revenue, there is serious cause for concern.

With this perspective in mind, let's take a closer look at how the analysis is done and where it should be focused. This is the subject of the next chapter. Then we will follow up with the "so what" part of the conversation, which asks: What does the analysis tells us and what should we do about it?

CHAPTER THREE CHECK-UP

1. Which vital signs do you think are the most difficult to understand? What can be done to make these easier to use?

2. If your company is having problems with profitability, how would you decide which section on the P&L needs to be improved?

3. If working capital is on a decreasing trend, what actions can be taken to improve it?

4. In what ways is the performance of the balance sheet important to the owner of the business?

5. What is more important, the status of a ratio or the direction in which the ratio is moving?

CHAPTER FOUR

Trend Reporting

You have to be able to tell if you're making progress.
-Jim Collins, Good to Great

Most business owners look at only a few numbers to see if their business is on track. First, they might look at gross revenue, which is a great starting point because, if sales are not working, everything else is secondary. Yet there is more to this story. The big challenge is getting a good understanding of what is really working and what is not. Looking at any one number in isolation will almost certainly lead to an incomplete understanding of the business. It takes seeing the numbers from multiple areas side by side to assess if things are in alignment and going in a healthy direction. This needs to be done on a continuous basis.

Few businesses actually have a formal budget planning and tracking process and even fewer have a formal process for trend analysis and forecasting. But when you take a close look at businesses that grow and become valuable, they are usually the ones that have figured this out. They have learned to use these financial disciplines as part of their routine management process. They know how to use metrics to determine what is working and what isn't. These numbers drive continuous course correction and their big strategic decisions.

The Value of Trend Reporting

Trend reporting can be an effective way to create a better and more complete picture of the overall health of your business. **Trend lines** are built by taking past and current performance and using them to project future performance. Ideally, trend reporting combines goal data with actual performance data to show you exactly how close you are, as of today, to being on target with your goals.

While budget reports can show your current status, they are not helpful with the bigger questions: Am I on track to hit a business goal? Am I moving at a pace that is over or under what's needed to hit the goal? Without trend information, it is very difficult to see where the problems are and where you need to make adjustments—until the target has been missed. Connecting the dots from where you are now to where you need to be in order to get to your destination is crucial to the management process. A good understanding of your current trend and how it compares to your *intended* trend helps spotlight areas where gaps exist, and where you need to make mid-course corrections in order to accomplish your goals.

Simplified, trends show your average movement over time. For example, if you were to graph monthly revenue over a period of six months, you would typically see a line with ups and downs from one month to the next. Just looking at this graph might give you a feel for your general direction but it can be hard to tell if the overall trend is getting better or worse. And, more importantly, it is very difficult to compare performance from one bumpy line to another bumpy line without converting the numbers to something comparable—something like basic growth rates.

Let's say you are looking at a graph of monthly revenue and a graph of monthly expenses and you just want to know if they are moving in a complimentary direction. It is easy to tell if revenues are greater than expenses but much harder to know if they are moving at the right rate. In fact, it is very possible to be on a collision course with expenses growing faster than revenue and not know it!

Now, just because you have an occasional month where revenue falls below expenses does not mean you are headed for disaster. Even less obvious is the case where revenue is always above expenses but the overall trends show a train wreck is coming—that's where the **trend lines** cross in the future. Most companies discover they are on a collision course when the wreck has occurred. It is generally impossible to fix at that point, and that is the end of the business. More than half of all new businesses have this train wreck in their first five years and go out of business.

Trend lines are the key to spotting problems early. They can show the comparison of revenues and expenses in a way that standard graphs cannot. **Trend lines** make data comparable and show when potential future problems will occur if the business stays on the **trend lines**. With this information a business owner can take corrective action early and avoid the **trend line** collision.

Trend analysis fits into a continuum of other kinds of analyses that are very important to running a business. By itself, it cannot do the complete job of performance analysis. At the same time, the data and reports provided by common accounting systems can't do the complete job either. The table below is intended to contrast the kinds of conclusions that can be derived by different levels of information and analysis.

Understanding the Numbers

Hierarchy of Financial Data	What the numbers tell us	What the numbers don't tell us
Transactions	Where money was spent or moved from one status to another	How does this impact the business? Do the transactions generate a profit or loss?
Account balances	The current status of an account reflecting accumulated transitions to-date	Is the balance good or bad in relation to other account balances? Is the condition getting better or worse?
Financial reports	Account balances and totals combined to show performance as of a specific point in time	Is the business as a whole improving or deteriorating? What parts of the business are working? (There are always areas in the business that are under-performing while others are at the top of their game.)

Graphic analysis	Visual data relationships and changes over time (e.g., bar charts, line charts, and pie charts)	Where is the business and each of the parts headed? Where will they be in the future?
Trend analysis (predictive analysis)	Performance over a period of time using smoothing techniques, which makes prediction of future direction a mathematical process	Individual **trend lines** provide important information but don't answer the question: How are multiple **trend lines** working together to help or hurt performance?
Trend analysis – multiple line comparisons	Combines **trend lines** to show how they are working together to help or hurt current and future performance	How does the performance of my business compare to my peers? Am I gaining ground or losing ground in my industry? Am I missing obvious opportunities that have been discovered by my peers?
Industry trend comparisons	Compare my trends to peer group trends, spotlights areas where I can make improvements proven by industry data to get better results.	Is the industry I'm part of making a shift that suggests contraction or expansion? Should I take a conservative or an aggressive posture in the months ahead?
Economy trend comparisons	Shows how my industry compares to the local, regional, national, and global economies; how the economy is performing now; how we expect it to perform in the months ahead; how likely this is to affect my industry and my business	What surprises lie ahead? Both good and bad surprises happen with roughly the same frequency. We tend to focus on potential dangers and too often miss good opportunities. It takes both caution and boldness to build a successful business.

As described above, all the elements of financial accounting and analysis play an important role. In many cases, the data at one level becomes a building block that enables the next higher level of analysis. As you consider the many ways you can analyze and understand your business, the one with the greatest potential for producing clarity is listed as "Trend analysis – multiple line comparisons." This is the basis for determining whether a company is fundamentally healthy or not.

For many business owners this may seem a bit foreign. But, when shown in a picture, it becomes an easy concept to grasp. The idea that multiple **trend lines** can spotlight problems becomes obvious when graphed. However, translating comparative **trend lines** and forecasts into a prioritized action plan is a bit more difficult. The big payoff comes from using **trend lines** as part of the routine monthly management process—that is where business transformation occurs. But, it will only happen when the whole team understands the picture and works together to close the gap between planned and actual **trend lines.**

The Mechanics of Financial Analysis

To get a better understanding of trend analysis, let's drill into the mechanics of trends and clarify ways to create and view trends. Following are definitions and illustrations of different forms of trends and related concepts:

- **Trend line** – typically this is a line through a series of points on a graph showing the average rate of increase or decrease over time. Technically this is a linear regression of the "least squares" line, which shows the "weighted average" over time.

Revenue – 24 months

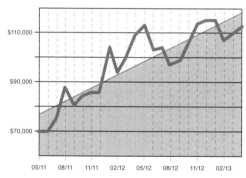

Actual Revenue - Dark Gray Line
Trend Line - Light Gray Line
Annual Growth - 24%
Growth Trend - 21%

- Growth Rate – in the above example "annual growth" is simply the amount of growth in the past 12 months over the total revenues in the prior 12 months. [(total revenue in past 12 months – total revenue in prior 12 months) / (total revenue in prior 12 months)]
- Trend Rate – shown as growth trend percentage above. This is similar to the growth rate. However, instead of using the actual monthly revenues, you substitute all the monthly values from the **trend line** and then compute the growth of the past 12 months over the total from the prior 12 months. There is a subtle difference between the growth and trend rates but it is an important distinction: the Trend Rate is a more accurate indicator of direction because it is weighted. This means it will reflect upward or downward pressure. For example, a Trend Rate will be lower than a simple Growth Rate when there is a current downward tendency or when there was an upward tendency early in the time-line.
- Long-term Trend – generally this should be a 24-month **trend line** so you can cancel out any effects from seasonality or year-end accounting adjustments. Ideally, a new long-term **trend line** should be computed every month so long-term trend changes can be monitored.
- Short-term Trend – generally the most recent six-month trend. A six-month trend can be highly influenced by seasonality and year-end accounting, so it should not be viewed in isolation. With that said, the short-term trend is where you will first see evidence of changes in direction and early warnings when something is off track.
- Acceleration and Deceleration – When a long-term trend is combined with its corresponding short-term trend, it can show if there is an upward or downward pressure on the long-term trend. Some amount of the short-term trend is simply the normal monthly or seasonal variation, but a close look can provide an early warning when the trend is really off track. If the short-term trend is actually showing an above normal increase or decrease, an early response can be very beneficial and can avert the sudden jarring most small businesses experience when business fluctuates.

- Leading Indicator – usually the short-term trend combined with enough context to spotlight emerging trends. In Corelytics, leading indicators include the short-term trend compared to the company's goals and industry benchmarks.
- Rolling Time Period – generally refers to a multiple-month time period ending in the most recent prior month. Most analysis will use a rolling six-month, 12-month or 24-month period. It takes 12- and 24-month time periods to cancel out the impact of seasonality and year-end accounting.
- Variation – to what degree there are upward and downward spikes in actual performance. For example, you might want to know how many months during a 24-month period experienced 10 percent or greater swings above or below the tong-term **trend line**. A company with more than 10 such spikes up or down (Unhealthy Company as shown below) would be considered volatile and would tend to have a lower value in the market, if it were being sold, compared to a similar company with fewer big swings (Healthy Company below).

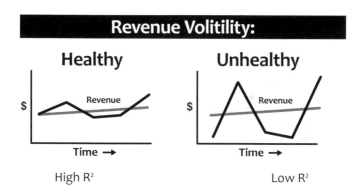

- R^2 - R-Squared or Coefficient of Determination is a number between 0 and 1.0 that describes how a **trend line** fits the underlying data. A value close to 1.0 indicates the **trend line** fits the data very well, while a value closer to 0 means the **trend line** does not fit the data very well. A high R^2 indicates the **trend line** can be a good predictor of the future. Excel has a built in function for calculating the R^2 for series of data (RSQ).

- Forecasts – extending a **trend line** or a combination of **trend lines** into the future. A simple forecast based on a single **trend line** can be very helpful but, by itself, will only tell a partial story. As explained above, the higher the R^2, the more likely a single **trend line** will be an accurate predictor of the future. Combining multiple lines can create an even better forecast. For example, Corelytics combines a long-term **trend line** and a short-term **trend line** to create a range of highly probable futures. This will be explained in more detail later.

- Benchmarks – most industry benchmarks are based on static performance data within a specific timeframe. For example, the benchmark might show average revenue growth from 2011 to 2012 along with the percent of revenue spent on payroll in 2012. Since Corelytics gets data updated monthly it is able to produce rolling 24-month benchmarks every month. This allows industry changes and benchmarks to be tracked month to month. This more dynamic form of benchmarks will ultimately become standard for small businesses much as it has been for large companies for decades. Seeing monthly fluctuations in industry benchmarks can help small business owners do much more precise planning and adjustment.

- Normalized Growth Rates – a mathematical process for calculating growth rates using a common base. Most often growth rates are computed by calculating how much growth occurred in a current period using the prior period as the starting point. The problem is that comparing multiple growth rates with different starting points will create a distorted view. Using a common starting point for two or more growth calculations eliminates the distortion and makes the actual growth comparable. For example, using the total asset value of a company as the starting point and then calculating the growth rates in multiple areas of the business relative to total assets will make these growth rates comparable and will answer the question: "How did each area we are comparing affect the total asset value of the business?"

- Normalized **trend lines** – a method for creating a common starting point for forecasts and goal **trend lines**. Our recommended approach is to use the long-term (24-month) **trend line** as the anchor point for forecasting and for establishing starting points for goal lines. Using actual performance data at a specific point in time creates radical swings in these starting points and creates meaningless forward projections.

The **trend line** illustration provided above shows an actual monthly revenue line with a lot of jagged ups and downs. The actual revenue line creates a general feel of an upward direction, but by itself does not give you a way to understand the speed and direction of overall change. If the graph only showed actual monthly revenue, you would notice there is an upward tendency, but you might not notice the drop in the last six months. The graph of actual revenue performance doesn't really give you any of the important handles needed to make business decisions. However, the year-over-year growth rate (annual growth) of 24 percent gives a more exact story; comparing that to the growth trend of 21 percent indicates there is a current downward pressure. Adding the leading indicator **trend line** (the trend for the last six months) creates a more complete picture, which could be an important call to action. Using this trend data and the graphs to visualize business performance creates a much more complete story and strong indicator of what lies ahead. This is the kind of information a management team can use to discuss and solve real business problems and then use to see if desired results are being achieved.

Understanding the Growth Rate of a Trend line

As previously described, a **trend line** is a simple concept requiring complex math. Fortunately, there are functions in Excel to calculate **trend lines**. In concept, a **trend line** is a straight line through a series of points that is the least distance from all points. Mathematicians refer to this as a "least squares" calculation, and practitioners call it a "linear regression." For business jockeys, it can simply be called the **trend line** because it is the most accurate depiction of a completely smoothed line that represents actual performance over a period of time. It is also the line most likely to be followed in the future if all else is held constant.

As soon as you have this figured out, it is important to know there can be a couple of problems with **trend lines**. First, they are going to bounce around a bit every time you add another month of data. The impact of new data is dampened significantly by the pre-existing data, but will be affected each month as new data arrives.

The second problem is a bit more subtle. When there is a big spike up or down early or late in a **trend line**, it will have a stronger influence on the **trend line** than spikes or dips toward the center. So, for example, it is possible to have a two-year graph of revenue that shows a five percent increase in revenue, but, because of a spike up early in the second year and a dip late in the same year, the trend could show a downward slope. In this case the **trend line** calculation would be negative while the annual growth rate would be positive. This can be confusing to people that don't work with statistics but it is explainable.

More importantly, the **trend line** is a better indicator of where growth is actually headed. If there were a rise early in the second year and a drop near the end, the more recent trend is downward and a good indicator of what is likely in the coming months. This subtle difference will show up with a **trend line** but would be completely invisible with a simple year-over-year percentage calculation.

Combining Long-term and Short-term Trends

If you really want to get a good understanding of where a business is heading, do a combination of long-term and short-term trends. When you connect the two, you get two important messages. First, the short-term trend (also called a leading indicator) is showing you which way your long-term trend is bending. If the short-term trend shows a slower rate than the long-term trend, it suggests an overall slowing trend in the future. On the other hand, if the short-term trend is growing at a faster rate than the long-term trend, it is an indication that you will probably experience growth above your historical long-term rate as you move forward. In essence, the short-term tells which way the long-term trend is likely to bend in the months ahead, assuming you continue doing the things you have been doing and the market continues at the same pace.

Example of 12-Month Forecast
With High Growth and Low Growth Scenarios

By hooking the short-term trend to the long-term **trend line**, you get a "Y" shaped branching line as shown above. The short-term branch either goes above the long-term line or it goes below. These lines show an area of high-growth and low-growth probabilities for your business. There is a very high probability that your business is going to land somewhere between the two scenarios in the coming 12 months.

The Corelytics team, in collaboration with students at the University of Washington, did a sample test of companies and found an 88 percent probability that each company would be somewhere within the range of its high growth and low-growth scenarios in the next 12 months, unless there was a major change in a company's business model. Though this was not a rigorous study, it did show that the combination of long-term and short-term **trend lines** can give pretty high certainty about where a company is headed. It should be mentioned that companies with highly seasonal patterns do not lend themselves to this particular forecasting method.

Of course, any company is capable of intentionally changing course and can use willpower to overcome the gravitational pull of **trend lines**.

However, it takes a lot of determination and often a great deal of money to do anything more than an incremental change that is almost certainly somewhere within the high and low scenario **trend lines.**

CHAPTER FOUR CHECK-UP

1. What can a **trend line** tell you that cannot be found in traditional financial statements?
2. What would cause a trend growth rate to be different than an annual growth rate?
3. What is the benefit of using a 24-month rolling time period for analysis rather than traditional fiscal year and fiscal quarter time periods for analysis?
4. What does the R-squared measurement tell you about a **trend line**? What is the highest score and what would that graph look like? What is the lowest score and what would that line look like?
5. What can be learned from combining a long-term **trend line** with a short-term **trend line** on the same graph?

CHAPTER FIVE

Effective Trend Line Analysis

Efficiency is doing better what is already being done.

-Peter Drucker

As we have discussed, looking at one **trend line** by itself certainly tells an important story, but putting **trend lines** together to see how they compare tells a much bigger story. For example, if you see revenues increasing at 10 percent per year, you might think you are on a great track—end of story. But wait—there's more! What if your expenses are trending up at 12 percent per year? Your current profits may look just fine today, but these **trend lines** are telling a very important story about where the business is headed.

The obvious story told by these two trends is that revenue and expenses are on a collision course. If they continue at this same rate, they will cross in the future and expenses will be greater than revenue. This is clearly not a sustainable combination of trends. But, what if expenses are intentionally high because you have been making an investment in the business that is leading to the higher growth in the future? If the **trend lines** are all about investment, the impact of the investment should begin to show up in leading indicators (short-term trends). The benefit of investment may take a few months to show up, but if it doesn't start showing desired results, management should start taking corrective action before major damage sets in. This is just one example of many combinations of **trend lines** that can show problem areas or can show the impact of changes made in the business.

Monitoring and managing these multiple **trend line** combinations can make a huge difference. Before we look more closely at various trend combinations and discuss how to spot healthy and unhealthy combinations, here's a caution to consider when comparing **trend lines**. Trend growth rates can be unclear or even meaningless when the **trend line** starts near or below zero. When the starting point is small or negative, just a little growth can generate a huge percentage rate of change. (See the discussion on normalized growth rates above in the previous chapter in the section entitled "The Mechanics of Financial Analysis" for a technique for addressing this problem.) The confusion occurs when you see a line with a very slight slope and a large percentage increase. This gets even more confusing when you compare a trend near zero with a **trend line** well above zero. For example, comparing the growth rate of profits and gross revenue will often create a confusing picture. In fact, you might see a big percentage increase in profits as compared to a very small increase in revenue and come away thinking things are looking great. But, on closer examination, you might see that the actual dollar increase in profits is very small, and, in fact, you could be generating less profit per dollar of revenue. This is where a bit of good judgment and understanding of both healthy and unhealthy trend combinations is required. It is also where comparing the slope of a **trend line** tells a more accurate story than does the percentage increase. That's why next up is a comparison of **trend line** slopes to better understand the health of the financial picture.

Healthy and Unhealthy Trends

It should be obvious that revenue must rise faster than expenses or the company is in trouble. However, since conventional financial statements don't show trend data, you may not see the problem until it is late in the game—often after expenses have exceeded revenues and the company is in a death spiral. The five mini-graphs below illustrate these healthy and unhealthy conditions.

You might assume that falling revenues are a bad thing but, as crazy as it sounds, it is actually a good thing if expenses are declining faster. Companies often dump a part of their business that is putting a drag on profitability, and this can be healthy. Companies that rid themselves of unprofitable customers or unprofitable lines of business often come back much stronger than before. This kind of pruning can be positive in the short run and position a company for growth in the long run.

The situation depicted in the bottom graph of the five shown below is not as clear as the four above it. The first observation should be that when revenues and expenses increase at the same rate, you have a company that is not getting traction—its wheels are spinning and the sand is flying but the car is not moving. It means that workload is increasing, more risk is being taken, more complexity is being built, and it is all for naught—there is no increase in profit. But there could be other not-so-obvious factors at play. Perhaps the company is making new investments in people, which may support further growth in the future without the need to continue hiring more people. But, generally, a short-term investment in future productivity will not have a big impact on a 24-month **trend line**, therefore it is unlikely that the graph with revenue and expenses traveling in parallel is a good story.

Revenue growth comparisons should also be done for all major expense categories including payroll, selling expenses, marketing, technology expenses, and others. Any time an expense line is growing faster than revenue it should be carefully examined. There will be times when a big jump in an expense category is appropriate. But when it is a surprise, this can be cause for alarm. There is no way to fix a company with expense trends greater than revenue without a major cash infusion and it's very hard to raise money when the business is upside down.

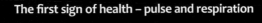

The first sign of health – pulse and respiration

Revenue Direction Changes

When you combine a long-term and a short-term **trend line**, you get a fork in the road that tells an important story. The branch of the fork representing a continuation of the long-term line is a prediction of the future if the company continues to do what it has been doing for the past 24 months (assuming we are using a 24-month **trend line**). Meanwhile, the short-term side of the fork shows the **trend line** forecasting the future if the company continues doing the same things it did over the past six months.

This is similar to our discussion about forecasting in the previous chapter, but here we are looking at directional changes in revenue. As we previously discussed, there is a high probability that actual future performance is going to be somewhere between the two lines of the fork. It is also important to know that when you have a short-term line dropping below the long-term line (in the two unhealthy charts), there is very little chance in the next 12 months that the company will achieve growth above the long-term line. In all probability, the company is on a falling

Effective Trend Line Analysis

trend that will require hard work to turn around. Conversely, a short-term line rising faster than the long-term line bodes very well. In all probability the next 12 months are going to produce results above the long-term line.

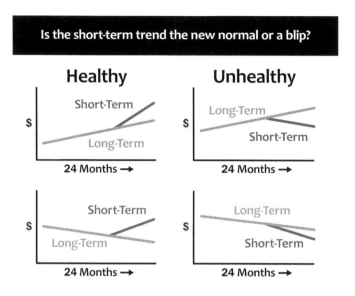

Benchmark Comparisons

The value of a company can be heavily influenced by how well it compares to industry benchmarks. It can be disappointing to discover your growing company is actually not keeping up with industry growth rates and as a result is losing value. Many companies think they are doing well just because they are growing. They have solid performance, are paying their bills, and even have money left over at the end of the month. But when it comes time to sell, they are in for a surprise: the company doing the valuation assessment tells them their value in the market is eroding because they are not keeping up with market growth rates. Of course, at that point it's too late. But if they had had the data earlier, there was certainly a lot they could have done.

Conversely, a company without any growth but holding steady may have high value in a market where the benchmarks are going downhill. Understanding market trends and benchmarks is crucial to putting your company's growth in context.

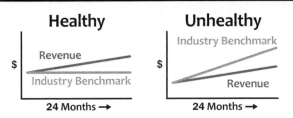

Understanding market trends and benchmarks is crucial to putting your company's growth in context.

Healthy

$ Revenue

Industry Benchmark

24 Months →

Unhealthy

Industry Benchmark

$ Revenue

24 Months →

Cash Trends

Cash trends also tell an important story; however, at best, it's only a partial story. In general, you would expect your month-end cash balances to trend upward if the company is growing. Unlike expense **trend lines**, if cash is falling while a company is growing, there is a strong indication something about growth is damaging the company by draining its resources and you need to look further for more clues. It is an important early warning sign when the cash trend is falling.

The first place to look when you find falling cash is receivables. If your customers are holding your cash and causing you to borrow to keep the engines running, you are in essence paying your customers to use your cash.

It's worthwhile to try clearing accounts receivable first. By making an effort to work with customers to clear invoices and resolve issues, many companies are able to collect these amounts they would have otherwise had to borrow to cover cash flow requirements. A relatively small cost and effort can yield a huge return on investment to get through bumps and back on a smooth track.

Jeff Hilton, Knowledge Circles
Read more: Appendix Contribution #114

However, if receivables are not going up as cash is going down, something else is draining cash. Potential causes can include an inventory buildup, balloon payments on debts, large incentive payments, staffing increases, and new systems investments. Any one of these could have a **trend line** showing they are taking more cash than can be supplied by

Effective Trend Line Analysis

revenue growth. Hopefully these expense increases are temporary or can be adjusted to fit cash availability. But if cash is being drained because of increases in COGS and you can see gross profit falling, you have a serious problem on your hands and should put a halt to growth until the underlying problem is solved.

Growth can drain cash. Cash starved but "profitable" companies go out of business every day.

Gross Profit Components

When revenue is growing, profits should also be increasing or your business is fundamentally not working. Generally speaking, the first thing business owners do when they see falling profits is to hunt for any cost that can be reduced. Unfortunately, cutting an obvious cost is probably the wrong action. The problem is most likely not in an obvious area or it would have been more conspicuous and would have been resolved a long time ago.

When revenues are going up and profits are coming down, the first thing to do is to isolate the source of the problem, which means eliminating the areas that are not the causes. One quick way to start zooming in on the problem is to look at the growth trend of COGS and SG&A expenses. One of the two is always going to be the primary cause of falling profit. If you cut the wrong one you can damage the business and, in all likelihood, will be back asking the same questions in the near future. Getting it right is important.

If COGS is going up at the same rate as revenue (or at a faster rate), you know you have found the problem. This is a big red flag signaling the need for an immediate slow down. Adding more revenue is just going to further increase direct costs and will drive the company into the ground. It is amazing how many companies have gone out of business because they grew their business and sunk their boat.

If COGS is growing too fast, there is some kind of problem with excessive costs or with prices set too low. But if COGS is falling as revenue increases and profits fall, the only other source of a problem is overheads. In this case, it is highly likely some overhead is actually a mislabeled direct cost because it is growing along with revenue growth. So, the solution is not to cut overheads but rather to correct the accounting of direct costs. If that's not the problem, then there is something going on in SG&A that is out of sync with the needs of the business and cuts are needed before the business chokes.

Everything Has a Trend

So far, we have limited our discussion of trends to numbers you would typically see on a balance sheet or P&L statement. However, this concept can and should be applied much more broadly. All KPIs and financial ratios also have **trend lines**, which should be included in the comparison process. They all help provide more perspective on business direction and can all become management "handles" used for monitoring, goal setting, and progress tracking.

For example, AR days (days of receivables outstanding) is a better non-financial metric for measuring of AR trends than is the trend in AR dollars. AR days is a ratio computed by taking the AR balance and dividing it by average monthly revenue divided by 30. This indicates how many days of revenue you have tied up in receivables. You would expect the **trend line** for the AR days to increase at about the same rate as the **trend line** for AR balances. But if revenue fluctuates a lot, AR days should follow revenue ups and downs pretty closely unless there is a collections problem.

One unique capability of Corelytics is its ability to compute AR days based on the actual revenue each month and the AR balance each month. This gives a very precise AR days number for each month. Most accounting systems would just compute the average revenue per month for the whole year resulting in a much less precise AR days metric for each month.

Converting the monthly AR days into a trend is just one more way to see if AR is running ahead of or behind sales. If AR is trending up at a faster rate than revenue, it tells you there is a fundamental problem with receivables. If this trend continues, it could dangerously reduce cash—and that's a problem everyone will see when it is too late.

Looking at internal trends is very important for understanding how the parts within your company are moving in relation to each other, but it is not the whole story. How is your company performing in comparison to your *peers*? This is where industry benchmarks play an important role.

When comparing financial performance to peer benchmarks, the main two things you want to know are: (1) their financial ratios and (2) their growth rates. There are dozens if not hundreds of numbers you might want to compare, but here's a pretty complete list to start with:

1. Revenue metrics
   a. Revenue growth – year over year and most recent quarter over quarter
   b. Revenue growth by LOB (lines of business)
   c. Revenue percentages by LOB (what percent is each LOB of total revenue)
   d. Revenue generated per FTE (full-time employee equivalent)
   e. Revenue generated per asset value – generally, total annual revenue divided by the total average asset value of the company during the year

f. Revenue from new sales

g. Revenue from established customers (when doing revenue comparisons be sure you are not including unusual one-time revenues from such things as the sale of office furniture being replaced, prize money from a contest, and many other random examples of revenue not part of your normal business operations)

2. Expense metrics

  a. Expense growth – year over year and most recent quarter over quarter

  b. Expense growth by LOB

  c. Expense as a percent of revenue

  d. Expense percentages by LOB (what percent is each LOB of total expense)

  e. Expense percentages of revenue by LOB

  f. Expense generated per FTE (full-time employee equivalent)

  g. Expense by category as a percent of revenue

    i. Payroll

    ii. Employee benefits

    iii. Contractors

    iv. Rent

    v. Infrastructure

    vi. Phone and Communication

    vii. Insurance

    viii. Interest

    ix. Sales

    x. Marketing

    xi. Meals and Entertainment

    xii. Taxes and Licenses

    xiii. Training and Certification

    xiv. Total SG&A (sales, general, and administration)

15. COGS (cost of goods sold, or direct costs associated with sale and delivery of products and services) metrics; each of the following should be reviewed for the business as a whole and also for each LOB

  a. COGS from new sales

  b. COGS from sales to established customers

    c. COGS labor

    d. COGS materials or cost of product sold

16. Profitability for the business as a whole and also for each LOB

    a. Gross profit

    b. Gross margin percent

    c. EBITDA (Earnings before interest, tax, depreciation and amortization)

    d. Net profit

5. Working Capital – Computed as short-term assets minus short-term liabilities

    a. Working capital growth rate

    b. Quick ratio (short-term assets minus inventory divided by short-term liabilities)

    c. AR Days (accounts receivable divided by average monthly revenue divided by 30)

6. Total assets and liabilities

    a. Debt to asset ratio (total liabilities divided by total assets)

    b. Long-term debt to long-term asset ratio

7. Equity

    a. Debt to equity ratio (total liabilities divided by total equity)

    b. Equity growth rate

8. Sales process

    a. New revenue generated per sales person

    b. Revenue retention and loss/cancellation

    c. Frequency of sales to established customers (repeat business)

    d. Sales funnel metrics

        i. New leads added

        ii. New leads converted to qualified prospects

        iii. Qualified prospects converted to sales opportunities

        iv. Sales opportunities converted to sales

Sales Metrics

The sales metrics listed above need to be tracked in terms of counts, percentages, and dollars. Ideally opportunities should have an estimated dollar potential; then the actual sale establishes the actual dollar value. The goal is to determine answers to these questions:

- How many new sales does it take to hit the monthly goal?
- How many opportunities does it take to generate the needed sales?
- How many qualified prospects does it take to generate the needed opportunities?
- How many new leads are required to generate the needed qualified prospects?

The answers to these questions will change depending on many factors such as the experience level of the sales person, promotional offerings being used, the quality of the leads, and the impact of marketing programs and messages used to support the selling process. Monitoring and tracking these numbers over time are important to developing an understanding of what elements are having impact. From an operations management perspective, it is important to have some version of these numbers defined as the monthly standard the sales team will have a set of numbers against which to perform. That way the marketing team will know if they are having the needed impact on new leads generated. From a benchmark perspective, the ideal numbers to compare against are ratios indicating standard conversion rates for your industry. Not many industries have this kind of data but there are peer groups and professional associations that share this information. Once you have this information, you should be able to determine answers to key questions that will help you monitor metrics such as:

- average cost of a lead
- average selling cost per new customer
- monthly conversion of leads to prospects per sales person
- monthly conversion of prospects to opportunities per salesperson
- monthly conversion of opportunities to closed sales per sales person
- monthly new revenue generated per sales person

These metrics ultimately help pinpoint where problems are occurring that are keeping you from hitting a monthly goal. Often the problem is not in the final closing step. The problem lies in another step leading up to the close, such as converting enough prospects to opportunities each month. It should also be noted that not all kinds of sales lend themselves to this kind of pipeline analysis. Strategic sales and big-ticket sales often have few target customers and many more steps in the selling process including quotes, general designs, pre-purchase testing, and so on. While the pipeline would look different, there should generally be something that can be expressed as a pipeline of activities that predictably relate to closed sales. These activities should be common within an industry and therefore comparable among companies in the same industry. If the data is not available, this is a fabulous opportunity for a professional association or a consultant that is an industry thought leader to pull together a group of companies that can build and share this data.

Operations Metrics

These metrics vary widely among industries and are crucial to managing internal performance. Setting goals and frequently monitoring progress toward those goals is the key to achieving optimal performance. Industry metrics are often produced by trade associations or consulting firms that specialize in a specific industry. Unlike financial metrics, operating metrics are very different from industry to industry and generally do not compare well. But in all cases, it is important to tie general operating metrics to financial metrics to get a complete understanding of financial implications.

Examples operating metrics include:

- Items produced
- Capacity utilization
- Total items produced divided by total direct production costs
- Items rejected and reworked
- Items delivered and accepted by customers
- Total cost per accepted item
- Total LOB profit per item
- Customer service requests received
- Customer service request average response time
- Customer service request average completion time
- Customer requests not closed within defined limit
- Total cost of customer support service function
- Total cost per completed request
- Total LOB profit per customer request

The idea here is to correlate operating metrics to bottom-line financial metrics. Most operations support systems just use standard costs and estimated profitability per item sold or service delivered because they don't usually have access to actual financial performance data. As a result there are often big surprises when operating reports don't agree with actual financial results. An annual deep dive analysis can at least help shed important light on what is working and what isn't and help create revisions to the standard data being used by the operations support system.

External Market Data

There are numerous sources for industry data that can be used to compare company performance to industry norms. However, most of the data provided by well-known business data publishers is highly flawed for small privately held companies. Most data publishers are great at benchmarking publicly held companies (companies listed on the stock exchanges and required to submit detailed financial reports for public access). Typical problems with data on small privately held companies are that the data is:

- Old – often six to 18 months old
- Not reliable – usually obtained from surveys and phone calls; the data often contains more opinion and wishful thinking than fact
- Grouped poorly – generally small and medium businesses are lumped together in a single set of statistics even though they have very different ratios and operating characteristics
- Classified incorrectly – most research data is organized using NAICS codes, which is very comprehensive but can easily be misused by businesses that can deliver multiple categories of products and services and, therefore, potentially fit the criteria for multiple codes
- Not granular enough – data is analyzed in calendar year increments so there is no information on seasonality or quarter-to-quarter trends

In addition, most industry data is not able to support short-term comparisons using trend data. Because there is generally no monthly or quarterly data available, the only way to establish a trend is to look at

Effective Trend Line Analysis

data over a three to five-year period. The longer term intervals are good for seeing macro level trends but not so good for supporting monthly and quarterly business planning. And since most market data is old, it has limited value in helping business owners detect current market trends that can have a huge short-term impact on their business.

It is also important to note that, even within a specific market niche or within an NAICS industry classification, companies of all sizes get lumped into a single category along with companies that have a variety of business models. All of these variations distort performance metrics and make businesses incomparable. When you lump businesses with very different characteristics together, you quickly get meaningless data for comparison purposes.

One of the unique capabilities of the Corelytics Financial Dashboard is its ability to generate benchmark data for very specific market segments and update this data frequently. And because Corelytics gets its data directly from accounting systems, it is much more accurate than survey data and much more reflective of what is happening in the market. Additionally, Corelytics uses a standard account structure and standard definitions for lines of business for each market, so data is comparable among the companies within an industry or a specific peer group.

In spite of the fact there are flaws in many of the industry data sources, it can still be beneficial to be aware of what data is out there and become familiar with what it shows. You should at least review this data occasionally because it is what your competitors are looking at.

Comparisons to the General Economy

Most owners of small businesses don't have time to evaluate the potential future impact the local or global economy has on their business. It's hard enough to get through the day and get the bank account reconciled occasionally. But as businesses grow and become economic dynamos, it becomes increasingly important to sync up with the broader economy.

Typically, large companies watch local and global economic conditions on a regular basis and tie their internal plans to changing conditions. This is probably not going to be a high priority for most small companies, but keeping the antenna up for news about economic conditions can be very beneficial. For small companies, this will be an informal process driven by company visionaries both internal and external to the company. The goal will be to identify trouble spots as well as to find opportunities that could open new doors. It will be up to the visionaries to use intuitive processes to translate these perceptions into strategies, goals, and actions within the company. Then the question will become, "How do we know if we are on track to achieve the goals defined by the vision, direction, and general strategies defined for the company?" This brings us back to the use of more structured processes, including trend analysis and **predictive analytics** to monitor progress and find the gaps needing focus and adjustments.

Conclusion

In summary, trends:

- are easy to understand
- show direction
- are a strong indication of future direction
- are easy to compare among peers
- show where underlying problems lie, which can't be seen in standard financial data

Monitoring internal business metrics and comparing them to industry metrics on a regular basis will help you spot areas where your business may be drifting off course relative to your industry. The goal is to spot these trends quickly and take corrective action as early as possible. The earlier corrective action is taken, the lower the cost, the easier it is to fix a problem, and the quicker you will see the benefit. Conversely, waiting until a problem is unbearable or extremely obvious can be devastating to a business. Problems that are allowed to build are not only expensive to fix, but are often damaging in many hidden ways. When problems escalate to the point they are visible to everyone, it often results in staff losing faith in management, customers losing faith in products and services, competition getting an opportunity to run ahead, and the business losing the opportunity to put profits to work to establish a stronger position in the market. If allowed to go too far, there may be no way back. All that to say, a course correction that should have been made early but that was allowed to drift can become uncorrectable.

CHAPTER FIVE CHECK-UP

1. What are the common problems with most market research data for small businesses? What are the potential problems that might result from using this data for planning?
2. What can be learned by combining a long-term trend with a short-term trend for COGS?
3. Under what circumstances would unhealthy **trend line** combinations actually hide a healthy situation?
4. Why should **trend lines** be updated and analyzed monthly instead of quarterly or annually?
5. If a company is growing and profitable, why would it matter if it is underperforming in comparison to its peers?

CHAPTER SIX

Diagnosis and Prescription

*You only have to do a very few things right in your life so long
as you don't do too many things wrong.*

- Warren Buffett

Business owners typically review financial performance as part of a monthly management routine. Operating reviews generally occur more often, sometimes weekly or even daily. Below is a series of steps that should be followed in the monthly financial review process. Big caution: There are always things to improve and the list is usually unending. The secret: Find the top three things you want to fix this month and then stop looking! If you focus on three performance improvements every month, you will make major progress over time. The worst thing you can do is: (1) do nothing or (2) try to do everything. That is where most business owners get hung up.

Your monthly financial review process should look something like this:

1. **Verify reasonability.** Take a quick look at the P&L and balance sheet to make sure there are no off-the-chart numbers. If something significant was booked incorrectly, you should be able to

spot it. Double check the activity on any questionable line item before diving into analysis.

2. **Compare to prior periods.** Look at financial statements for the last two months and determine if there are any major changes in the current data that look unreasonable. If you are using a financial dashboard, check performance numbers against the dashboard to find trends that are headed in the wrong direction.

It is important to get the books closed as soon as possible after the last day of the month. The sooner you get started reviewing performance and setting goals for the new month, the better your performance will be. Every day counts.

Usually there are a number of items that should be cleaned up before the books can be "closed" for the prior month. However, you don't need to wait until all items are finalized in order to start reviewing financial performance. Some companies wait up to two weeks to get every question answered and every adjustment completed before they start reviewing performance. This completely destroys their ability to start taking corrective actions early. Timeliness and a sense of urgency are critical to building forward momentum. One of the beauties of a financial dashboard is that you can review performance early and often without waiting for the books to be officially closed.

Timeliness and a sense of urgency are critical to building forward momentum.

Problems and Opportunities

There will always be problems to solve and opportunities waiting to be seized. Make sure the monthly review process has a balanced diet of both problems and opportunities. In reality, most problems are really opportunities waiting to be discovered. But you can also fall into the trap of confusing problems and opportunities and giving them the wrong handle. If you're an idealist, you are liable to call everything an

Diagnosis and Prescription

opportunity and confuse your team by not knowing the difference. If you are a skeptic or a cynic, you are likely to identify everything as a problem and can smother your team with pessimism. Getting the balance right is a real mark of leadership.

Example P&L Trend Analysis

All P&L line items and totals should be analyzed in the form of **trend lines**. These **trend lines** should be compared to each other to find alignment problems. They should be compared to industry benchmarks in order to see if your business is keeping pace with the industry. Goals should also be set for growth rates and for percent of revenue targets.

Example taken from the Corelytics Financial Dashboard

The above trend analysis shows that gross margin dollars (same as gross profit) fell by 1.95 percent over a 24-month period. This trend would not be visible simply by looking at the actual performance data (the heavy black jagged line). In fact, it would be potentially misleading to look at just the last two months where the actual data shows an upward bend in the line. It would be easy to think of that as an improvement, but, in the bigger picture, it is really just returning to the **trend line** from a four-month dip.

Just as important is the fact that the trend is nowhere near the goal line or industry benchmark line. This picture needs to be shared with the management team so everyone understands the problem and has the opportunity to participate in finding a solution.

Symptoms versus Problems

Most issues that show up on the P&L are usually symptoms of a deeper problem. Quite often the real problem will not be obvious and may take effort to dig out. A well-structured Chart of Accounts (COA) can help a lot, but even an imperfect one can tell a sufficiently complete story.

It can be tempting at this point to blame problems on data organization in the accounting system. There will always be room for improving the data, but don't wait for data perfection! Very often there will be two answers to a problem: (1) get the data straightened out and (2) use the data you have to make decisions about short-term solutions. Rarely should problem solving and decision-making be put on hold while data is being perfected but sometimes that is the only choice. The bottom line is that all problems, even small problems, need to be solved in the context of the big picture. Often the big picture context is enough to determine what actions are needed even when the data is inconclusive.

Ideally, the monthly review process should start with current performance trends. Next, move to longer-term performance trends and then compare them all to industry trends. Then drill into specifics with the "big picture" vision/mission/goals as the backdrop to deciding what you need to accomplish next. When you compare goals to actual performance, the first question is, "Why are we not hitting our goals (if the goals are not being hit)?" Once there is agreement on "why," you are then in a position to ask, "How do we close the gap?"

Prescriptive Action

Actions should be related to goals and to your progress against those goals. There should be a few goals to track all year long, combined with a variety of goals that may be part of a short-term focus, and then dropped once progress is made. For example, your long-term goals might be to: (1) increase revenue by 15 percent this year and (2) achieve a 38 percent gross margin. Then, every month you need to inform management of your progress toward the company goals. In addition, you should set monthly goals for the top three priorities you spot when you do your P&L review. It's not enough to say, "We want to improve this area" without being specific about how much improvement you are looking for.

One cautionary tale is about prescribing "sales" as the solution— here lies a dangerous trap. If you think sales are the major measure of success, you could get sucked into the trap of going after sales at any cost. A very large percentage of company failures are the result of going after sales first and then finding out that the company was digging a hole from which it could not escape.

Here are examples of ways to use combinations of P&L **trend lines** of revenues, expenses, ratios and totals to see problems and opportunities:

Example P&L Decisions that Improve Performance

	Example Scenarios			
Conditions	1	2	3	4
Revenue Trend	Up	Up	Down	Down
Gross Margin Trend	Down	Up	Flat	Up
Overhead Trend	Flat/Down	Flat/Down	Flat	Flat
Actions				
Increase Sales	No	Yes	Yes	Yes
Increase Prices	Yes	No	No	No
Decrease COGS	Yes	No	No	No
Decrease Overheads	No	No	Yes	No

It is important to be sure profits are improving as sales volume is improving. If profits don't rise when revenue is growing, there is a high probability that something is fundamentally wrong with the company's financial structure, and the business is going to go further downhill if the problem persists.

Surprisingly, some companies can be much more profitable by *cutting* revenue. This may sound counter-intuitive, but not all products and services are equally profitable, just as not all customers are equally profitable. Some businesses make a lot of money on most of their customers but lose a lot of profit as a result of a few very squeaky wheels. Those customers can require a great deal of hand holding and special attention. For many companies, if they could just figure out where to trim off money-losing customers or money-losing products and services, their profits would go up and they would have a much brighter future. But who wants to reduce revenues? This becomes much easier to solve when the business owner can see clearly that he or she is losing money in a specific area within the business. He/she will find it easy to make such cuts when they can see the damage being done to the business.

With these thoughts in mind, here are a few secrets to building a financial monitoring process that will keep a company on track:

1. Develop a list of metrics that get reviewed every month in order to prevent performance problems from building.

2. Analyze performance metrics in combination. For example, look at revenue and profitability together, not in isolation.

3. Convert all metrics to trends. Recognize that the current status has very little meaning by itself. Understanding trends is the only way to know if a number is headed in the right or wrong direction.

4. Use rolling 24-month and six-month trends to see if your **trend lines** are headed in the right direction and in what direction they are turning.

5. Monthly reviews should continuously include a review of:
   a. strategic direction
   b. sales performance
   c. operating performance
   d. financial performance

6. Monthly reviews should also include a combination of internal and external data. If a given market is growing at a rate of 10 percent annually and a company in that market is growing at five percent, the company is actually losing ground and may be on a path to extinction.

7. The monthly review process should always conclude with the identification of the top few big priorities. Picking too many priorities will only ensure that nothing will get fixed. Picking a few each month

makes it easier for the whole team to get on board and become part of the solution.

Benefits of Vital Signs Management

To put a final touch on the discussion about vital signs, let's summarize briefly the benefits you should gain from a good management process:

- early warning when some aspect of the business is headed in the wrong direction; ideally this will occur well before the problem becomes large
- lower cost of solving problems because early detection and early correction costs a lot less than when a problem becomes full blown
- the whole organization becomes attuned to a new way of thinking, which leads to a much greater sense of responsibility and understanding of what it means to be proactive; this becomes part of your business culture
- reduced organizational drama because you are putting out small fires rather than large ones
- better overall customer experience because they aren't subjected to major corrective actions
- company ability to take advantage of opportunity much more quickly when it arises
- greater employee trust, satisfaction and retention

Goals and gaps

Creating a goal **trend line** is a high-impact way to compare actual progress to planned progress. By displaying a **trend line** that takes you from actual performance at some point in the past to a goal in the future, you can easily observe the path that will take you to your goal. Then, if you add to the graph your actual performance **trend line**, you can determine if there is a gap between the two lines. If the goal line is above the actual performance line, you will be able see the gap. You will get a clear picture of the amount of improvement required to lift performance up to the goal line.

This approach is very different from setting budgets at the beginning of the year and doing a routine budget status review. The obvious problem with a budget review is that you really can't get a picture of the gaps and size of the monthly adjustment required to close the gap.

The Gap is the Difference between the Goal and the Trend

To be fair, the purpose of budget management is somewhat different than a goal management process. Budget development is often a line item specific process in which management works backward from a destination dollar amount and then figures out how to make each spending line item add up to the target amount. It usually takes a certain amount of guessing and force fitting, but, in the end, it all adds up to the desired target. The problem is that most budgets tend to be overly detailed and not a good vehicle for discussing financial progress with the management team. This usually results in the management team not receiving any detail on progress or on areas where budgets need to get tightened. Corrective actions often happen late in the budget cycle when desperate measures are needed to hit their budget.

Goal management using **trend line** comparisons, plan versus actual, should not be viewed as a replacement for budget management. They can, however, be complementary. Goal management is a condensed way to show where management wants to go with revenue and spending without getting tangled up in a detailed budget. When the team can see big picture progress from month to month, it becomes easier to see how their actions are making the gaps bigger or smaller. Then the team can play a meaningful role in hitting goals and supporting the overall budget plan. As we will discuss in Chapter 8, collaboration with the team to achieve goals and to take corrective actions is a well-documented best practice and a very powerful way to achieve alignment and top-notch performance.

While we are discussing goals, let's point out that there are many potential financial goals beyond revenue and expenses that are not part of typical budgeting. Businesses should have goals for decreasing debt, increasing assets, building equity value, making investments, and perhaps acquiring other companies. Most of these goals are centered on balance sheet accounts and are generally not shared with the broader management team. Yet there are times when some goals should be shared and made part of the team review process. We will expand on that point in Chapter 8.

All balance sheet goals, just like P&L goals, should be viewed as **trend lines** so they can be compared to actual performance **trend lines**. Corelytics, for example, allows trends, actual performance, and goals to be compared for all standard elements of the balance sheet. This data is automatically updated in seconds as part of the routine dashboard update process. A quick spin through the major screens sheds light on gaps and problems requiring attention. The differences between goals and actual performance are the keys to spotting gaps in all areas of the business.

Caution When Using Trends and Goals

Goals as used in the dashboard are mathematical projections with a starting date and a growth rate, which creates a goal growth line into the future. Goals as defined in the Corelytics Dashboard are not tied to a specific dollar budget. The **trend line** shows the average actual performance over a period of time and the goal line shows where the **trend line** would be if the company were achieving its defined goal.

When computing a forecast, the goal line is "normalized" to the current **trend line** so you can see what the next 12 months will look like at your current performance level versus the goal line. The picture will change each month as new performance data is added. The re-calculated 12-month forecast will show the **trend line** moving towards the goal line or moving away if the gap is getting bigger. Since the goal line begins on the **trend line**, it will move from month to month as new data is added and the **trend line** moves up or down. This will cause the 12-month forecast to change from month to month; however, the goal will always retain the same growth percentage unless changed by the owner. When explaining this to the management team, the important message is that the goal line is directional and not intended to land on a specific number. The important thing to watch is the gap between the goal line and the current **trend line,** and then make every effort to close it.

Another caution when planning growth goals is in regards to the math behind percentages. If you were to say you wanted to grow your business by 12 percent in the coming year, translating this into a one percent growth goal for each month introduces a math error. A one percent monthly growth actually produces a 12.6 percent increase in 12 months because of compounding. For most purposes, it is not important to adjust for compounding until you get to very large percentages. Even a 50 percent annual increase split across 12 months only produces an 8.8 percent error, which is almost certainly much less than the variance created by monthly swings. If anything, splitting the 12-month goal into individual monthly goals will only increase the final goal and everybody wins if either goal is hit! The same math error concept applies to converting annual goals to quarterly goals, but the error is smaller and less relevant. So, rather than creating a complex description of the math, we tend to leave it out of our calculations.

Vital Signs Summary

Vital signs play an important role in many aspects of business management. They should be central to strategic and tactical planning as well as integral to early warning processes. Without them, it becomes easy to take short cuts that can be damaging to the business. With the proper monitoring of vital sign metrics, it becomes much more apparent what actions are needed to create sustainable business performance.

Monitoring your company's vital signs can help you maintain a steady course as you move your business toward defined goals.

Monitoring your company's vital signs can help you maintain a steady course as you move your business toward defined goals. And by keeping those metrics visible, everyone stays aware of what is working and what is not and of what they need to do to contribute to success.

Of course, none of this is automatic, and it all takes a lot of effort to realize the full benefit. But it takes more than data to achieve success. It requires management disciplines, well-defined processes, and the necessary steering mechanisms so that management can hit a strategic bullseye with a high degree of certainty.

CHAPTER SIX CHECK-UP

1. Who should participate in the monthly diagnosis and prescription process? What should their roles be?
2. How can you tell the difference between a symptom and an underlying problem?
3. Would you expect to see more volatility in a short-term trend (leading indicator) or a long-term trend (lagging indicator)? Why? Which is best for forecasting the future?
4. What is a gap, as described in this chapter, and what should be done when you find one?
5. When is growing revenue a bad idea?

CHAPTER SEVEN

Planning

Drive thy business or it will drive thee.

-Benjamin Franklin

Putting strategic plans, dashboards, performance analysis, task plans, and operating reports into the blender and producing a business road map is as much an art form as it is a science. In the end, it is up to the business owner/leader to distill the essence of this concoction and serve it to the management team in a way that they can swallow, digest, and ultimately be inspired to meaningful action.

This is a delicate undertaking. It sounds a lot like alchemy—the ancient mythical process of turning rocks into gold. If there is *too much* information or if it is unclear, the team will come away confused and unfocused. If there is *not enough* information, the management team will create its own explanations to fill in the picture, causing rumor mills and creating an environment of uncertainty.

That's why, in this chapter, we look at the process of pulling the pieces together with a healthy dose of reality in order to create a clear picture for the owner and for the management team. This becomes the framework that drives the selection of priorities and areas of focus for the company. In addition, we will look at the way the planning process can set the stage for ongoing learning, for fine tuning business focus, and for building a high-performance company. Chapter 8, then, will explore ways the management team can work the plan to deliver the results that matter most to businesses.

Realities, Barriers, and Solutions

Let's face it: analysis of financial and operating metrics is rarely the strong suit of entrepreneurs. Most are not driven by skills in financial analysis and operating metrics. They launch their businesses because they have a passion for some product or service they want to bring to the market. Once they begin building their businesses, however, they soon realize, often to their surprise and disappointment, that a great deal of analysis and problem solving are required to make a business hum. Some entrepreneurs resist doing needed analysis and planning. But done, it must be. Eventually, if they want to survive, they will either hand the responsibility over to someone else or buck up and do it themselves. If they delay too long, they will discover there is no room left for needed corrections and will have no choice but to shut their doors.

In more structured companies, planning is done on a predictable schedule and the whole team knows that adjusting the plan is a continuous, living process. In contrast, early stage companies, where everything relies on the owners' instincts, or in small businesses, where a few people wear many hats, this process tends to occur at more random intervals and tends to lack process and follow-through.

Ultimately, owners must find an approach that will get the job done and produce needed results. One high-impact approach is to get some professional reinforcements. This could include joining a peer group for owners and CEOs, hiring a consultant to provide monthly analytical expertise (perhaps a "fractional CFO"), hiring a business analyst or operations manager, or building a board of advisors that participates in business analysis and planning. Some combination of these actions can do a lot to strengthen the planning process, but, ultimately, the owner still has to make the final decisions.

The peer group landscape has changed with the availability of consolidated and real-time financial data. Peers and experts have to come in and ask the tough questions. A peer group makes it comfortable and gives you confidence to navigate the tough decisions and evolutions of a business.

Josh Peterson, Bering McKinley
Read more: Appendix #111, Peer Groups

To get the best results from limited time, owners should set aside dedicated blocks of time with the single purpose of business review and planning. Even if most of this work is delegated to others, some will always need to be performed by the owner. The more this work can be pre-scheduled and structured, the more likely it is to get done and the less disruptive it will feel to the owner and the organization. Additionally, just as important as structure and process are automated information systems and good analytical tools. Good tools can eliminate the time drain dealing with data collection and analysis and allow the owner to focus more on vision, goal setting, priorities, and planning.

In summary, best results occur when:

- planning and analysis are done on a regularly scheduled and frequent basis
- the process is structured
- information systems and analytical tools are used to minimize manual data collection and analysis
- the owner spends more time on priority setting and planning than on data acquisition and analysis
- the owner involves the team in the planning process; everyone gets on the same page

The complete monthly cycle should feel like a heartbeat. There will likely be slight variations at quarter-end and at year-end, but the basic structure should be the same month in and month out. As companies get more agile there may be a series of mid-month reviews on targeted functions that need the tightest controls. Regardless of how the work gets done, the monthly process should include the following:

1. Collect and analyze the data.
2. Determine where focus is most needed.
   a. the most important problems to be fixed
   b. the most important opportunities to be seized
3. Adjust or set general direction, goals, and priorities .
4. Communicate directions, goals, and priorities to the organization; engage in a collaborative problem solving and action planning process.
5. Document agreed upon solutions and task plans; adjust job responsibilities where necessary.
6. Track progress and make needed adjustments.
7. Return to step one and repeat cycle.

Planning with the Team in Mind

Before we dive further into the planning process, let's take a look at the psychology of what we are trying to accomplish. If we get the planning right but the delivery is wrong, the end result can be way off track and damaging to the business. So, let's discuss a few pointers on what should be accomplished in the plan in order to get the best traction and outcomes. The ultimate goal of the plan is to serve three main purposes:

1. Gain a clear understanding of what is happening in the business.
2. Set the vision and direction for the company.
3. Clearly communicate priorities and define areas of focus for the organization.

The ultimate outcomes achieved by a business have more to do with how people perceive and respond to direction and less to do with the accuracy and correctness of the plan.

There is an important subtlety we will underscore repeatedly in this chapter and throughout the book: The ultimate outcomes achieved by a business have more to do with how people perceive and respond to direction and less to do with the accuracy and correctness of the plan. Many owners get this part backwards and can't understand why it is such a struggle to move the team forward. All you need is a correct and clear plan, right? Not true!

Actually, the way the plan is communicated to the team will have a major impact on how the team responds and how they commit to needed actions and changes. To refine this further, there are two basic alternatives when presenting the plan to the team: (1) present the goals and priorities along with the specific actions the owner wants the team to take, or (2) present the goals and priorities and then ask the team to participate in a problem solving discussion wherein the team defines the actions that need to be taken. In other words, the business owner or senior manager can choose to tell the team what it will do, or they can invite the team to collaborate on key business issues and jointly decide on needed actions. We will discuss the psychology of these two approaches in more detail in Chapter 8, "Activating Your Team."

For now, let's acknowledge it takes a blend of both; however, collaboration creates a greater sense of team commitment and a higher probability of success. Knowing that collaboration is an important part of the process will help us think through what needs to be accomplished in the planning process. Given that collaboration is crucial, this chapter will focus on a planning process with team collaboration in mind. Chapter 8 will deal with the process of getting the management team engaged and on the right track.

Planning with Process in Mind

As we have discussed in earlier chapters, standardized processes used by a company are the keys to driving repeatable action and to business performance. So, if a company is not achieving its desired results, the first question should be, "Do we have a problem with our processes?" There are only three possible answers to this question, plus an infinite number of blends of these answers:

1. We don't have a clearly defined process – it does not exist.
2. The process does not produce the needed outcome – it doesn't work.
3. Staff are not able to execute the process correctly – staff can't do it.

One or more of these will explain why a company is off track. Fixing the wrong problem can be damaging to a company. For example, replacing people when you have a process that doesn't work will generally only make matters worse. Also, bear in mind that the process for hiring the right people may be what is broken—i.e., a process that is not working. When the team and the processes are working correctly there should be no gap between the track the company is actually on and the intended track. If there is a gap, something is not working.

Notice that none of these three basic problems are the fault of the staff. If top management blames the staff, they are setting themselves up to have repeat problems. Top management is responsible for ensuring the right processes are in place and the right people are being asked to follow the processes. Again, just replacing people will not fix process problems unless, of course, you are looking for a person capable of creating and managing process.

Top management is responsible for ensuring the right processes are in place and the right people are being asked to follow the processes.

One more piece to this puzzle: when staff understands the process and are following the process correctly and the desired results are still not being produced, the only thing left is the process itself. If the process is not working there are two possible reasons: *either the process is flawed or the expected outcome is wrong.* Both of these are management issues. Here again it is very possible to draw the wrong conclusions and you could do damage by fixing the part that is not broken.

When there is a difference between actual and intended tracks, just realizing there is a difference is the all-important first step. The next step is to make decisions about what actions are needed to move from the current track to the desired track. This means either changes to processes or people. Then the real work begins. The processes of monitoring, managing, and adjusting are what put things on a track that can achieve the desired results. Assessments of actual and intended results along with monitoring business process metrics must be conducted continuously. Without constant feedback and correction any results achieved will be purely accidental.

All processes should include some form of information sharing and feedback; however, the information must have purpose and meaning. Information and insight have value when they help you get traction and move the business forward. This is how organization alignment is achieved. Remember, though, it is a continuously moving target and requires continuous improvement. The defining difference between companies that stay small and the companies that are able to grow and build economic value is how effectively their processes work and how well information is used to integrate people and processes

With this backdrop it should be clear that planning is all about process, people, and information. Of course, resources and more specifically finances are part of this equation, but they are really there to support the process, people, and information elements of the plan. By boiling this down to its essence it becomes easier to ask the simple question: what should be in the plan?

The Living Plan

Consulting firms and business schools often promote a business planning concept that can be a total waste of time and money. The classic idea is that a plan is a document organized like a book with a complete table of contents outlining all the building blocks that comprise the business. It describes the company and where it is headed, complete with organization, finance, product, service, sales, marketing, and operating plans. And don't forget to include the market and competition assessment plan. This can be a 50 to 100-page document.

At the opposite end of the spectrum is the "One-Page Plan," which is highly condensed and very easy to understand.[8] This concept goes straight to the point with mission, vision, goals, and milestones and is easy for everyone to digest. The danger with both of these concepts is they can remain static and end up on someone's shelf, never to become part of the management process. While I much prefer the one-page plan because it is easy for the management team to absorb and align with, the plan needs to go one step further and become part of a monthly review process where key elements change every month. The goals and mission should remain the same, but the primary areas of focus, top priorities, and major milestones need to constantly change. Hopefully the change will be slight from month to month, but if it's not changing and adapting, it is not moving with the business and is therefore irrelevant.

The Agile Plan

Here's where we can stir in some additional concepts from Eric Ries's book, *The Lean Startup*, that make planning a highly dynamic process. Eric takes key concepts from the world of lean manufacturing and lessons from Toyota and applies them to business development and planning. His book includes concepts like MVP (minimum viable product) to get an early jump into the market and test ideas to see what works in the real world. He talks about making "pivots"—rapid adaptations to lessons learned in the market. He also proposes BML (build-measure-learn) as a method for analyzing results and knowing when you are on or off track. These concepts can save companies a lot of time and money. They convert the learning process to a short interval cycle followed by quick-response adaptations and then back to the market with the next iteration. Central to the message is keeping the number of variables for each new iteration to a manageable minimum. With too many variables being changed at one time, the plan becomes difficult to manage, making it hard to know which changes are working and which are not.

My recommendation is to identify three top priorities every month and make a serious push on them with everyone involved to the extent possible. Of course, there will be a lot more going on than this, but the big three should get everyone's attention and be drilled into bedrock. This part of the planning process will be discussed further in the next chapter.

Planning for Action

Now let's look a bit deeper into what it takes to make the monthly planning cycle work best. The first step, regardless of who does it, is to review the numbers and reports that show how the organization is functioning. The most fundamental metrics should come from financial data generally found in accounting systems. Ultimately, all operating results get translated into financial performance data that can be quantified and monitored. Financial data can point to areas where operating problems exist and make it possible to understand the relative priority of topics needing attention.

If there are defined goals or industry benchmarks it becomes much easier to see gaps and spot performance problems. Sometimes problems will arise in areas where there are no established metrics. Then it will be necessary to define new data collection processes along with processes for monitoring and managing activities. The goal is to build information that can be used by the owner for strategic planning and by the team for detailed action planning and performance tracking. The goal for the owner and the team as a whole is to get a solid understanding of how things *are* progressing in comparison to how they *should* be progressing.

Comparing Trends, Goals, Benchmarks, and Forecasts

In many ways, managing company performance data is like managing a stock portfolio. There are lots of moving parts, of which some are established, some are new, some are stable, and some are at high risk. Responding to every fluctuation in your stock portfolio would be overreacting and would get expensive very quickly. In the same way, reacting to every fluctuation in your various business metrics would drive everybody crazy, and could be costly both in monetary terms and in terms of team psyche. However, if you find multiple indicators pointing to an off-track condition, you now have multiple reasons (corroborating evidence) for sounding the alarm, and a much greater probability of being on target. At that point you are responding to something with broader meaning and not simply making knee-jerk decisions. When there is a broader rationale, it becomes easier for everyone to understand and support a needed correction.

Let's take the stock portfolio analogy a step further. You may have experienced the disappointment of looking at your investments and seeing some doing very well while others looked bad. Overall, the combined good and bad performers make the total portfolio look pretty mediocre. That's when your broker steps in and says, "Don't be disappointed, it's all about diversification." But, while you never want to be completely reliant on a single stock or even on a single sector, diversification is not an excuse for lack luster performance. Here's where the broker has the wrong picture. Smart investing should include diversification but that doesn't mean you should intentionally pick poor investments. Smart diversification means a blend of different investments that spread risk in a way that leads to an overall positive outcome. We won't solve this here, but settling for a blend of investments that includes losers is not smart. In the same way, allowing your business to harbor loser functions is not smart. This means you have to know how to spot the loser areas.

We have observed companies that knowingly allow some parts of their business to underperform, rationalizing it by saying they must offer loss leaders, or door openers, in order to get the higher value sales opportunities. Or they may view the low performing areas as something they need to offer as part of a "complete" solution expected by their customers. All of these are important considerations, but the thought process needs to go further. The question should be: how do you stretch the team to figure out solutions for making problem areas perform better? There are usually no silver bullets, but by showing the team the numbers and letting them see the performance problem and by actually asking them to help find a solution, you can move everyone away from "default thinking." We will cover more on team motivation in Chapter 8. The key point here is that by using various forms of measurement and comparison along with internal and external data, a compelling story can be developed and a logical goal can be set to launch new awareness and an invigorated sense of direction in all areas of the business—all of which leads to top notch results for the business.

Going back to our analogy, if your stock portfolio is performing below the market as a whole, you know you have a problem unless you are intentionally going after a highly conservative, low-risk, and low-return portfolio. But even a low risk portfolio can be compared to benchmarks for similar profiles to see if performance is above or below market norms for that investment profile. It is the comparisons that create perspective and help the owner decide where to focus and contribute to the story that will drive team response.

Small businesses, unlike large companies, usually skip the step of using industry benchmarks to monitor growth and performance. We have seen hundreds of businesses that thought they were doing just fine until they saw their peers doing better. It can be a real surprise when the business owner finds out his or her 10 percent annual growth is half the average growth rate being experienced by companies in that market. In reality, a company getting 10 percent growth in a 20 percent market is losing ground. This often translates into falling out of touch and potentially becoming irrelevant in the market. In today's hyper economy and global reach, this can happen quickly. But it's still a chilling reality punch when a more in-touch competitor steps in and grabs customers and market share when everyone thought they were safe from intrusion.

Slow growth by itself is not a problem. It's when a company is not keeping pace in its market that there is cause for concern. The process of natural selection in an evolving ecosystem will tend to push slower, out-of-touch players to the margin where they will fade away. Similarly, the guys that are way out in front of the market have a different kind of concern. While this can be a fabulous problem to have, the front runners are often the guys that have "overheating engines" and when they hit a significant bump in the road they discover they can't keep up the momentum and don't have a solid and sustainable footing. The next thing you know they hit a bump that causes them to fly apart, at which point there is probably no way to recover. Of course, the ones that do make it big and keep the momentum going are the rare ones you hear about that everybody wants to emulate. But no company continues on an unending growth path. Even Microsoft, which was once the envied growth engine, has had flat stock values for many years and is struggling to build a new identity and avoid atrophy.

All businesses need to constantly monitor performance and identify the areas requiring the most attention—playing their best game with the team they have. There are always problems to be found and fixed. There is always some area in the business that is underperforming. And there are often team members that are not a good fit. Understanding where performance problems are coming from is the real trick. Rarely are problems company-wide but some are. Figuring out which problems are company-wide and which are confined to a specific area in the business, perhaps a specific LOB, is the first step in zooming in and understanding where improvements are needed. Fixing problems that have little benefit can be a waste of time.

The big challenge is to understand how all the moving parts fit together. It generally requires a hunt for the patterns with multiple clues pointing to the same problem area. Market benchmarks, peer group data, current actual performance data, and planned performance targets all combine to paint a more complete picture of where problems and opportunities lie.

LOB Perspectives

As companies grow, it is common to split various products and services into separate lines of business (LOBs). There are many ways to define lines of business, so we need to explore this further to make sure the concept is conducive to planning and ongoing management. A key concept to remember is that LOBs are "a business within a business," which means they have all elements of a business including their own revenue, direct costs, overheads, and profitability. By understanding financial performance at the LOB level, you can tune each LOB, resulting in overall improvements in the combined business. Companies that don't manage at the LOB level are forced to diagnose problems in aggregate, often making adjustments far too blunt to fix the areas actually needing to be fixed. When you can zoom in on problems at the LOB level, you can have much greater assurance you are actually fixing something that is going to be beneficial to the whole.

For most companies, individual LOBs have very different performance characteristics. An LOB for product sales is going to perform very differently from an LOB that is all about service or maintenance. The costs and margins are different and the overall profitability is going to be different. Separating revenues, COGS, and overhead expenses by LOB is a crucial step in understanding LOB performance and potential problem areas.

Before we go further, we need to be clear that small profits in one LOB do not automatically signal you have a problem. But, if that LOB with small profits should be generating a bigger profit according to industry standards, then it is time to take a closer look. There still may be plenty of intentional reasons for the performance you are getting, but make sure it's part of the plan and not an accident.

An additional benefit of dividing a company into LOBs is the logical structure it provides for assigning management responsibilities. LOBs create a logical framework for performance measurement and incentive compensation. In the early stages of company development, it is common to have staff working across LOB boundaries. But over time, as LOB volume increases, it is natural to split responsibilities along LOB lines. Then, as competencies are developed in each LOB, the business can expand by replicating its successful LOB template in another geographic location. In some cases, owners will build an LOB and then sell it off keeping the rest of the company and continuing to build with a more narrowly focused business model. In any case, the skills and management processes required to successfully manage multiple LOBs are what is needed to make a business "scalable" and able to grow.

LOB performance analysis requires that revenues and expenses are identified and posted correctly in the accounting system. If this part is sloppy, there is no way to adequately manage performance. Some companies use departmental accounting (class accounting if you use QuickBooks) to split out LOB data. A common problem is defining too many departments or LOBs. Some companies take this way too far; They end up with many departments and way too much detail to manage. The result is a lack of precision, not more. Adding to the confusion, the literature on this topic is remarkably inconsistent. So, here we adopt definitions taught in a typical business school:

- LOB – line of business; an area within a company with its own distinguishable revenues and direct costs and a common subdivision within the industry in which it operates. Some companies will create LOBs unique to their business with no relationship to industry standard LOBs. These highly unique LOBs can be useful for internal management purposes but make it impossible to compare LOB performance and metrics to industry benchmarks. One way to maintain both industry standard LOBs and unique internal LOBs is to use a financial dashboard such as Corelytics to track the industry standard LOBs and the accounting system to track company-unique LOBs. This allows the best of both worlds.

- Revenue Center – generally a subdivision of an LOB with a focus on a specific product or service or family of products and services. These often don't have completely distinguishable direct costs and therefore are calculated or derived from other numbers. Generally a business will have a few core revenue centers and everything else is left unassigned. Revenue centers are sometimes used as the basis for incentive compensation and may be used to track special marketing programs where a vendor participates in cost sharing and co-marketing expenses.
- LOB Profitability – since LOBs typically have identifiable direct costs, it is generally easy to compute gross profit. Overheads are usually allocated to each LOB based on a formula, generally a percentage of revenue. This allows each LOB to have a complete bottom line analysis and makes it very clear how an LOB is contributing to or detracting from the performance of the company as a whole. Generally, LOBs are defined to encompass all aspects of a company so the sum of activity of all LOBs is equal to the total for the company. This is an important assumption if overhead expenses are going to be split out to each LOB based on percentage of revenue.
- Revenue Center Profitability – typically this analysis stops with gross profit per revenue center. Most companies tracking revenue centers will not attempt to have every revenue source be attributed to a revenue center.

Occasionally companies will use LOBs as a way to describe divisions or multi-location businesses. This not a standard way to use the definition. Instead, an LOB should be thought of as a way to view a certain type of business activity that can cut across multiple divisions or business locations. So, in the case of a retailer with 10 stores and a central office, the stores would not be considered LOBs. They could be business units, locations, divisions, offices, or sites, but not LOBs. Let's say each location sold products and customer training classes and also did custom fitting and alterations. Each of these areas might be considered LOBs. LOB performance would be tracked in each store and also combined in consolidated company reports. If this company was using Corelytics, each store manager would get his or her own dashboard and would be able to see his or her store's total performance as well as the performance of each LOB. They could set financial goals for their store and for each LOB in the store and could monitor progress toward their goals. At the same time, the central office would be able to monitor the performance of each store as well as the combined performance of all stores. Corporate could also monitor the combined performance of each LOB company-wide. For larger chains or groups, the central organization would also be able to get benchmarks derived from their own stores along with industry benchmarks. This enables the organization as a whole to compare its internal peer groups and promote best-in-class performance.

Example Income Statement with Three LOBs

Jerry's Tech Company
LOB Income Statement (P&L)
For Quarter Ending June 30, 2013

Income	Managed Services	% of Rev	Product Sales	% of Rev	Projects	% of Rev	Total	% of Rev
Sales	280,000	33%	235,000	28%	330,000	39%	845,200	100%
Cost of Goods and Services Sold								
Product Costs	0	0%	180,000	21%	0	0%	180,000	21%
Technical Staff	160,000	13%	5,000	1%	75,000	9%	24,000	28%
Technical Contractors	35,000	4%	0	0%	85,000	10%	120,000	14%
Commissions Paid	0	0%	45,0000	5.3%	0	0%	45,0000	5.3%
Total COGS	195,000	23%	230,000	27%	160,000	19%	585,000	69%
Gross Profit	85,000		5,000		170,200		260,200	
Expenses								
Marketing	8,282	1.0%	6,951	0.8%	9,767	1.2%	25,000	3.0%
Infrastructure	3,975	0.5%	3,336	0.4%	4,688	0.6%	12,000	1.4%
Depreciation & Amortization	1,988	0.2%	1,668	0.2%	2,344	0.3%	6,000	0.7%
Salaries	9,276	1.1%	7,785	0.9%	10,939	1.3%	28,000	3.3%
Utilities	298	0.0%	250	0.0%	352	0.0%	900	0.1%
Rent	1,656	0.2%	1,390	0.2%	1,953	0.2%	5,000	0.6%
Interest	265	0.0%	222	0.0%	313	0.0%	800	0.1%
Taxes	29,503	3.1%	22,243	2.6%	31,254	3.7%	80,000	9.5%
Total Expenses	52,243	6.3%	43,847	5.2%	61,610	7.3%	157,700	18.7%
Net Income - From Operations	32,757	4%	-38,847	-5%	108,590	13%	102,500	12%
LOB Net Contributions		32%		-38%		106%		

Industry LOB Benchmarks

For industries where LOB benchmarks are available, it can be very helpful to compare your LOB performance to industry-specific LOB data. Unfortunately, there are additional complexities to understand when using industry LOB data. Companies in the same industry often have different mixes or different proportions of business coming from their LOBs. These proportion differences can result in completely different performance patterns and very different results. For example, in the restaurant business, those specializing in a comprehensive bar experience look very different from a fast food café or a restaurant specializing in catering. There are many restaurants that do all these things to some extent but the mix and area of emphasis is different, resulting in entirely different business models that are not comparable. Care must be taken when simply looking for catering benchmarks so that comparisons are not being made to restaurants where this is a minimal or occasional part of the business as compared to one where it is a central focus. But once you have benchmarks for truly comparable business models, it can be extremely useful to track and compare them.

Finding the Gaps

When assessing performance of a business, there are two major areas where performance gaps can exist: (1) a gap between a goal and actual performance, and (2) a gap between a benchmark and actual performance. A gap can exist with any measurement that has a **trend line** and a goal line. This includes any measured financial or operating metric with an associated goal or industry benchmark. There could be a gap between a revenue growth goal set at 15 percent and the actual growth rate of 10 percent. Or there could be a gap between the goal for payroll set at 35 percent or revenue and actual performance at 40 percent. But, as we have discussed, finding that a gap exists is just the first step; closing a gap can take multiple steps and be very challenging.

The all-important first step is to do a survey of gaps. The second step is to identify which gaps you want to focus on first. It's not always going to be the biggest gap that requires the most immediate attention. A large gap in a new area of the business may just show that the company is going through a learning curve and the results are as expected. A small gap, on the other hand, may exist in a stable bedrock part of the business where a small shortfall is going to have big impact on the business and corrective action is highly urgent.

In most companies, there will be more gaps than time and resources to address them, so decisions need to be made and priorities set. Aside from the fact that you can't fix everything and you certainly can't do it all at once, there is another important consideration. When a defined gap involves the work efforts of many people in an organization, the process of correction may need to be broken into a series of steps over a period of time.

Our standard recommendation is to focus on three gaps each month to take to the management team for discussion and action. Some gaps can be addressed with little fanfare and unceremoniously resolved by a single individual. These should be handled with minimal discussion and involvement of the management team. For example, if working capital is falling and the quick ratio is below a target level, it may be obvious that some short-term debt could be moved to long-term debt. This can be a conversation between the owner and an accountant and the bank— and the problem is solved. This would not be one the management team should spend time on.

It takes good judgment to know when a problem should be brought to the management team. Some gaps are best addressed by the owner and some should just be ignored. Management should focus on just a few gaps at a time or they run the risk of creating an unproductive frenzy. Sorting and prioritization is part of the monthly assessment process and, if well facilitated, will keep efforts on a stable and consistent track. Once decisions have been made as to which gaps should be taken to the management team, it is time to put some basic discussion documentation together and get ready for the meeting.

But we are not ready yet! Finding gaps related to goals and benchmarks is only the first step in the review. The second step is to search for **trend lines** headed for a collision in the future. You may have already found the problem trends by looking for gaps. Very often a **trend line** with no gap is assumed to be a safe bet, yet there could still be a potential disaster in the making. Even without an obvious gap showing, the **trend line** could be headed in an unhealthy direction relative to another **trend lines**. (Refer back to the discussion in Chapter 5 on healthy and unhealthy **trend line** combinations). Only after gaps and potential unhealthy conditions are reviewed should priorities be set and preparations made for the management team review. Sorting through the various performance metrics to find the top three priorities is an ideal function to delegate to an advisor or consultant.

Steps to Effective Analysis and Planning

Following is a proposed outline of the major steps in the analysis, planning, and preparation for management decision-making and team collaboration on business performance. We will use the Corelytics Dashboard as a way to illustrate the use of an analytical tool that eliminates the need for time consuming data analysis.

1. Start with the dashboard that calculates short-term and long-term trends for all financial variables in a business.

    a. Look for early-warning signs of potential future problems.

        i. Start with leading indicators that show performance below goals (shown as red in Corelytics).

        ii. Drill down to long-term **trend lines** to determine if problems with leading indicators indicate emerging new problems or a normal performance "blip".

        iii. Look for **trend line** conflicts. For example, are total expenses growing faster than revenue? (More of these "healthy" and "unhealthy" **trend line** combinations were discussed in Chapter 5, "Effective Trend Analysis.")

    b. Review operating metrics, KPIs and financial ratios (collectively called metrics).

        i. Look for metrics that are performing below recommended thresholds.

        ii. Review metrics **trend lines** to see which ones are improving and which ones are having problems over time.

    c. Identify the "Big Three" priorities.

        i. Select the **trend lines** that are showing the biggest problems—unhealthy financial **trend line** combinations that will have the biggest negative impact on the company in the near future or metrics and KPIs showing the biggest declines.

        ii. Single out areas showing exceptionally strong performance because they may call for more rapid expansion than had been previously planned. Areas of exceptional performance may become the basis for redefining the business or possible geographic expansion through acquisitions or other actions that have not been part of the planning process.

d. Make a list of other areas that are important but not top priority. Keep a running list of problem areas and high-performance hot spots not selected in the Big Three. There may be persistent topics on this list that can be addressed outside of the monthly management team process.

2. Review top priorities from prior month.

a. Evaluate progress in priority areas. Are current numbers showing signs of improvement? Is there evidence that traction is occurring? Is the traction enough to warrant removing the topic from the Big Three?

b. Determine if any of last month's top priorities continue as high priority this month. Is there reason to believe continued focus is crucial to achieving defined goals? Can previous hot items be dropped and replaced by more pressing items?

3. Consider strategic plan and priorities.

a. Do any goals need to be modified?

b. Are any special reminders of strategic direction needed?

c. What are the strategic priorities that should be highlighted at every management meeting?

4. Prepare management team meeting materials.

a. Summary of progress from prior month

b. Summary of top three priorities for coming month

   i. Show actual, goal, benchmark, and forecast if available.

   ii. Describe the gap between goal and actual performance.

c. Presentation of any goal changes and relationship to strategic plan

d. Agenda for management meeting

   i. Recap of business strategies and general direction

   ii. Assessment of progress since last month

   iii. Current performance graphs

   iv. Changes or adjustments to goals

   v. Priorities for next month

   vi. Summary

      1. Top priorities

      2. Revised goals

      3. List of items not yet in Big Three status

Conclusion

The assessment process involves a lot of heavy lifting. For smaller companies, it will fall to the owner to do most of the work. As the company grows, it becomes increasingly important to have more people involved in the assessment process. As we get ready to move into Chapter 8, "Activating Your Team," the final caution is to make sure that delegating assessment is not the same as deciding how problems are going to be solved. This can quickly shut down the collaboration process if the people with responsibility for delivering results are taken out of the planning loop. They will soon become disconnected and ultimately converted from active participants into passive actors.

Moving from assessment to activating the team is where the magic happens, and that's the topic of our next chapter.

 **CHAPTER SEVEN CHECK-UP**

1. How frequently should planning be done in a small business?
2. How is agile planning different from traditional planning? Why is it important?
3. Why would a business owner want to use a dashboard to check business status if the accounting books have not been closed for the month? What are the risks? How significant are the risks? What are the benefits of getting results before the books are closed?
4. What role should the company team play in the planning process?
5. What are the conditions that would cause an issue to be considered as one of the "Big Three" priorities for monthly management attention and focus?

CHAPTER EIGHT

Activating Your Team

It is only as we develop others that we permanently succeed.

-Harvey S. Firestone

Our research shows that less than 30 percent of small businesses share meaningful financial data with their staff. Is it any wonder that these same companies feel a disconnect between management and staff? Is there any surprise that small businesses struggle to stay afloat?

Building a team and getting its members to pull in the same direction is the key to business success. You can do a lot of things right, but if the team isn't working together in a cohesive way it is very likely that the business will fail. The big question is: how much financial data should be shared with company employees? We know that sharing income statements and balance sheets with staff creates more questions than answers. These traditional financial statements are important but not very helpful for most management decisions and much less helpful for staff. This is where financial dashboard graphics with summary financial data can play an important role. Dashboard trends and graphs can be used to portray a picture of business performance that everyone can understand.

When the picture shows the track you are on right next to the track on which you want to be traveling, the big "aha!" moment arrives for everyone. Once this is clear, the next step is to convert understanding into action that can move the company to the intended track.

In this chapter we will focus on information that should be shared with the team as well as the processes that drive information sharing, action planning, and results delivery. Here is a summary level list of the steps that should be continuously repeated to put a company on the right track and keep it there over time. This applies to small and large organizations within any business or industry.

Management Process Overview

Management Process	Team Involvement
1. Evaluate business performance.	1. Monitor individual and team metrics.
2. Set/adjust goals and priorities.	2. Brainstorm solutions to gaps.
3. Meet with the team to review performance and plan for the coming weeks. a. Update metrics to be monitored. b. Assign due dates and owners to new tasks and corrective actions.	3. Recommend multiple alternative solutions to management.
4. Track and report status.	4. Take ownership of assigned actions.
5. Make corrections and adjustments. a. Take corrective actions on tasks and initiatives that are not hitting targets. b. Review results of completed tasks to ensure quality; make corrections where needed.	5. Anticipate potential issues and identify potential solutions (always bring potential solutions when raising an issue).
6. Return to step 1 above.	6. Ask for help early, not on the due date.

This is a very basic description of the essential management steps. A more extensive version of this outline was presented near the end of

Activating Your Team

Chapter 7, "Planning." We will elaborate on how these steps relate to team involvement in the pages ahead. But, before we do that, we need to point out that if any of these steps are skipped, the management team is likely to fall out of sync with the needs of the business and business performance will not be optimal.

At the same time, there should be a corporate culture in place that is receptive and responsive to this cycle. Team involvement needs to be cultivated and encouraged over time. If the team is resistant to change, the management process will be a grind and results are likely to be poor. There are many good books dealing with corporate culture that should be on the owner's / manager's reading list. Building a team driven management process can make a huge difference.

Our focus at this point is on creating and following a structured monthly process that will bring management and team members together to drive the business forward.

Managing the Review Process

To make the review process work most effectively, all team players need to come together on a routine and structured basis. To make this come alive, here is a list of recommended structural elements:

1. Management Review Meeting Frequency – monthly on a fixed day and time such as the first Wednesday of every month at 8:00 a.m.
2. Meeting Agenda – the meeting should have a standardized agenda ("standing agenda") so everyone knows what they need to bring to the meeting and what they need to accomplish.
3. Action Logs – a list of tasks or initiatives that is updated prior to the meeting. Action logs should contain target completion dates, a designated responsible person who may or may not be the person actually doing the task, and a brief status description that is updated for every meeting.
4. Issue Logs – a list of raised issues that can't be resolved during the meeting. Issues are usually questions or areas of concern without an immediate answer but which need to be researched or explored further. Issues may turn into tasks once they are understood. This log is a great way to park questions and concerns requiring follow-up but which should not take up meeting time for discussion.

5. Metrics and Trends Performance Summaries – these are the main focus of review meetings.
6. Task Management Follow-up – a routine administrative process for updating the action log and the issue log. Progress and status updates should be made available to the team as they occur between meetings.

These are the basic elements that should be part of an ongoing management process. There are many refinements that can be added over time but, if these basic elements are not functioning, it is likely the reviews will not be focused and results will be unpredictable.

It is likely that hot topics will emerge as annual business cycles roll around, which could push the regular monthly review process to the side. Actions such as quarterly and annual tax filings, regulatory reporting, budget planning, board meetings, and other contractual obligations will take priority. However, the underlying monthly process should not be dismissed because of these quarterly and annual actions. Keeping a steady rhythm of monthly review and tuning is a well-known best practice. When the stride is broken it can be difficult to restart.

Secrets to Traction

Now that we have defined what the management review process is and how it should be organized, let's dive into best practices that can lead to top quality outcomes. Here are six key areas that can make or break the management process:

1. Key business questions to be answered every month
2. Identifying who should participate in the review process
3. Information to share with the team
4. Strategies for accountability and results
5. Meeting facilitation
6. Keeping stakeholders informed

Let's explore these topics and a few related ones, further.

Activating Your Team

Management Review Preparation

In preparation for the monthly progress review meeting, the business owner or executive manager driving the review process should walk through a checklist of key questions. Think of it like a pilot readying an aircraft for take-off and going through a standard checklist procedure to insure no critical element is overlooked. Even though the pilot knows all the steps and has repeated them many times, the checklist provides structure and ensures the process is being followed. Without structure, managers who are constantly being pulled in a thousand directions are going to skip key steps and take shortcuts to keep things moving. For most small businesses, it is appropriate to have just a few structured processes and leave room for creative management, remembering at the same time that processes need to be expanded and more structured as a company grows. This becomes the framework for holding a growing business together.

Following are key financial performance questions that should be answered every month by the owner of the company. Even though these questions have a lot of finance and accounting content, they should not be answered by accountants and finance managers. Their views are important, but the owner needs to provide an operational and strategic spin to these questions.

> *If you bring in a professional to manage your accounting, you have to be able to understand if they are doing a good job for you. When you choose an advisor or business coach, choose one who comes with strong references and evidence of objective performance.*
>
> *Making the Jump into Small Business Ownership*, 2013
> – David Nilssen & Jeff Levy
> www.makingthejumpbook.com

Monthly Review Questions Checklist

In preparation for the monthly management review, the owner, the financial manager, and, ideally, their trusted business advisor should step through this checklist to look at problems and opportunities. From here they determine high priorities and the key messages that need to be delivered to the management team about directions and goals. These might include:

1. Do we have any glaring new performance problems? Do the Corelytics Leading Indicators show any radical movements in the most current month? Which leading indicators are red and therefore need further investigation?

2. Is revenue growth meeting our goal? Does the 24-month revenue trend show we are on track? Do we need to make a major correction?

3. What's the revenue forecast for the next 12 months? Is there a potential collision with revenue and expenses in our forecast? Are we on track for a good year-end?

4. Do we have an unusual spike in expenses distorting our picture? Do we need to make adjustments to get a clearer picture?

5. Is gross margin growing faster than revenue? If not, we have a potential ticking time-bomb and we can't "make it up in volume."

6. Are overheads growing faster than revenue? If SG&A is growing at or above the rate of revenue growth, we probably have COGS mixed in with overheads and will not be able to fine-tune pricing for products and services. (We will then have bogus gross margin data!) If SG&A is correct and growing faster than revenue, the company has an "economy of scale" problem that needs to be addressed.

7. Is payroll or other major expense growing faster than revenue? If so, these need careful management. Runaway expenses can drain fuel very quickly. Intentional investments are a different story but they have to be tied to a measurable increase in revenue or the company will be losing ground.

8. Is cash keeping up with growth? If cash doesn't grow along with revenue growth, we can be forced off track even if everything else is working perfectly.

9. Are we building financial strength? If working capital and the quick ratio are not improving over time, we are losing traction. If the company is growing and losing financial strength, there is a fundamental problem that needs to be corrected before growth continues.

Activating Your Team

10. Do we have an LOB that is hurting the business? That LOB can put stress on part of the business engine and cause it to burn out.

After these questions are answered and if all of the above are "green lights," there are two more "bonus questions" to be asked:

11. How do I compare with my peers? Am I falling behind or moving ahead of the industry? Industry benchmarks are the key to answering this question.
12. Do I need to adjust goals to make them more realistic or to address future changes and opportunities?

Setting Priorities

Then there's the big question: What are the top three priorities I want my team to focus on this month? As we know, there will always be more work to do than time and resources will allow. Something is not going to get done. If you create the perfect list of tasks but some things simply won't get done, who is going to decide which tasks are to be dropped? If there is no attempt to define the top priorities, the people doing the work will decide what gets accomplished (or not), usually based on personal preferences and convenience. So, if company leadership wants to define the tasks that get priority attention, they need to set the priorities. It certainly never works to say or assume everything is a top priority. That simply has no credibility and will not create focus. Defining the top three priorities each month has a sense of logic and is generally at the right level for creating a meaningful sense of focus.

Defining the top three priorities each month has a sense of logic and is generally at the right level for creating a meaningful sense of focus.

When the above checklist becomes part of a monthly routine, it can be done very quickly, which can be transformative to companies that focus attention on the loudest "squeaky wheels" or that think of progress reviews as a quarterly or annual process. Most of the real brick walls that companies hit will not make any squeaky wheel sounds—until you actually hit them. Companies conducting only quarterly or annual reviews can get way off track and have a tough time recovering if steering adjustments aren't happening at shorter intervals.

Who Should Participate in the Review Process?

The quick answer is everyone in the company. Unfortunately, this is not feasible as a company grows. For very small companies, everyone in the company might be on the team. As companies grow, it will be impossible and impractical to have everyone in the company participate in management planning meetings. Management meetings will tend to become more exclusive and most of the operating, technical, and administrative staff will not be asked to attend. However, it is important to include everyone involved in managing people and resources. Clearly these are the people that need to understand where the company is headed and what it needs to accomplish in order to be successful. If the managers are not on the same page, the impact will be felt throughout the company.

Another way to think about this is to ask who will be responsible for getting the work done. This is not necessarily the person doing the work or even the person supervising the person doing the work; it is the person that has the responsibility for ensuring the work gets done and done right. This could be a manager four levels up from the worker or the manager that is actually going to do a specific task. But, most importantly, it is the person accountable for getting the work done. As a best practice, there should never be more than one person assigned as the accountable lead. There may be multiple people involved in delivering a given task but only one person accountable for getting the job done. The concept of "single point of accountability" is addressed in many business books and is a well-defined best practice by the Project Management Institute (www.pmi.org).

Information Needed by the Team

If you don't give your team the information they need for a complete and accurate picture, they will simply fill in the picture with their own imagination. This happens naturally. We all do it. We do this with art, music, personal relationships, books, and conversations, for example. We take the information we are given, add our own interpretation, and come up with our own version of a more complete picture. We stir in our own impressions, spice it with imagination, add a few assumptions, and next thing you know we have our own version of the complete picture. The more abstract the input, the more creative we are with the interpretation. The more we create, the less likely the resulting picture is going to be the same for any two people. And it is very unlikely it will match reality.

Business leaders cannot afford for their team members to create their own picture of where the company is and where it is headed. This creates unpredictable results and can be very destructive. The more the team has a correct understanding of how the business is performing and the more aligned it is with the strategic direction of the company, the more likely the team will produce coherent and meaningful results. There's nothing wrong with creativity—except when it results in confusion. Creativity in the wrong setting can cause people to work at cross-purposes and undermine the business.

Confusion and conflict generally lead to one outcome: dis-integration. When company leaders provide a more complete picture and a structured process for making change, many of these problems disappear.

There is one more thing to consider. Not all information is helpful. In fact, there is a danger of giving confusing, conflicting, or too much information. This is potentially just as bad as not giving any information at all. Finding the right balance and the right method for sharing information can make a huge difference.

Information to Share with the Team

With this backdrop on the importance of information, let's broadly highlight the kinds of information needed by your employees and management team:

1. Operating data
2. Performance feedback
3. Planning data

Operating data includes everything from policies and procedures to customer data, orders, deliveries, products, production, and services. Most routine operating data necessary to support customers and to produce products should be provided in real time as the work is being done. More summarized data on work produced, orders delivered, and revenue generated should be provided weekly and monthly.

Data that is provided daily and weekly is generally more tactical and operational. This helps management get needed work done and spot immediate problems needing to be fixed. This is not where the more complex decisions are made.

It's the monthly and quarterly summaries that show progress toward strategic plans and operating goals. This is where top management looks at summarized data to find "off track" conditions and then works with the management team to make necessary adjustments. Adjustments at this level may involve such actions as restructuring company processes, making new investments in infrastructure, making organizational changes, and sometimes discontinuing lines of business that are hurting overall business performance. This is where the monthly management review process comes into play.

Getting Your Team on the Same Page

Providing data in the simplest and yet most complete way is the ideal approach and should include graphics illustrating the trends for all dollar and operating metrics data. Some supporting data tables and detailed reports can be helpful, but they can obscure the big picture and should not be used as primary communication tools. The graphs and supporting data should include the following:

1. Progress evaluation – compare planned versus actual performance for the past month and for the past 24 months; review in terms of dollar performance and in terms of **trend lines** that show actual trends as compared to the goal-based **trend lines**. Where possible, general industry and market benchmarks **trend lines** should be included.
   a. Overall goals and metrics
   b. Last month's priority areas
      i. Status of action items
      ii. Roadblocks and issues identified

Activating Your Team

  c. Areas needing priority attention in the coming month
    i. Sales
    ii. Margins
    iii. Costs
    iv. Expenses
    v. Cash
    vi. Staff productivity
    vii. LOB performance
2. Problems and performance gaps
3. Top priorities as defined by owners and top management
4. Adjustments and new directions as defined by top management
5. Problems and gaps to be addressed by the broader management team
6. Management team decisions
  a. Actions needed to close the performance gaps for top priorities
    i. Assigned accountable manager
    ii. Target completion date

The keys to a successful monthly management review process include:

1. Measurements – KPIs, operating metrics, and financial performance data; expressed in short-term and long-term trends
2. Review – a structured recurring process that continually aligns owners, managers, and staff
3. Visibility – access to comprehensive financial performance data that tells the whole story
4. Collaboration – top management working with the management team to solve problems and make business adjustments, not unilateral decisions coming from the top
5. Delegated responsibility – giving management team members the responsibility to deliver the solutions they recommend for closing performance gaps
6. Ownership of results / consequences – single point of accountability for agreed upon actions combined with a continuous review of progress and results

As an organization expands, the CEO needs to shift his or her role to provide vision, set priorities, and facilitate the management process. This transition can be difficult, especially when the CEO may have the answers. Even worse, the CEO ends up being the "owner" of the imposed solutions, which can lead to lukewarm commitment from the rest of the team. When the CEO stops short of dispensing answers and, instead, creates alignment and agreement on direction and priorities, a completely different dynamic occurs. When members of the management team are given ownership of problems and issues along with the responsibility of finding solutions, a much different level of commitment follows. As individual managers come up with solutions and have the authority for implementing them, the outcome is much more likely to be positive.

Jeff Rogers, Principal, One Accord Partners
Read more: Appendix Contribution #130

Assembling the Performance Picture

Following is a list of steps that make preparation for the monthly performance review fairly simple. The goal is to deliver a full picture along with a focus on priorities.

1. Choose three top priority messages to share with the team each month. This may take a bit of time exploring trend data to find the areas that need the most attention. The leading indicators and long-term trend graphs are color coded in the Corelytics Financial Dashboard to streamline this process. There is a big red highlight on areas that are performing at less than goal, and a yellow highlight in areas that are close but not quite at goal. This is a big time saver for users of the dashboard.

2. For each graph chosen, display the actual, trend, goal, and benchmark lines. You may not have all this data available on some graphs, but when possible it should all be included.

3. Copy the graph and the key numbers displayed to a PowerPoint slide. You can use the free Snipping Tool that is included in Windows to highlight and copy any portion of the screen you wish.

Activating Your Team

4. Add a couple of comments to each slide describing your concern about what you are seeing in the selected graphs.
5. Produce a couple of selected graphs to tell the overall company story, such as the company's two-year revenue graph, the revenue forecast graph or the gross margin graph. These can be used to highlight overall company performance but will probably not be the graphs used to drill into the three top priorities.
6. Present the three chosen priority graphs each month and ask the team to help you figure out a solution to the problems you are trying to solve.

Delegating Responsibility

The major point here is this: don't simply hand your team the answer to the top priority problems. Instead, let them come up with their own solutions. When they do, they will have a much greater sense of ownership of the solutions and will be much more committed to achieving the needed results.

Many business owners make the mistake of stating the problem and then providing the answer. There is nothing left for the team to do but to listen and agree. This leads to a very unhealthy sense of reliance on senior management and generally results in half-hearted commitments. When team members are encouraged to come up with their own answers and deliver against the solutions they recommend, the probability of meaningful progress is greatly enhanced.

Sometimes the right solution might be to change the goal rather than close a perceived performance gap. Sometimes the answer might be to focus on another problem that is the root cause of the gap. But in no case should the team dismiss with the benchmark numbers that your peers are achieving. If you are performing at less than benchmarks, you know you are below average and need to improve or agree that improvement in this area is not a high priority. There are usually many "80/20 solutions" where just doing a smart 20 percent of the perfect solution can produce 80 percent of the potential improvements. That can often get you to par or better in comparison to the benchmarks for your peer group.

Bottom line: get the whole team on board and committed to the success of the company. Let them all see the big picture so they understand what is working and what is not. Elicit their solutions to problems. When everyone is on the same page and pulling in the same direction, you can have phenomenal success.

Meeting Facilitation

Rarely is the CEO of a company the best person to lead the review sessions. In fact, the more the CEO can be a participant and not a keeper of the meeting agenda, the more likely the discussion will have deep value to everyone. It is difficult for a meeting organizer and agenda cop to also engage in big thinking. This is an important reason to shop for a business coach or advisor to play this role.

Many professional associations recognize the importance of helping their members get good quality advisory services because this is one of many ways they bring value to their members. It is common for them to provide forums where their members can shop for experts that can help with various aspects of business performance.

Professional associations play a crucial part in the business ecosystem — they help build and grow the industry workforce, and also help keep it accountable through certification, standards, and best practices. They foster an exchange of business and technology ideas and find a common voice when it comes to ensuring their market thrives and that the highest standards are upheld. They bring expertise from various branches of the industry to define regional and global benchmarks in order to successfully apply them to their respective operations.

David Labuskes, CTS, RCDD, Executive Director and CEO,
InfoComm International
Read more: Appendix Contribution #126

Finding the Right Business Advisor

No professional athlete would consider being without a trainer or coach. This is not because the athlete doesn't know what needs to be done, but rather because his or her focus needs to be on execution while the coach focuses on fine-tuning the process and providing perspective and encouragement.

In the same way, no professional business owner should be without an advisor. It's not that the owner can't figure things out, but an advisor brings perspective, asks key questions, and can help organize priorities. The advisor becomes an accountability partner.

Finding the right advisor is usually more difficult than finding the right employee. There needs to be a good match in intellect, cultural background, personality, and a wealth of relevant experience. Sometimes the ideal person is a professional advisor or consultant. In other cases, the ideal person may be employed elsewhere and is interested in serving more as a mentor with a minimal time commitment. Whatever the case, the advisor can be an extremely valuable resource to the owner and ideally to the whole management team.

With that in mind, let's take a short side trip into setting the right criteria and expectations when selecting an advisor. This person can be a key part of the team and can play an important role in building a monthly review process that generates real traction.

If you bring in a professional to manage your accounting, you have to be able to understand if they are doing a good job for you. When you choose an advisor or business coach, choose one who comes with strong references and evidence of objective performance.

Making the Jump into Small Business Ownership, 2013 –
David Nilssen & Jeff Levy
www.makingthejumpbook.com

The New Breed of Trusted Advisor

Bringing in outside help, including consultants, trainers, accountants, and bankers (which we will refer to collectively as advisors), is a factor to which many executives have attributed their success. And now the market is changing, and advisors are getting even smarter and delivering more value for their services. A new breed of advisor is emerging from accounting firms, consulting firms, banks, and other business service companies. They establish a close relationship with the company owner and play a role in the monthly management review and priority setting process. They tend to be a business expert in some area of specialization with a competency in planning and analysis. They also tend to be great at reading and interpreting metrics and effective sounding boards for top management. The right advisor can help the business owner navigate business analysis and identify areas needing priority attention.

Additionally, there is a recent trend for advisors to take advantage of technology that allows them to stay on top of their clients' metrics and operating data and proactively alert owners to issues requiring attention. The Corelytics Financial Dashboard is a tool that can play an important role in this process. To get the best results, the advisor should use tools such as these that do the heavy analytics, allowing them to focus on synthesis and interpretation. If the tools also support forecasting and scenario modeling, all the better.

The technology used by the advisor can help make his or her service less expensive and yet more valuable. It can provide the advisor already-analyzed data so they can reduce or eliminate the time spent on data collection and analysis and go straight to interpretation and prioritizing—the most valuable part of their service. With the right tools, they can provide expert opinions in a shorter timeframe and pack a lot more benefit into a small price tag.

Small businesses often only keep track of yesterday's business. Big businesses hire planners and are prepared for tomorrow. Now, savvy small business bookkeepers with new technologies can forecast 'tomorrow's business'. The challenge for accountants today is moving from theory to practice.

Shelly Robbins, Accounting Technology Expert, Founder The QuickSource
www.thequicksource.com

As we discuss the role of the advisor, here is one cardinal rule: the advisor should not play the role of "the guy with the answers." It is important to repeat a point made earlier about how issues and priorities should be handled in the monthly team review process. The team needs to own the solutions and the delivery of solutions. The owner and the advisor need to tee up the priorities and direction, but the minute they start dispensing answers they let the rest of the team off the hook. Over time this becomes demotivating and builds dysfunctional dependencies. Experienced advisors know they have much greater impact when they facilitate and help move awareness forward, and they stop just short of dumping answers.

Demand for this kind of advisor is growing and is becoming part of the monthly management cycle for many companies. The typical advisory relationship is the one-hour per month phone call in which the advisor and the business owner view the dashboard in a shared web meeting, zooming in on the top three areas of priority. Much like the monthly management review process discussed earlier in this chapter, the advisor can discuss the results achieved in the prior month, help set priorities for the new month, and suggest which trend charts should be used in the next management team meeting. It is amazing how much can be accomplished in a small amount of time when all the analysis is done ahead of time. This is great way to get everybody on the same page and build greater visibility.

Certified QuickBooks ProAdvisors are able to provide top level services to clients because they are always up to date and have a variety of training outside the product-practice management, best practices when working with clients, and even helping accounting professionals to stay ahead of the curve with new technology.

Stacy Kildal, Advanced Certified QuickBooks ProAdvisor,
Co-Host of RadioFreeQB.com
findaproadvisor.com

Keeping Stakeholders Informed

There are also external players that should be considered a part of the extended management team. These could include accountants, bankers, lenders, attorneys, brokers, investors, strategic business partners, outsourced experts, and business advisors. They are great resources on which companies depend at various points in time.

Most businesses tend to think of these outside players as "being there when you need them" and having no role until needed. An alternative approach is to think of these players as resources that can play an important role on a continuous basis. They can provide helpful insights and solutions on an ongoing basis as a business grows and faces new challenges.

For example, having closer ties to a banker can really pay off. As you know, the worst time to get a loan is when you really need it. The best time is when you don't. By having your banker become a part of your financial performance review cycle, he or she can help you anticipate future needs, set up lines of credit that will be available when you need them, and then be there to help you through the tough spots, which every company experiences from time to time. But if the banker is kept at arms-length, he or she will be unprepared to help when you need it the most. Providing monthly or quarterly financial performance metrics and progress toward defined goals is a great way to keep the connection strong and the banker ready to serve as your advocate within the bank. There is no way to get this kind of support from your banker if you keep him or her in the dark.

Visibility and honesty is the hallmark of any great banking relationship from the banker and from the client. Covenants are there to create a discussion. My best clients are the ones that, if there's an issue or a problem they see coming, they come to me first and go, "Hey here's where we're at. Here's what we think the problem is. Here's how we're going to solve it. We need your help to work through this problem." That's the perfect client.

Don Brown, Vice President and Senior Relationship Manager, KeyBank
Read More: Appendix Contribution #116

A similar case could be built for your accountant. Many companies tend to think of their accountant as a technician who helps with the

Activating Your Team

accounting system, creates reports, and does the taxes. There is usually much more an accountant can do, but he or she should be brought into the management loop in order to provide broader services. A common mistake made by many businesses is to think that because the accountant has the financial data, he or she must therefore understand the business. However, when the accountant is brought into the planning and monthly review circle, he or she can get a more complete picture and contribute in many meaningful ways that neither the business owner nor the accountant usually think about independently.

One word of caution: there is a big difference between accountants that are good at bookkeeping and those that are good at analysis and planning. The ones that are good at bookkeeping are more focused on a retrospective view of the business and making sure that records are correct, reports are accurate, and the rules are being followed. In contrast, accountants that are good at analyzing and financial planning are a very different breed. They think in broader business strokes and are more interested in thinking ahead. They understand business dynamics and can help with modeling and forecasting and defining future resource requirements.

There are a lot of good accountants who can help with tax compliance issues and basic financial reporting, that's old school accounting. Today's business owners need an accountant who understands managerial accounting and how to apply those principles (business acumen) to improve the overall performance of an organization.

Edi Osborne, Mentor Plus and Author, *Firm Forward*
on www.amazon.com
Read more: Appendix Contribution #118

Many business owners don't know the difference between the two, and most accountants don't know how to tell the business owner how to best use their expertise. In some cases, the accountant aspires to be more involved in the planning process but his or her real expertise is in the retrospective management of accounting data. This all adds extra challenges to the business owner trying to make the right choices. However, when the right relationship is established, the most important thing the business owner can do is keep the lines of communication open and keep the "trusted advisor" current on an ongoing basis. When the advisor receives regular updates on goals, priorities, and progress, he or she can often play an important role in finding solutions and providing important insights.

Conclusion

When you consider the broader mission of all companies, which is to serve their shareholders and provide products and services to their target market, the picture of who's on the management team becomes much larger. Many benefits can be gained by having external experts in the inner circle. With the right information and the right management processes, teams can get highly motivated and produce high performance results beating industry benchmarks and exceeding company goals. That's the kind of company everybody wants to work for.

 **CHAPTER EIGHT CHECK-UP**

1. How often should a management team get information on financial performance?
2. To what depth should the management team understand the owner's financial priorities? What kind of information should they be given to help with this understanding?
3. Who is responsible for identifying areas needing high priority attention? Who is responsible for finding and delivering solutions to financial performance gaps?

Activating Your Team

4. Who are the external stakeholders that should receive company performance data? Why would you want them to have this data? How often should they get information on company performance?

5. What does "single point of accountability" mean?

6. Why would a management team care about peer performance and industry benchmarks?

CHAPTER NINE

Decisions: Cash Management

Rule No. 1: Never lose money.
Rule No. 2: Never forget Rule No. 1.

- Warren Buffet

Cash is the lifeblood of your company. Managing cash ("cash flow") is as essential to the running of your business as blood flow is to the life of your body! When managed well, no one will notice. When done poorly, everyone will notice and there will be lots of unhappiness. In a worst case scenario, problems with cash flow management will grind a business to a halt. Companies that appear profitable on paper go out of business every day because they simply cannot get the cash they need to stay alive. Being profitable and generating cash are two very important aspects of running a business. Though they are closely related, you can succeed at one and fail at the other and grind the business to a halt.

Many small businesses stay small simply because of the way they manage their cash. In order to grow, cash management must move from a short-term tactical process to a more strategic long-term management process. This chapter will examine the difference between tactical and strategic cash management and will discuss how cash management can make or break a business.

Cash Flow Basics

The first priority of cash management is to make sure bills get paid and the company doesn't run out of cash. This may require prioritizing bills so the most important items are paid first—so any shortage of cash does not impact the most important aspects of the business. Generally payroll is one of those top priority areas. Some bills can be paid late and have minimal impact on the company, but a late payroll could be devastating to the morale and commitment of company employees. This level of cash management is considered to be "tactical cash management."

As companies grow and have predictable and dependable flows of cash, the challenge changes. The questions become more centered on how cash can be used to get more long-term benefit for the company. This may involve investments, acquisitions, expansions, and other strategic decisions. This may also include using bank lines of credit, borrowing against company assets, and potentially bringing in funds from the sale of company stock. This level of planning cash requirements is referred to as "strategic cash management." Strategic cash management assumes that tactical cash management is continuing but is delegated to accounting staff and no longer a focus for the owner.

Tactical	Strategic
• Prioritize bill payment • Collect receivables • Reduce costs • 30-day cash plan • Find creative solutions to getting early payment	• Adjust prices » lower to increase volume » higher to increase margin » track "price elasticity" • Set and track goals • 90-day cash plan • Manage LOC
Make ends meet	**Achieve goals**

Cash Management Realities

Whether or not a company uses the tactical and strategic cash management approach depends largely on its level of cash reserve. A two to three-month cash reserve makes it possible to take a "forecast and monitor" approach, which is longer term and therefore more strategic in nature. If cash is tight and the company is operating close to the line, meaning they have little or no reserve, a tight tactical cash control approach is necessary. Many small business owners operate in the tight cash control mode all the time—some have never known any other possibility. In a worst-case tactical scenario, bills get paid in priority order as cash comes in the door in hand-to-mouth fashion.

Even companies that usually operate with a healthy reserve will experience times of tight cash flow. They may even have a near death experience and need to get very tactical with cash management until they recover. Conversely, companies will occasionally have a spike in cash availability and have the opportunity to become strategic and put this money to wise use. The goal should be to keep the company in a position of adequate cash reserve so the owner can be more strategic in management of the business on an ongoing basis.

It is also important to recognize that companies operating close to the line have much less value in the market. Companies with great revenue growth and poor cash position create the impression of underpricing their services or of having poor internal controls. All of this communicates that the company is a "fixer upper" and not a premium value company.

Companies with a good history of cash balances and a cash **trend line** that matches or exceeds the rate of revenue growth attain a premium value in the market. The work required to elicit a premium value for your company is much less than you might think, but it must be sustained on a continuing basis to be perceived as "real."

Understanding when to think tactically and when to think strategically is crucial, regardless of how new or how well established your company might be. These are two important ways to think about your business and both will play an important role as your cash position cycles through highs and lows.

Tactical Cash Management Process

When operating with little or no cash reserve:

1. Build/update the list of pending payments due.
   a. Put in priority order.
   b. Compute running total on each line item (see example).
   c. Determine cash availability cut-off points and payment dates.
      i. Determine cash currently available and what can be paid now.
      ii. Determine cash expected to come in within the next 30 days and when additional payments can be made.

      Caution: Do not pay this month's low priority items with cash needed to pay next month's high priority items. For example, say you receive a big project payment this month and you have already paid your high priority obligations and now you could pay low priority obligations. Before you take that step, take a look at next month's expected revenues and make sure you have enough expected cash to cover all high priorities due next month. It could be a good idea to pay down your line of credit now and then tap in again next month when the cash is needed. But it would not be a good idea to pay down credit card balances if next month's cash forecast looks like it won't cover high priority obligations. You cannot easily tap into credit cards to pay most bills if you are running short of needed cash.

      iii. Maintain a minimum cash reserve for unexpected or un-planned requirements.

      Tip: look for opportunities to make split payments if you are unable to cover all top priorities. For example, if you have a vendor to whom you owe $5,000, contact them and let them know you can pay $2,500 now and $2,500 in three weeks when you receive payment for a large project that is near completion. Most companies will appreciate the heads-up and will waive penalties as a show of good faith. If they are not willing to go with a split payment, don't press it if there is another vendor that might be more flexible. If they agree, show the two payment amounts on the pending list with the first payment showing higher on the priority list and the second showing lower on the list (below the cut-off line).

2. Manage credit sources.
   a. Track amounts available on the company's LOC.
   b. Determine availability on credit cards (General rule, don't use credit cards as a source of cash if you can avoid it; only use credit cards as a convenient means of payment and pay off the balance every month. Getting hooked on credit cards as a source of cash can be a slippery slope from which there is often no way back.)
   c. Determine amount of credit sources required to pay highest priority obligations.

      Tip: Check to see if your bank will give you an overdraft line of credit. This is often different than a regular business line of credit. It is usually attached to your checking account and will cover payments that would otherwise be treated as NSF (insufficient funds in your account). This avoids overdraft penalties and enables you to manage cash more easily when you are getting close to zero balance. Some banks will let you roll an overdraft LOC into your regular LOC but they may require an account manager's approval.

3. Manage relationships with people and companies to which you owe money.
   a. Notify selected individuals and companies of planned delays in their payments.
   b. Determine if a partial payment can be made.

Worst-case scenario: If your foreseeable cash requirements do not cover your operating costs, it's time to make the tough decisions. Don't keep digging a deeper hole. You may need to downsize, sell your customer base, or close down. These are not fun things to think about, but if you cannot generate enough cash to cover your obligations, you will not solve the problem by denying it exists. Major changes must be made.

Be cautiously aware that wide swings in average monthly cash balances put a business at risk. Just like with revenue, business owners need to find ways to smooth out large peaks and valleys in average cash balances. Strategies for smoothing out cash flow include:

- Pay selected bills weekly and not monthly; spread payments out during the month.
- Pay off credit cards whenever cash is available (in excess of needed reserve for current priority bills).
- Create customer contracts that provide multiple interim payments rather than one or two big payments when projects last longer than two months.
- Pay off LOC frequently whenever there is cash availability—this will help your lender give you a higher credit score.

Tactical Cash Management Tracking

Tactical cash flow planning is typically done for 30 days at a time and updated weekly and sometimes daily. The easiest way to do this is to construct a spreadsheet such as the one shown below only with more detailed line items. You can engage an accountant to create this spreadsheet or do it yourself. What is essential is that you have a good accounting system for tracking actual income, cash receipts, and expenditures (amounts paid and due).

The objective of the 30-day plan is to make sure that the highest priority expenses get paid first and that bills are not paid until cash is available.

The following table illustrates a 30-day plan that lists payments due in priority order. As cash becomes available the bills on the list get paid. If cash is not sufficient to pay all the bills, the lowest priority bills will not be paid or more likely will be paid late.

Sample Pending Payments Due

Payment Recipient	Amount	Running Total
Top priorities – must pay		
- Payroll	40,000	40,000
- Taxes	6,000	46,000
- Benefits	5,000	51,000
- Utilities	1,500	52,500
- Credit card and LOC minimums	1,000	53,500
- Critical suppliers	10,000	63,500
- Low priority suppliers on hold	0	63,500
High priorities – should pay		
- Contractors	2,500	66,000
- Rent	8,000	74,000
- Owner base pay	5,000	79,000
- Staff incentive pay – obligations	2,000	81,000
- High priority suppliers	3,000	84,000

Example of tactical short-term payment planning. The line indicates the payments that will be made given the current availability of cash. In this case, let's say there is currently $80,000 available for paying bills.

Example: The Average IT Service Company

According to market statistics produced by Corelytics, the typical IT service company maintains an average cash balance equal to 16 percent of average monthly sales. Most companies rely heavily on credit cards to make purchases to avoid using cash. This is living close to the edge and leaves a company in a very vulnerable position, often finding itself one bad deal away from shutdown.

An ideal average cash balance would be the equivalent of two months of sales, although very few companies actually do this. With more cash, business owners have more flexibility and can focus on business growth and expansion. With a small cash balance, the focus, by necessity, is on figuring out which bills to pay.

This is one more way to invoke the old adage: "Owners need to spend more time working ON their business rather than working IN their business." When the business owner is focused on deciding which bills need to be paid first, he or she, by definition, is working IN the business. There is not time or resources to do anything else.

Building good cash management disciplines and procedures make it possible to delegate the process that can free up the owner to work on more strategic issues. However, there is a danger to this way of thinking. If the owner completely delegates cash management to the bookkeeper, there is a risk of losing touch with the decisions that drive cash reserve. Even with good procedures, if cash is tight, it is probably going to require owner involvement to make critical choices. So, in reality, the combination of having a solid cash reserve and clear procedures makes it possible to delegate routine accounting activities and move the focus to the bigger picture.

A financial dashboard is a good approach to monitoring overall monthly cash position and cash **trend line** to make sure cash is moving in a positive direction. But a dashboard is not a solution for managing a list of pending payments and making sure bills are paid in priority order. When balances are headed in a positive direction it becomes clear that internal processes are working and the business is gaining ground, then it is safe to focus energies into growing the business, building long-range plans, and developing the asset value of the company.

Strategic Cash Management

This more advanced form of cash management assumes an adequate cash reserve usually ranging from one to three times average monthly revenue. Here the owner is more involved in longer range planning and will usually delegate the monthly bill payment process to the accounting staff. In all cases, the owner should remain part of the bill payment authorization process.

At this level a more comprehensive 90-day cash management plan can be used to oversee cash as shown below. The objective of a 90-day cash flow management plan is to ensure the timing of cash outflows is consistent with cash inflows. When companies have an established revenue flow it is much easier and more appropriate to use the 90-day plan approach. It does, however, require that cash be predictable and generally sufficient to cover the normal monthly commitments.

Cash flow planning with this type of reporting is intended to highlight the timing and any differences between cash outflow for payments and cash inflow from income collections.

Cash Management Three-Month Report

Cash Inflows:	Month 1	Month 2	Month 3
Customer Payments	$20,000	$35,000	$18,000
Other Income	$1,500	$800	$1,200
Total Cash Inflow:	$21,500	$35,800	$19,200
Cash Outflows:			
Hardware Purchases	$12,100	$6,400	$15,800
Salaries	$12,000	$12,600	$13,000
Other Expenses	$6,500	$6,900	$6,750
Total Cash Outflow:	$30,600	$25,900	$35,550
Net Cash Flow:	($9,100)	$9,900	($16,350)

In this table shown above, there is a $9,100 shortfall in the cash forecast for Month One. Since Month Two has a positive net cash flow greater than the shortfall in Month One, the likely solution will be to hold some lower priority payments until Month Two. Management could also choose to use its line of credit (LOC) in Month One to pay all bills and then pay off the LOC in Month Two. But Month Three is looking like a bigger problem. It is showing a predicted drop in cash receipts and a large expenditure for hardware. In total, this is a larger cash obligation than the company can handle with routine income. This may be a situation where the company decides to defer the planned hardware purchase or perhaps borrow from the bank in order to spread out the payments over time. Several options are available but they usually take some advanced planning in order to make the necessary arrangements for them to occur.

Strategic Cash Management Processes

1. Three-month cash planning worksheet – This worksheet should show the categories and line items for expenses and revenues for the current and following two months. At the bottom is the total cash remaining after netting projected cash receipts and cash expenditures. This worksheet should include line items for planned investments and cash you plan to borrow. As companies grow, this reporting process becomes more critical to ensure cash requirements do not outrun cash receipts and the flow of new investments fits the cash capacity of the company.

2. **Trend line** comparisons (revenue trends versus cash trends) - Every month a new cash **trend line** (based on end-of-month cash balances) and a new revenue **trend line** should be computed. Comparing these **trend lines** reveals a lot about the overall health of the business. If the revenue **trend line** is increasing and the cash line is not increasing at a similar or better rate, you may have a serious problem. Companies that try to grow aggressively and that have falling cash balances are on a path to disaster.

3. Budgeting – Small company budgets do not need to be as complicated as large companies. Often it is enough to just have total quarterly spending limits by category. For example, you may set a maximum for marketing spending so your marketing team knows what they

have to work with. This tells them how much money the company is willing to allocate to marketing. From there, the marketing team can prioritize spending within its defined limits. More detailed budgets by category and department become more important as a company grows. But regardless of the level of detail, budgeting is crucial for pushing decision-making down into the organization.

A more sophisticated version of budgeting ties spending limits to revenue. For example, you might attach marketing spending in a specific line of business to eight percent of the revenue received in the quarter for that line of business. So, if revenues come in above plan, the team can increase spending to further build momentum.

4. Spending approval process – In addition to budgets, there should be rules limiting how much a manager can spend without approval. For example, you might say any purchase over $2,000 needs to be approved by the department manager and over $5,000 must be approved by the CEO. Approvals should also be required for purchases that are over budget or that place unusual contractual requirements on the company regardless of the dollar amount.

5. LOC usage plan – The line of credit should only be used under specific conditions. For example, it should not be used to finance capital purchases. Company policy on this should be defined and documented so everyone understands this.

6. Investment planning – A best practice is to create a mini-plan for each major investment. The investment plan should identify when the investment will be made, how it should impact revenues, and how and when the investment will be recovered. Most business owners don't bother with this, but when cash runs low they wish they had.

All big companies learn that there are endless investment opportunities. Clearly choices must be made and many potential investments will need to be dismissed. The process for setting priorities and making choices is the difficult part. The best approach is to consider new investment opportunities as a portfolio containing a balance of short-term and long-term investments combined with low-risk/low-yield and high-risk/high-yield investments.

High-risk/high-yield investments:

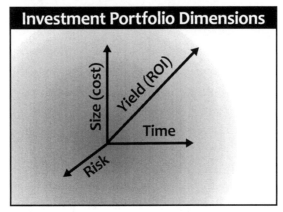

Organizing a list of potential investments into categories and then selecting some investments from each category is a better approach than just picking all investments sharing the same characteristics. Ideally investment opportunities are ranked and prioritized in each investment category and only the most beneficial investments should be accepted from each category. A balanced portfolio of investments generally has a much better outcome over time. This also helps get those short-term, low-cost, low-hanging-fruit opportunities mixed in with long-term investments in a balanced way.

Most large companies also know it is easy to forecast an investment yield; however, all too often investments do not live up to their hype. By monitoring each major investment and tracking results, management can learn what type of investments work and where they need to place their bets. At a minimum, each investment should have a plan that includes:

    a. Cash requirements

    b. Revenue impact

    c. ROI and payback analysis

7. Cash benchmark comparisons – Watching cash, debt, inventory, and other measurements as a percentage of sales can be a very important way to spot problems within your business. The two important benchmarks for cash are:

Decisions: Cash Management

a. Cash balance as a percent of average monthly revenue

b. Cash balance growth rate compared to revenue growth rate

8. Goal setting for cash balances – Setting goals and then tracking actual performance against goals is a highly effective way to get results. Management should set goals in many areas within a company and track actual performance. It is difficult to know where to take corrective action and even more difficult to know if the corrections are working without this process. When you set goals for cash and actually track these goals, management processes will improve, which ultimately leads to improvements in company finances. At a minimum, goals should be set for:

a. Monthly cash balance as a percent of revenue

b. Monthly cash balance growth rate

9. When to tap credit cards and LOC (line of credit) - Credit cards should not be used as a way to generate cash; instead, they should only be used as a convenient way to make purchases. They should then be paid off completely at the end of the billing cycle. The reality is, of course, that many companies let credit card balances build. This is an expensive way to borrow money because of the high interest rates and because credit card borrowing can become a slippery slope with no solid footing.

Ideally, the LOC is what should be used during slow months or seasonal swings in revenue. It should be fully paid off in two to four months and carry a zero balance several months out of the year. Banks will look at how often the LOC is paid down to zero to determine if a company is a good credit risk going forward. The worst problem is using the LOC to finance capital purchases or make infrastructure purchases. It is much better to use long-term debt (a long-term loan) for such purposes and preserve your ability to use the LOC when it is most needed.

Example of Cash Trend Monitoring

In this chart taken from the Corelytics Financial Dashboard, you can see a very strong cash growth **trend line** along with a couple of areas of concern. This is the kind of trend data companies should monitor every month.

Example Cash Trend Analysis

Balance Accounts

LOB: [Combined ▼]   View by: [Month ▼]

[Cash ▼]

Avg./mo.	Avg. Mo. Expense
$85,122	**$58,085**
Prior year: $68,232	Avg. Mo. Revenue
	$66,517

▓ based on 12 past months

Yearly Increases

Actual	Goal	Expenses
24.8%	**n/a**	**18.4%**
	> update goals	Revenue
		27.4%

Cash (% of Rev.)

Actual	Goal	Benchmarks
128%	**n/a**	**n/a**
	> update goals	

Legend: ▓ Revenue ▓ Expenses ☑ Acct. Rate ☑ Rev. Rate ☑ Exp. Rate

Example taken from the Corelytics Financial Dashboard

Observations:

1. Cash is growing at 95.1 percent (seen over the past 12 months) while revenue is growing at 23.9 percent. This is a very positive indication that growth is beneficial to this company. (This is not always true.)

2. Monthly cash balance is averaging 247 percent of average monthly revenue. That is approximately two and a half months of revenue. This allows the company to manage strategically and be in a great position for strategic investments in additional growth.

3. The company is not meeting its goal for a cash balance of 300 percent of revenue. Management may want to be even more aggressive in managing cash flows to achieve this goal. You can see from the dark line in the graph that monthly cash balances have taken a hit in the last few months. In this particular case, the dip in cash was the result of management deciding to add a couple of new engineers. That put a bit of cash drain on the company but is expected to further increase revenues and cash in the months ahead.

4. One area of concern in this chart is the relationship between the growth rate of revenue and expenses. This chart is showing expenses rising at 27.5 percent—a bit faster than revenue, which is rising at 23.9 percent. This isn't an alarming situation especially since we know the company hired a couple of new staff in the past few months. This should result in revenues outpacing expenses in a few months. However, this is an important indicator of company health and requires management attention if revenue doesn't soon outpace expenses. It's also important to note that you cannot see these trends unfolding just by reading P&L statements and balance sheets. Cash problems can be building and can go unnoticed until a big problem occurs and more painful corrections are required.

Cash Flow Using Company Assets

Another set of cash flow techniques deals with your own company assets—for example, whether you buy or lease things like vehicles and property or office space.

First, your vehicles could be leased instead of being purchased outright and that would avoid using cash. Even assets that you already own can be put in a bank's lease back program or they could be used as collateral in a long-term loan (That is, you can pledge them against a bank loan.). Leasing or borrowing against assets increases your cash position and can typically be done at a lower rate than with unsecured loans. It is generally much easier to lease when acquiring new equipment or vehicles but it is also possible to lease used equipment or vehicles or even lease-back equipment or vehicles that you have already paid for. There are sophisticated discounted cash flow models available for determining when leasing provides greater value than owning.

Renting or leasing office space can have short-term cash flow benefits as compared to buying space. But if you own your office building or office condo, you can finance it to the extent you have equity. Typically real estate will give you the best financing rates of all money borrowing options. However, unless you own the property outright, you will have a first mortgage on the property. That means the bank (or lender) has precedence, or first rights to the property, if you don't make payments and they have to foreclose.

Utilizing second mortgages and LOCs is another method of generating additional cash; however, they typically have higher rates of interest than first mortgages. The difference between a straight second mortgage and a real estate line of credit is simply that the real estate line of credit (RLOC) can be tapped up to a limit and you are charged on what is outstanding versus taking out a full mortgage amount. This allows you to manage the amount of cash you pull out at any point in time. You can pay back the RLOC and then pull cash out later when a new need arises.

Staffing Cash Flow Alternatives

Now let's talk about cash flow techniques related to staff compensation. There are a few things you can do in this area to enhance cash flow.

The first option to consider is outsourcing some areas of work. Outsourcing, while it might increase total costs, may help cash flow in the short-term. Taking advantage of 30 to 60-day invoice payment cycles can help cash flow. Ideally you should time the payment of contract resources to coincide with payments from your clients. If you hire the equivalent help on an internal payroll, at a minimum you have to pay them within 30 days. If you decide to use contracted help on a large contract, you might negotiate payment to the contractors to occur when you get paid—a great technique to enhance cash flow. You do need to exercise care in terms of whether you are using an employee as a worker versus an independent contractor—the IRS continues to crack down on this rule. In general, if you have outsourced staff that is full-time for an extended period, you really need to examine these rules or you can be caught with penalties and back taxes.

As for salaries and bonuses, the more you pay in year-end bonuses versus salaries during the year, the more this will enhance cash flow. Senior level employees are better targets for this type of payment, as opposed to more junior employees who are typically living paycheck to paycheck. Obviously, pay for performance and commissions instead of fixed salaries tend to help cash flow. And, although many owners don't want to go here, equity in lieu of salary obviously helps cash flow.

An established employee benefits plan is one area that you don't want to take creative shortcuts with to conserve cash. Pulling back on benefits once they have been granted is a very damaging action and should only be a very last resort. It is much better not to offer them in the first place. When cash is tight, delaying payments to insurance companies can be very damaging as they can shut your coverage down pretty quickly if you get behind in payments, creating significant legal risks and, of course, employee dissatisfaction.

Inventory

From a cash flow perspective, you should minimize inventory whenever possible. Ideally you should not carry any. To the extent you do carry inventory, it might as well be cash sitting on shelves! Inventory eats cash.

For the inventory you DO carry, be sure to monitor the inventory "turns." To do this, note how frequently each inventory item is used and replenished each quarter or year. Any inventory that is not "turning" routinely should be eliminated by selling, donating, or disposing of it. Getting rid of unused inventory will not free up cash unless you sell it. But taking a loss by converting obsolete inventory into cash can be a smart way to generate cash. The longer it sits, the less cash it will generate.

Taxes & Dealing with the Government

There are a number of ways to manage tax and fee payments to improve cash flow, but great care must be taken not to let this turn into a disaster. The IRS and government agencies in general are not very forgiving. You can get into more trouble and increase costs beyond any benefit gained by delaying government payments! But let's explore further.

First, one of the fastest ways to get into trouble with the government is by not paying employer taxes. Employer taxes include Federal Withholding, State Withholding, FICA, Unemployment, and any local withholding taxes. I'll even throw 401K contributions into this category. Don't mess with these payments—pay them on time!

Sales and use taxes are another area not worth messing with. The one place you can "manage" government tax payments is estimated federal income taxes—the quarterly payments based on estimated annual revenue. Work with your tax accountant to stay within the law on this topic. In general, your quarterly estimated tax payments must be equal to your prior year's tax obligation or equal to this year's expected obligation whichever is greater if you are filing an estimate. If your tax accountant believes you will pay less in taxes in the current year than last year, you may be able to reduce your tax payment and increase your cash flow. However, if you do this and then discover you owe more than estimated, you could get hit with a penalty, so care is required.

Property taxes (and other miscellaneous government fees) should be paid on their due dates, as late payments generally garner penalties large enough to make them not worth delaying.

Following is a summary of your tax-related obligations that generally consume cash:

- Employment Taxes (Federal and State Withholding, FICA, Unemployment, etc.) – Don't mess with these
- Sales and Use Taxes – Don't mess with these, either!
- Estimated Federal Income Taxes – Use a tax accountant to find ways to minimize these payments
- Property Taxes, Permit Fees, etc. – Pay when due

Unsecured Loans, Credit Cards, & Personal Loans

Let's talk now about unsecured loans, personal pledges, and credit cards. First we will cover credit card use. One option is for employees to use their personal credit cards and then reimburse them for expenses. This will spread out cash flow and, if the employees retain the miles or "points" or whatever perks they get for using the cards, they may be happy about this.

You can also take out a company credit card. If you do this and pay off the card at the end of the month, there's no interest and you have cash flow for an additional 30 days or so. Remember, though, that credit cards are very expensive if you don't pay on time.

While it is not desirable to many people, you may be able to obtain a personal credit line from a bank, savings and loan, or credit union. If you personally, as a company officer or director, pledge on a company credit line, you should think of it as a personal credit line because the issuer (i.e., bank, savings and loan, or credit union) will come after YOU if it is not paid, just like any personal loan.

Again not very desirable to many people is the option of pledging your personal assets, your home, other real estate, your automobile, or other personal assets on a loan. Generally, asset-backed loans have better interest rates than unsecured credit lines or credit cards. While these loans may be for business purposes, you are personally liable for these loans regardless of the kind of business you have setup.

For all personal loans, credit cards, etc., you need to shop around, as there is a myriad of options, terms, and rates for these.

Following is a summary of your credit options:

Credit Cards
- Employee personal credit cards and then reimburse
- Company credit cards – pay on time if possible

Loans
- Personal credit lines / personal pledges on company credit lines
- Home equity, second mortgages, and other personal asset backed loans

Metrics that Matter Most

Most business owners have at least heard about the basic financial metrics used by banks and lenders: Quick Ratios, AR turns, Inventory Turns, Assets to Liabilities. All of those metrics are important but most often they are seen as a static number at a specific point in time. Below we can see two cases emerge with two fundamentally different views:

Susan	Eric
Susan owns a dance studio and just wants to keep a sustainable, solid business.	Eric owns a popular top-performing franchise.
Independent owner, family business. Lives next door to her studio. Works hard to keep happy employees. Plans to pass it on to her daughter. She uses the Corelytics dashboard to keep visibility on all areas of the business where costs tend to creep up and which have caught her by surprise in the past.	Wants to grow his footprint, add more offices and divisions, and ensure that his growth can be sustained and optimized. All franchisees track financial trends in Corelytics and compare their performance to group averages. They all aspire to be fast-growth companies.

Susan	Eric
Metrics that matter to Susan:	**Metrics that matter to Eric:**
• Stability of revenue • Maintenance of gross margin– Her ability to generate gross margin is equated to her ability to generate compensation for herself and her employees and do promotional programs. • *"I need to make sure I'm getting sufficient revenue out of my existing engine to cover ever-increasing costs."*	• Percentage Revenue Growth Rate • Creating a widening difference between gross profit and revenue as the business grows. (If you grow and your margin doesn't grow faster, the business is headed for trouble). Growing financial leverage builds business value. • *"I'm trying to build a continuously improving engine. Better efficiency fuels the development of a bigger and more efficient engine. It's an exciting cycle."*
Exit strategy – Family asset, stable, dependable. Structured management process has built-in alerts and controls so that it will be easy to transition to a new owner. The processes and structure are cookbook: someone else can follow the "recipe" and be just as successful as she was.	**Exit strategy** - Merged or acquired with high-value. Buyers will be attracted by the ability to generate "free cash" (cash not required to sustain operations) and by the ability to generate an ROI on the acquisition price. Visibility on all monthly performance data decreases risk to the investor and adds value.
Sand traps and opportunities – Susan needs to continue her revenue and expense vigil, but she needs to move more focus to her balance sheet. Her business could quickly move from being a family asset to becoming a liability if the strength of the balance sheet is not managed. Building a strong and growing owner's equity and building a continuously improving assets-to-liabilities ratio are key to building overall financial strength.	**Sand traps and opportunities** – Too many franchisors let their franchisees sink or swim. This happens mostly because the franchise owner doesn't have visibility on all the moving parts of each franchisee's business. Eric is on a track where he has the visibility and can reach out to individual franchisees and help them take specific actions to improve their business. Eric wins when his franchisees win. The value of his franchise network can outperform the many thousands of lackluster franchise networks flooding the market giving him a strong advantage.

Conclusion

While cash is crucial, it does not operate in a vacuum. It is completely connected to everything else in the ecosystem within a company and in its external operating environment. If something is going wrong with operating costs or if growth is outstripping company resources, the problem will show up in a shortage of cash.

These problems and many more like them can be monitored and managed, thus avoiding extreme problems. If left unmonitored, there is no way for a company to stay ahead of the curve; and sooner or later, when problems become so obvious that they cannot be ignored, it may be too late to take corrective action. Cash trends serve as a "canary in the mine shaft," alerting business owners to early warning signs well before big problems occur. The secret is to monitor and manage cash trends and not overly fixate on the continual normal monthly peaks and valleys that can hide the real direction in which the company is traveling.

Business management is a continuous process of adjustment and change. Cash management is just one of many such topics. Along the way, every business encounters major decisions and big changes that are more than simple, small, course corrections. The big decisions combined with the many smaller but continuous adjustment decisions determine the success of the company and of the people integral to its journey. In the next chapter we will look at the milestone decisions all businesses will face if they stay on a growth track.

CHAPTER NINE CHECK-UP

1. Under what circumstances would strategic cash management techniques not be appropriate for a business?
2. Under what circumstances are personally guaranteed loans appropriate? What are the risks?
3. How does inventory affect cash flow? What management decisions can be made to keep inventory from putting a drag on cash?
4. Why should a business owner leave cash in the company when they can reduce income taxes by taking it out as bonuses?
5. What is the importance of "free cash?"

CHAPTER TEN

Decisions: Strategic Pivots

Whenever you see a successful business,
someone once made a courageous decision.

-Peter Drucker

Business owners make decisions every day—often several times per hour. Most decisions simply require a quick answer based on gut feel and you're done. Should we buy a coffee pot or a coffee service? Should we subscribe to an industry news service? How are we going to cover the phones when our admin person is on vacation? Should we replace the desk with a broken leg? The list of daily routine questions and decisions is continuous and unending. Very few of these will have a significant impact on the business, but neglecting them can create logjams and distractions that can slow a business to a crawl. These decisions need to be made quickly, taking as little time and attention from top management as possible.

It's the big decisions that make a business move forward and that take a lot of time and consideration. When routine decisions take all or most of the time of top management, they crowd out the more important decisions. Big decisions are what define a company, its direction, and how it operates within its market. Unfortunately, there is usually much less clamor for big decisions than for routine decisions. The well-worn phrase "tyranny of the urgent" comes to mind. There tend to be many squeaky wheels vying for attention around routine decisions and fewer people tuned in to the big ones. When big decisions are being neglected, fewer people notice—until it becomes apparent the business is not moving forward.

The big problem with large, impactful decisions is often the decision process itself. When big decisions are treated the same as routine decisions, things can become erratic and fall apart. Knee-jerk decisions at the routine level can be just fine and are great for moving things forward quickly. But when a decision has broader strategic impact, the thought process must be very different.

Big decisions usually have some number of prerequisites that must be understood and addressed before the decision can be finalized. In fact, these prerequisites often define what is actually possible and how it can be achieved. Let's say you've decided you want to buy a business and merge it into your company. Before you get too far into the process, you'll want to have a business broker (and possibly an attorney and accountant) help you. Now, you may already have an attorney and an accountant but they may not be experienced with acquisitions; allowing them go through their learning curve with your company could be a mistake!

The steps you take in this process will be different if you start with a buying opportunity that found you, rather than you searching for a company to buy. Both paths require a lot of exploration and many questions answered before any final deal can be made. In any case, jumping to a final deal before completing the prerequisite work can be an expensive mistake. It can take a lot more time and money to correct a big decision that was not well thought out than it would to do the job right in the first place. Most business people know this intuitively, but they often fall into the trap of wanting to make big decisions the same way they make routine decisions. It may feel like progress is being made but it just takes a few big mistakes to do permanent damage to a company.

Know Where You Are in the Process

One major consideration for big decisions is "stage appropriateness." For example, a new company that is just learning how to create management processes is probably not in a good position to go out and buy another company and merge operations. But, a new company with seasoned experts on the team might make this an easy win.

Bottom line: Stage of evolution plays a major role in determining what strategies will work to move a business forward. If a company dives into big decisions and bold strategies at the wrong time in its evolution, the chances of achieving a successful outcome are very low if not impossible. The goal is not to slow down the decision process but rather to make it more complete. You may remember that sinking feeling after a hasty decision on a big purchase where you knew you did the wrong thing right after the deal was done. It is referred to as "buyer's remorse." If you had just applied a bit more effort to the investigation and thought process you could have avoided a bad decision or made a few critical changes to the final agreement.

How many times have you seen someone spend the next 10 years wishing they hadn't made a hasty decision? It's not always the decision that was wrong; it may be the actions taken after the decision. Even a perfect decision can have a bad outcome if not implemented well. But take solace here—even bad decisions can have a great outcome! If the actions following the decision compensate or correct for errors in the decision process, all may end well. My preference, and the much safer course, is a combination of a good decision and a good implementation.

One of the prerequisites for almost all major decisions is to obtain key business metrics. These metrics need to be understood from three perspectives: (1) the metrics of the business prior to the decision, (2) the likely impact of the strategic decision on current metrics, and (3) the expected new metrics that will result when the planned action is fully operational. With that in mind, we will now draw on the company development stages described in Chapter Two and the metrics and vital signs described in Chapters Three and Four to frame the major strategic decisions that the typical growing company will face during its evolution along with the metrics needed to secure the best outcomes. Please know there are many exceptions and variations to these decisions and guidelines. The intent is to give you a thought process that moves away from gut feel and wishful thinking and sets the stage for a methodical approach with a higher probability of success.

Forming a Company

Perspective

This is probably the most irrational thing a person can do, according to conventional wisdom. But for those that defy the odds and refuse to be influenced by conventional wisdom, there can be big rewards. Just bear in mind that more than half of new businesses are gone by year five.[9] Of those that remain, the vast majority get stuck and are unable to grow past some barrier they encounter. Small companies usually don't fully understand the barriers that stop them from growing or that keep them from being a sustainable and profitable business. When the company has good metrics there is a much higher probability the owner and team will make well-informed decisions that ultimately lead to success.

Prerequisites

Time, energy, enthusiasm, vision, and commitment are critical elements for moving forward. Information on the market, competition, market demand, viable pricing, the cost of building and delivering the proposed products and services, and an understanding of how much investment is needed are all part of the research required to achieve specific goals. Knowing trends, competitors, and major market changes are important to understanding how your new business will fit in. It is also extremely beneficial to have working experience in your chosen market along with credentials and expertise that will help you quickly build credibility with employees, customers, and potential investors.

Key metrics and vital signs

Industry benchmarks for business growth rates are a key starting point. A growing industry is ideal; a shrinking industry is going to be tough. It is also useful to know the typical revenues for small companies in the target market in your geographic area. Data on the average number of customers serves to generate target revenues, and typical prices is key to building a plan and a financial model that will attract investors and team members.

Going to Market
Perspective
Business plans created at start-up are purely hopes and guesses backed up by market data. As a business builds momentum, the importance of planning becomes greater and the opportunity to do more fact-based projections becomes more of a reality. Unfortunately, most owners of small businesses do not do formalized planning, and very often it is the lack of planning that causes a company to stall. When a business owner sets goals and builds plans for achieving those goals, the probability of hitting them increases dramatically. In other words, companies that do not set and manage goals are likely to drift and achieve limited success.

Prerequisites
Specific goals and supporting rationale—market research data—competitive analysis—general implementation plans including resource requirements for continuation of existing operations plus resources required for growth and for new expansion—identification of needed capital for required investment including plans for repayment or compensation for investors—identification of potential external capital resources

Key metrics and vital signs
Growth rates (short-term and long-term)—company capacity to generate needed capital for investment—growth rates required to achieve defined goals—gross profit and net profit percentage requirements to support planned growth and expansion

Bringing on Investors
Perspective
Bringing in external investors is often the only way a company is going to get started or move to the next level of performance. Growth based

on internally generated resources ("bootstrapping") is usually a slower process. A slow and methodical growth path may be more stable and have fewer risks, but the downside is that the market opportunities can pass you by. In volatile markets, slow growth can render a company unresponsive to the needs and opportunities of the marketplace. Clearly in this scenario there are advantages to bringing in external financing; however, it does create many new obligations to investors and can lead to a loss of control of the business.

Before you go too far down this path, be sure you understand what kinds of companies are viable to investors. For example, most service companies will not attract the typical outside investor. For the most part, investors are looking for companies with assets like products and intellectual property, along with an opportunity for major growth. A company with the potential to generate $50 million in annual revenue will only attract small investors. Companies with a potential for $100 to $500 million in annual revenues begin to get interesting to professional investors, while it takes a $1 billion annual revenue potential to attract most venture capital firms.

Prerequisites

First, it is important that everything about the company be squeaky clean before any legal deals are done with investors. Potential legal problems, incomplete records, disputes, or hidden financial obligations—any major holes in the company—need to be cleaned up and resolved first. When you bring in investors you will be signing "representations and warranties" about the condition of your business. You certainly do not want to leave out any critical items, which can be the basis for a lawsuit. At the same time, you don't want to show a list of exposures that will scare away your investors. It will be important to have your accounting firm and attorney help you identify areas of necessary house cleaning before you get too far down this road. You may find there are issues that cannot be resolved easily and may therefore prevent you from moving forward with outside investment.

Key metrics and vital signs

When prospective investors are performing due diligence and getting to know the company, they will want to understand the plan for growth, the cost of delivering the planned growth, and the funding required to make the growth happen. They will also want to know how they are going to recoup their investment and obtain a return on their investment. Some of the explanation will be narrative but a big part of it will be the numbers. Key metrics include projected annual revenue growth rates, expense ratios, cash requirements per year, gross margins, and forecasted long-term profitability. Ultimately, there will be some form of "liquidity event," which is where the investors finally get their reward. This event could be in the form of selling the business to another company or taking the company public, which means creating an initial public offering (IPO) and getting the company listed on a public stock exchange. All of these are major potential payoff moments for investors and owners.

Getting a Bank Line of Credit

Perspective

First, it is important to recognize that banks generally only extend line of credit (LOC) loans to support operations that generate short-term revenues. LOCs should not be seen as a way to raise capital required to build a business over time. In fact, most banks will want to see that you will be able to pay back the line of credit in less than a year as a result of high probability sales. If the line of credit is not likely to be paid off within one year, it is likely that it is not really an operating loan but rather a long-term capital investment. Bankers will sniff that out quickly and won't go there. One exception is SBA loans. Since all SBA loans are actually made by banks and guaranteed by the Federal Small Business Administration, they do have a few different rules. It is possible to get an SBA loan for funding capital expansion and to establish a long-term (multiple-year) repayment plan. These can be a great way to get a small business started, but there has to be strong evidence that the proposed plan is not just a long-shot gamble. Also remember that it is important to work on building a relationship with a bank and establishing a line of credit before the need arises. Again, the worst time to get an extended LOC is when you are desperately in need of cash.

A big misconception with the SBA is that anybody can walk in and get an SBA loan and that's not true. You have to demonstrate that you have management expertise in the industry and that you can generate that cash based on a projection. I would suggest you make sure you can speak to your numbers. I've seen people bring me projections and, when asked a couple questions about them, they have no clue what I'm talking about because they let their CPA do all the work and didn't even take a look at them. That's not where you should be. You need to understand your numbers even if you're not a numbers person; it's something you need to deal with if you're going to be a business owner, and you're going to grow your business to be all you want it to be.

Jennifer Ringenbach, SBA Specialist, KeyBank
Read more: Appendix Contribution #115

Prerequisites

Be aware that SBA loans and regular bank LOC loans are going to require business owners to personally guarantee the loan. This usually means they will need to use their personal assets such as home, car, and other major assets as collateral. It will also be a requirement to have a business plan, a financial forecast, and two years of tax returns and financial statements to get the process started. Banks and other lenders are also going to want the details on all existing loans and other debts of the company and owner.

Key metrics and vital signs

All the major metrics come into play when applying for a loan. Most banks will have 10 to 20 different ratios they will want to see up front and also monitor throughout the life of the loan. These include ratios such as quick ratio, assets to liabilities, assets to equity, long-term debt to total assets, total debt to equity, receivables to sales, inventory to sales, gross margin, net profit, revenue growth, and total working capital. Then they will want to see the business plan, projected growth rates, projected profitability, and any other expected future needs for capital.

Getting Market Validation

Perspective

This is often a step skipped by small businesses. If the company can grow enough to get off the ground, there becomes little reason to seek input from the market. In fact, most entrepreneurs tend to avoid input from others because they are pursuing a vision most other people would see as illogical. So the entrepreneur is going to think the average person is "just not going to get it" and therefore has no valid input to offer. But, like many of other paradoxes in the world of entrepreneurship, input from the potential target market is absolutely vital even if those individuals don't see the bigger vision. If the market doesn't see the need for the proposed product or service, it is time to do some serious reevaluation. Getting market validation is critical to getting outside investors, strategic partners and highly experienced and qualified team members.

Prerequisites

Market validation should be a structured process involving scoring and quantification of market perceptions. This process is usually best done by a professional marketer, but there are many consultants and advisors qualified to help set up this process. In some cases market validation can also be provided by awards and recognition in the market from thought leaders, leading vendors, and professional associations.

Key metrics and vital signs

The metrics for this process are mostly going to be in the form of scores indicating to what extent prospective customers agree or disagree with structured statements or ranking of choices on a list. One key area of validation lies with pricing. This requires careful planning so that a bell-shaped curve will result, highlighting a central tendency. If the test is just "yes/no" on price testing, it is likely that important perceptions are not being gathered or considered. The goal is to gain market evidence that can substantiate the existence of a market for a proposed product or service at a price that will sustain the business that delivers the product or service.

Transitioning from Operator to Manager

Perspective

This is the process of moving from founder to executive manager or from expert to administrator. Most entrepreneurs and business founders are resistant to this change. If this transition does not occur, it is likely the business will find an upper limit to its growth and will stop at that point. The ideal book to read to get a more in depth perspective on this concept is *The E-Myth* (see appendix for details).

Prerequisites

It usually takes an external expert to help with this transition. It is rare that a founder or entrepreneur will perceive the need to make this change and even more rare that they will take the correct actions to enable it to occur.

Key metrics and vital signs

The ideal strategy for this transition is to set some specific goals for the business that would not be possible to attain given the company's history or current management approach. These goals should be in the form of growth metrics such as annual or quarterly revenue growth goals, profitability goals, and other business performance metrics. In addition, there should be operating metrics such as conversion of leads to customers, units of production, reduction of defects, and decreasing customer complaints. All of these goals should be "stretch goals" that can only be attained by radically changing the way decisions are made and management processes are executed.

Transforming to Growth Mode

Perspective

When a company has looked at all its options and comes to the realization it is not on the right track to achieve its desired growth, this can be the start of a critical turning point. Sometimes investors or other stakeholders impose these turning points; sometimes they are the result of a methodical examination of the current performance and growth rates. This is also a point where an outside expert or advisor can be a big help.

The idea of redefining the business or reshaping its mission is a very tough thing to do. If this process is not done well, there is a high probability the company will go backward instead of forward.

Prerequisites

Usually a transformation includes extensive business planning and some level of market testing and validation. In addition, there are usually significant organizational changes required. The company may need new skills and expertise to move in the new direction. All of that will require recruitment, hiring, training, and creation of new processes.

Key metrics and vital signs

A major transformation requires metrics and results tracking at all levels. This would include baseline sales and marketing metrics as well as financial and operational goals and performance tracking. Measurements and monitoring become even more important once a transition is underway.

Adding a New LOB

Perspective

Generally adding a new line of business is not a disruptive action and can be done in incremental steps. The big danger is that a new line of business often becomes the "new shiny object" that distracts everyone from the other business activities needing to be managed. So, when a new LOB is added, it is often wise to put extra measurements in place on the existing LOBs to help ensure the new business does not disrupt or damage existing business.

Prerequisites

A new LOB should be introduced in much the same way as launching any major change in a business. It should have its own business plan with goals, milestone dates, and management processes. A new LOB should have a defined manager responsible for achieving the planned results. The plan itself should include a number of phases that create management decision checkpoints so adjustments can be made as early as possible.

Key metrics and vital signs

A new line of business should have a full suite of financial goals including revenue generation and growth rates, direct cost ratios, and gross profit attainment. The set goals should be coupled with productivity goals, customer satisfaction goals, quality of service goals, and other operating metrics. The tracking process should be more extensive during the early stages and then simplified once it is clear the new LOB is stable and is meeting its planned goals. Unfortunately, many companies start out with light measurements and only add new ones when they see that something is in trouble. This can make it increasingly difficult to get the job done. This backward approach generally allows significant problems to build early on, which are much more expensive to correct as rollout advances.

Ending Unprofitable Business

Perspective

This is often a very hard thing to do, partially because of emotional attachment but also because there is often a lack of information indicating exactly where the performance problem lies. Without specific data there is a tendency for denial. When each LOB in a company is required to carry its own weight and contribute to overall performance in clear and measurable ways, it can be easy to see which business units are creating a drag on the company and what actions are appropriate. There are many cases where an underperforming LOB will be retained as a loss leader or door opener, enabling a more profitable LOB to get access to a flow of customers. But rarely does a loss leader need to be a drain on a company. When loss leaders are not managed well (i.e., they are not expected to perform at some minimum level), they can become toxic and lead to sloppy management and cynical staff. When it becomes clear it is more damaging to keep a business unit going than it would be to shut it down, it is important to take action quickly and not let the situation become even more damaging.

Prerequisites

As with any major transition, a plan needs to be implemented to ensure existing business units continue to function. The detailed impact of a discontinuance should be considered and resolved before the planned termination, as it usually takes some time to think through all the implications. Many of the business processes may not be documented or may have evolved informally and are not visible to management. As the review process is conducted, there are often discoveries that might change the thinking as to how (or even if) the termination should be done. Sometimes these discoveries result in ideas that can solve problems assumed to be unsolvable! Needless to say this investigation should be done with an open mind.

Key metrics and vital signs

When one business unit is dismantled, it is important that extra measures be put in place for monitoring and managing the remaining areas of the business. By early and proactive monitoring, new potential problems can be caught early and corrective actions taken before major damage is done. The metrics involved should be the full range of financial and operational metrics including business unit growth rates, direct costs, gross margins, and various productivity and quality measurements. If unexpected changes occur during the planned termination of the non-performing business unit, it may be a sign an unexpected connection exists and action should be taken quickly. Most companies do this backwards by not putting metrics monitoring in place until a problem becomes obvious. This is both expensive and damaging when done in reverse order.

Acquiring a Company
Perspective

Acquiring another company can be one of the most disruptive experiences in the life of a company. Many successful companies will see acquisition as a great way to grow faster and add new skills, talents, and customers in the process. But for many such companies, once they have acquired one or two other companies they decide the process of integration is too difficult. They then change the strategy to grow incrementally with the newly combined organization. In some cases, they never succeed at fully absorbing the acquired companies and are left in a weaker position than before the acquisition. There are often many good reasons on paper to do an acquisition, but the actual experience is usually quite different than expected.

When evaluating the value, the key metrics we used were primarily around percentage of revenue (MRR) and service revenue and then non-MRR service revenue and 'other revenue (product and the like).' So, those were the key metrics along with talent and financial position, profitability, and culture.

Jamison West, Arterian (formerly)
Read more: Appendix Contribution #119

Prerequisites

The most successful acquisitions have tight plans and measurements, leaving little opportunity for the process to spin out of control. If there is heavy focus on delivering specific, visible, and measured results, there is less room for creative interpretation or internal conflict. Ambiguity is the enemy of acquisitions. If the integration process is not tight and the new operations environment not well monitored and managed, people will slip through the cracks and processes will fall apart. This is usually not intentional, but simply a consequence of the disorientation resulting from two cultures being pushed together.

Key metrics and vital signs

Like most of the above major transitions, a full range of financial and operational metrics should be employed. Over-managing in the early stages and then cutting back as goals and milestones are met is the best strategy.

Taking on a Partner

Perspective

The assumption here is that two separate companies decide to work together to achieve mutual benefit. This could be a sales channel relationship or an outsourced service such as IT infrastructure management. It might be a co-marketing arrangement or a combination product arrangement, to name a few possibilities. In any case, there is some contractual relationship defined and some outcome that both parties wish to achieve.

Usually these are intended to be long-term relationships, but sometimes they are initiated for a specific project and then terminated. The last instance would usually not be viewed as a partnership but more so as a joint project relationship. In all instances, there is some legal agreement and some specific plan to be achieved. Some companies will have multiple partnership arrangements and the process of building and maintaining these relationships becomes a core competency. The first partnerships are the hardest and usually suffer the most mistakes.

The emergence of strategic alliances as alternatives to going it alone is apparent everywhere. Equally apparent is the failure of most to make these alliances work. In fact, an ongoing strategic alliance requires both partners to maintain control and be unafraid to risk or they will fail. There are three factors to blame for this failure: lack of frequent reporting, limited financial visibility, and inadequate metrics and forecast disclosure.

Terry Wyman, Northwest Strategic Ventures
Read more: Appendix Contribution #129

It's important to have a different set of eyes looking at what you're doing as a reality check. With American football, you see the coach on the sideline with a massive binder, thick with plays but the quarterback has a very simple flip-up wristband from which he can call plays. Similarly, one or two slides of a playbook for different types of partners in your ecosystem is sometimes all that is required. One might look at the financial implications of that relationship and what solutions you may be working on jointly, but more importantly at the relationships. Relationship is really the cornerstone of that playbook. What's the whole point of this relationship? Where is it taking us? Where do we want to go with it?

Gareth Wade, Principal, One Accord Partners
Read more: Appendix Contribution #125

Prerequisites

The key to success is the legal agreement and an operations management procedure. Sometimes these documents are combined. The legal agreement should be specific as to the purpose of the relationship—how the organizations will work together, the means by which fees and compensation will flow, a plan for handling exceptions, how the deal can be terminated, and a process for protecting the intellectual property and proprietary interests of both parties. The operating procedures are less obvious. Operating procedures should define workflows, exception handling, roles and responsibilities, lines of communication, and reporting requirements. The operating agreement should anticipate that there will be learning and discovery during the course of the relationship and should define a process for reviewing and fine tuning processes, goals, and measurements.

Key metrics and vital signs

Specific financial and operating goals need to be defined specific to the partnership arrangement. To the extent possible, goals should be set pertaining to business performance including revenues, costs, margins, and overall profitability. In addition, metrics should be defined to monitor and measure failures, problems, help requests, and other indicators of quality and delivery of support.

Re-branding
Perspective

Growing companies are likely to restructure their branding and identity in the market multiple times as they evolve. Sometimes this is in response to competition or because of new market conditions, but most often it is because of changes in product and service offerings. Re-branding can be disruptive and can take a company way off track if not managed well.

Re-branding is often just the tip of the iceberg that includes changes in operations, production, delivery and pricing of products and services. Often there are new procedures for answering phones and emails, new customer support processes, and new organization structures— the potential list goes on. If all of the affected parts of the company don't move in unison, it could result in market confusion, partner confusion, and, of course, employee confusion. This is a company transition that requires careful and exhaustive planning and execution.

Prerequisites

Re-branding is normally done to help a company better engage its market and improve business performance. A plan and business model dealing with all elements of the changes needs to be prepared and reviewed with all impacted staff well in advance of implementation. There will likely be a significant amount of external communication in the transition, which requires all related internal changes to be in place at the right time in order to converge correctly. You can't be half-hearted about this effort; it is difficult to do a pilot test on a re-branding rollout just like it's not easy to be half pregnant! It is usually an "all in" implementation with no way back.

Key metrics and vital signs

It is particularly important to monitor the performance of all existing business activities not expected to change because of the re-branding right along with the areas that are impacted by the change. If re-branding has broader negative implications than expected, the sooner problems can be detected the better. Metrics should not only include planned and actual revenues, costs, margins, and profits, but also a range of metrics to help verify that customers are happy and not confused. These could be satisfaction surveys or random follow-up phone calls. Early warnings and early adjustments are the key to success.

Geographic Expansion

Perspective

For businesses serving customers in geographic proximity, growth often means putting service and product support operations in new locations in order to gain and serve new customers. Even though more and more companies are moving to a virtual model, there are many businesses lacking that option. Dentists, restaurants, groceries, technology product installers, construction companies, and many other businesses need to be close to their customers. Most of these businesses are happy to get incremental growth in the single geographic area in which they operate. For others, expansion requires adding new locations. When expansion becomes a routine part of a growth strategy, it must become a core competency with well-defined processes. As the competency evolves, it can become relatively easy to build a large number of locations on a very predictable basis.

Prerequisites

Geographic expansion has one requirement unique to all of the above major strategic directions outlined. It is the art and science of selecting optimal locations from which to serve customers and operate the business. This requires unique expertise and experience as there are many considerations beyond just gaining access to more customers. There are a variety of issues such as economic considerations, travel between locations, access to employees with the right skills, proximity to competitors and access to suppliers. An often-neglected consideration is taxing jurisdiction boundaries; very often there are significant differences in local tax rates within just a few blocks. All of this requires a business plan, operating procedures, and ongoing monitoring.

Key metrics and vital signs

When adding locations it is important to monitor all the basic business performance metrics of each location as a separate business unit, and then monitor the combined company as a single business. To make it more complex, each location will probably have multiple LOBs that need to be monitored and managed individually and collectively. This becomes a multi-dimensional reporting and analysis challenge, but can be very profitable as new efficiencies are learned by top performing locations and shared with all locations.

Franchising

Perspective

This is not for everyone, but is a potential path for businesses that can be easily replicated. Franchising is significantly more complicated than most people realize, with many complex legal requirements placed on franchisors that make it especially challenging. But the big advantage is that entrepreneurs use their own money to buy the license and fund operations at the franchisee location. The most important concept in franchising is the creation of a complete business template and procedures manual enabling franchisees to follow the guidelines and be assured they will achieve the planned results.

Prerequisites

Franchisors need to create the plan and business model for the franchise as a whole and also for the individual franchisee. Here it is important to create a process franchisees can use to track their own progress against specific goals that change during the ramp up phase. Then a different process is needed for established franchisees that can help them stretch as they grow their business and build a solid ongoing operation. The whole secret is to build a few early successes in order to attract additional interested prospective franchisees and turn the franchise network into a business engine that leverages off of its own best practices.

Key metrics and vital signs

Metrics for franchises call for almost everything in the book. This includes all the basic financial metrics, revenue, COGS, gross profit, overheads, cash, short-term assets and liabilities, long-term assets and liabilities, and owner's equity—all in terms of dollars, ratios, and growth rates. All of these should have goals, **trend lines**, forecasts, and comparisons of planned and actual performance. Then there is the complete set of operating goals, trends, and actual performance comparisons—all of which are unique for each franchise network. The more franchisees can see how they compare to top performers in their franchise network, the more they will see where they need to tune their business and the more they will steer it in the right direction. This means more financial traction generated for the franchisor.

Outsourcing
Perspective

Outsourcing is an important decision for every business. Where outsourcing used to be an exception, the tide is shifting in the opposite direction. Business owners are learning it can be cheaper and more efficient to outsource many business processes and just focus on the critical few competencies that make their business unique. They can outsource everything from accounting, HR, web site development and management, marketing programs to e-commerce, online catalogs, telesales, computer infrastructure, IT management, specialty writing—and the list goes on. The things that can't be outsourced are vision, direction, leadership, and ongoing business management. However, even those can be handled by turn-around experts and consultants if necessary. With all these options there are many choices to be made and lots of coordination needed. And when you decide to use outsourced services the question becomes, "How do you budget and manage the various levels of spending and services that each of these options offer?" This approach offers a lot of flexibility along with many ways to make mistakes and spend money unnecessarily.

The increasingly mobile and distributed workforce is pressuring traditional organizational structures to evolve and forcing businesses to rethink the way they view their employees. Technology enables them to work on their terms— from where and when they want. The result is a tendency towards less hierarchical organizations and teams. Although the projects themselves are ambiguous, the financials and resourcing do not have to be. Real-time insight into how much of the project budget has been used and whether the right resources have been allocated is essential when organizing creative thinkers. Time-tracking and resource-planning software can offer this insight, but all team members are given access so everyone understands what impact this work has on the overall project.

Martijn van Tilburg, CEO 10,000ft, www.10000ft.com
Read more: Appendix Contribution #127

Prerequisites

Outsourcing takes research, comparisons, selections, contracts, ramp-up, quality-of-service management, and ongoing oversight of results, or else things can quickly get off track.

Key metrics and vital signs

There is certainly a financial element to outsourcing, but the critical element is SLAs (service level agreements) that determine the level of responsiveness provided by the outsourced service provider. When you outsource IT services, you can require 24/7 systems monitoring with full systems redundancy so you never have an outage. Or for a whole lot less money you can have a 10/5 coverage plan with one-hour responses to problems and 24-hour maximum resolution of complex problems. You would probably want 24/7 on your ecommerce web site, but 8/5 would probably be fine for general business email systems support.

Once all the performance metrics have been defined for all outsourced services, the next goal is to monitor and manage compliance. **Predictive analytics** applied to SLAs can play an important role here. If you can track usage patterns and forecast growth, you can negotiate expanded services before the need arises and stay a step ahead. This is also a great basis for budget planning for the outsourced services used by the company.

Protecting Your Intellectual Property
Perspective

Protecting IP is something that needs to be done early on in the life of a company. Doing it after the fact creates an exposure that sometimes cannot be corrected after the fact. There are many options for protecting the critical information of a company. There are patents, trademarks, and service marks that provide different levels of protection. Copyright and trade secret protections are most appropriate for brands and titles of products and services. The cheapest options are covered by non-disclosure agreements and may turn out to be the most important and the most valuable.

Trade secrets are anything you want to keep secret and protect so you build value in some concept not shared with anyone outside a specific group of your confidants. The idea is that each person who is given access to this information signs a confidentiality agreement giving you exclusive legal rights to what you have shared with them. This increases the value in your trade secret. There are many other strategies with subtle differences, but the purpose here is to urge you to think through what you need to protect and then verify you have contracts and agreements in place to ensure your exclusive rights are protected.

Prerequisites

It is important to think of IP as an asset. But there aren't very many ways to get IP translated into an asset that can be recorded on the company's financial statements. However, IP can translate into significant value when it comes time to sell the company.

Key metrics and vital signs

This item doesn't really have any associated metrics, but it is part of a company valuation assessment when potential buyers are doing their due diligence review.

Selling a Part of Your Company

Perspective

Companies that have built a solid business have more options than simply selling the whole company. For example, the owner might do a "leveraged buyout" deal with the management team, allowing the team to buy out the owner over some defined period of time. This could take many years and could spread the payment out in a very tax advantaged way. And if the management team doesn't meet certain payment and performance criteria, the original owner could get the business back for some fractional cost. Or it might be possible to sell 30 percent of the company to an outside investor who ultimately wants the option to buy the whole thing at some predefined value formula. Or maybe you just want to put your key employees on a stock option plan. There are many options that can generate additional commitment and some that can generate early cash while setting the stage for a full buyout later on.

Prerequisites

All of the required work is the same as if you were preparing to sell the whole company as described above. The big difference is that you will continue running the company for some period of time when the sale

Decisions: Strategic Pivots

is done in stages. You can expect to have a fairly complex set of performance metrics to track and you will need to constantly be prepared to take action when any party does not meet its minimum performance obligations.

Key metrics and vital signs

As with the above, this requires the full set of financial and operating metrics.

Selling Your Company

Perspective

This is a momentous occasion—a lifetime of work culminating in one complex transaction. The problem is that most business owners don't plan ahead for this possibility. Then one day something happens that makes it mandatory for them to sell their business. Very often it has nothing to do with the business itself. It could be due to a sudden health issue, a divorce, a sudden change in the local economy, or a family financial crises. If the owner has built his or her business with the idea that it will be ready to sell whenever the right opportunity arises or when an unexpected situation occurs, he or she has a huge advantage over the person that just waits until the time comes. In fact, very often businesses that have not prepared will find they are worth very little or nothing and they generally can't change that with just a few months of lead time.

On the other hand, companies that have prepared and made all the right moves to maximize their value can obtain huge benefits when the time comes to sell. Ideally all small businesses should find a business coach to help them put their house in order and keep it that way. That would be far better than buying an insurance policy and a great way to manage risk. At a minimum, a business owner should assume it will take two years to make the moves necessary to maximize value. It would be even better to plan five years out. The longer the planning horizon and the more aggressive the plan, the greater the value and return on the owner's investment.

A special note on **exit planning** and **tax planning** is appropriate here. Many successful company sales end up generating unnecessary taxes that can erase the value of the sale. It is just as important to plan what you are going to do with the proceeds of a sale as it is to plan for the sale in the first place. If done right, there are many ways to multiply the benefit of the sale and avoid unnecessary taxes.

All, or most of, your business assets can be lost to taxes during a succession transfer. This is money that could otherwise be directed to philanthropy with some planning. It requires knowledge of the code, where you not only can save a significant tax outlay but contribute in a way that directs money to your personal passions.

Chuck Albers, Dynamic Affluence Group
Read more: Appendix #117

Prerequisites

This is all about basic business planning with an added twist. The goal is to build a plan tuned to maximize value. The steps to be taken will be unique for each industry, but, very broadly, the goal is to build a track record showing stable and steadily growing revenues, expenses that are growing at a slower rate than revenue, gross profit that is growing steadily faster than revenue growth, and an ability to generate cash in excess of what is required to pay ongoing operating bills (often called "free cash"). Then there are the goals of building a management team that can run the business without the owner being present, create processes everyone understands and follows, obtain solid long-term customer contracts, and more. All these actions combined can make a huge difference in what a prospective buyer will pay for a business.

Key metrics and vital signs

It is important to manage the full range of business metrics, including both financial and operating numbers. It is also important that you know what potential buyers are going to look for and how they will conduct due diligence before agreeing on a price. If you know ahead of time, you can take action to ensure you get top results. If you and your coach are watching the progress of your company, you can gradually make the key

Decisions: Strategic Pivots

moves that make big jumps in business value. Just be aware that business brokers working with business buyers put a huge emphasis on trend analysis and future growth forecasting. The price a buyer is willing to pay is a combination of the profits they can earn now combined with the potential profit they can earn in the future. If the trends show a good match between growth and spending, the forecasting will show a very attractive future for the new buyer. A steady and consistent business model will always have greater value than a business with big peaks and valleys.

Be aware that business brokers working with business buyers put a huge emphasis on trend analysis and future growth forecasting.

Conclusion

If you don't understand your metrics and vital signs before, during, and after a major transition, you are likely to resort to gut feel and get unsatisfactory results. The odds of success are greatly increased when a business has a good handle on the numbers. The metrics become your steering mechanism and allow you to adjust your course as events unfold. Big decisions and big changes need good steering mechanisms to minimize risk and improve the probability of success. Keeping the vital signs and goals visible and making continuous steering adjustments are key to arriving safe and sound at a desired destination.

CHAPTER TEN CHECK-UP

1. When should an owner begin planning for the sale of his/her company?

2. What are the ways a business owner might grow his/her company?

3. Should all companies care about IP? Is IP the same for all companies? What are the most common forms of IP?

4. What are the advantages and disadvantages of bringing in outside investment?

5. In what situations will outsourcing be good for a company and in what situations would it not be appropriate?

CHAPTER ELEVEN

Making a Move

---

*Good business leaders create a vision, articulate the vision,
passionately own the vision, and relentlessly drive it to completion.*

-Jack Welch

There are moves and then there are MOVES. Business owners and senior managers are constantly making decisions and taking actions that keep a company moving. Along the way there are major moves that may adjust the course or even set a new direction. These are often referred to as *strategic decisions* because of their long-term impact. In this chapter we want to build on the list of major decisions discussed in Chapter 10 by outlining the process by which major decisions get implemented and produce results.

First, let's be clear as to why this is important. We make decisions because we want to achieve specific goals or outcomes. However, no result occurs in a vacuum. Any desired outcome must sit on top of some existing reality. Even for a brand new startup, there is a beginning point that includes the skills, reputation, history, and resources the founders bring to launch the new business. If it is an established business taking a new direction, the existing business will in some way be part of (or at least the starting point for) the new direction.

Another way to look at it is through the eyes of the entrepreneur. Remember, one of the attributes of an entrepreneur is the ability to suspend common beliefs that tend to limit creativity and avoid risk. The entrepreneur will ignore conventional wisdom and make a leap of faith into some new opportunity with the confidence that he/she will eventually be able to figure it out. Entrepreneurs are driven by visions of future outcomes that can bypass issues of practicality. This is good news and bad news. Sometimes the big leap of faith is ill-informed and really just wishful thinking that has little real hope of achieving a good outcome. In many cases, a little bit of intelligent investigation will make it clear that the hot new idea is not realistic even for the most optimistic entrepreneur.

But as we think about applying a bit of reasoning and analysis to the entrepreneur's thought process, it is important to know that many of the greatest success stories have come from new ideas that would never have stood the test of research and investigation.

The idea of selling books on the web was already an idea that had been tried and failed before Jeff Bezos decided to build Amazon.com. When he started Amazon, there were many reasons to believe he would fail as many others had. In fact, it would never have worked if he hadn't made significant changes to his original concept—changes he hadn't even considered when he first started.

When Jeff started Amazon, he had no idea it would become a platform for e-commerce that would rock the world. He just wanted to build a cool online book selling company. As he began to see what worked and what did not, he redefined his vision many times along the way. I'm sure the idea of the Amazon Web Service (AWS) was never in his wildest dreams when he launched the company in 1994. But with the launch of AWS in 2006, Amazon has been a force in driving cloud computing, which is having a transformative influence on information technology equivalent to the Internet. As the company continues to evolve, it will probably look very different in another five to ten years.

As we think about the decision-making process and what it takes to turn bold new decisions into reality, we must agree on one thing: it is impossible to put entrepreneurial thinking in a bottle. We are not going

Making a Move

to reduce it to a formula or a canned process. It is creative. It's about taking ideas in new directions. Sometimes it begins with old ideas and giving them new life. Sometimes it begins by creating a fresh never-before-thought-of idea and popping it into existence. This takes a spark of imagination that is probably in everybody but is usually thought of as "dreaming." Most of the time the "dreamers" that come up with these hot ideas lack the conviction and willpower to create a new reality.

While you consider how the Amazon story might apply to you, remember there are a number of pitfalls into which entrepreneurs can fall. Bad things happen. As you read the steps below, keep in mind that the goal is to get a good handle on the major business milestones way ahead of time so you can minimize your personal risk and move through these hurdles quickly.

Making Your Vision a Reality

I recently had a conversation with a business owner who confessed,

I had to make a decision. I had a vendor and an employee standing there waiting for me to pull the trigger. Were we going to add a new monitoring service for our clients or not? This was a big decision. I knew this could cost us big time and we really didn't have money to spare. I also knew that everyone else was doing it and if we wanted to keep up with our competitors we needed to take action. So I swallowed hard and said yes. I told my employee to work with the vendor. I signed the order, and went back to my pending list of dilemmas that needed my immediate attention.

The business owner went on to say,

Two weeks later I asked my employee where we were with the new monitoring software. The answer I got was a shock to me. The purchase was completed, the software was installed, but no further action had been taken. It was just sitting there. The software was incurring a monthly cost but not doing anything for the business. My first thought was, What's wrong with you people? Do I have to spell everything out for you?

But I pulled back from the edge and simply told my employee to make this a priority and get it operational for selected clients. So I'm hoping that next time I check there will be something happening that makes this a positive decision for our business.

It's not hard to see some obvious problems with the business owner's thought process. My advice would have been to take the following three steps:

1. **Decide what you are trying to accomplish.** If you can't be clear on this point, team members are going to come up with their own ideas and you will very likely have multiple definitions of success floating around.

2. **Define specific goals and timelines.** This should include target dates and target sales or customer volumes and other measures that clearly show what is expected. There should also be some form of analysis showing what the investment needs to accomplish in order to pay for itself and create a "net benefit." This means that the financial benefits should be greater than the costs.

3. **Schedule progress reviews.** Without a structured review process, it is likely that things will drift off track and other priorities will take over. These can be short meetings, but an actual meeting (not just an email update) will go a long way to focus attention and solve problems that can stay hidden until something breaks.

True confession: I made plenty of decisions just like this over the years. It's pretty common for even the best managers to make impulsive decisions and then discover that wishful thinking wasn't enough to achieve a good outcome. It's easy to give advice and describe exactly how a decision process should work, but it's much harder to actually take all the right steps to do this. Sometimes there just isn't enough time in the day to get everything done right.

With that backdrop, let's take a closer look at the ideal process for making major business decisions. All decisions have two parts: (1) evaluation - arriving at a decision and (2) action - turning the decision into reality. If either part is missing or not done well, desired results will not be achieved. Decisions can be made and declared for the world to hear, but if the right follow-up action doesn't happen the decision is nothing more than an idea without substance. Declaring bold new decisions can create the sensation of forward momentum. But, in actuality, if there is no action, nothing happens. Or worse yet, there can be lots of arm waving and activity that looks like action, but if there is no traction, it leads to the same results—an idea with no substance. Many entrepreneurs and idea-people are great at arriving at a decision. In fact, many entrepreneurs think the decision is done when they make a declaration. They expect everything else to happen automatically and they move on to the next issue or adventure.

In fairness, this process of making quick decisions and moving on to the next topic is fine for routine operating issues, assuming there is a team in place to turn the decision into action. In any business there are routine situations or questions where the business leader just needs to make a decision so everyone can move forward. Gut instinct is often just fine for these decisions—questions such as, "When is the due date for a specific task?" "Who should do the task?" "Who should return a customer call?" and "Where shall we meet for lunch?" If you spend more than a nanosecond on these issues and questions, you will run out of time to do the important jobs.

Careful thought must be given to strategic decisions with large and long-lasting impact on the company. As we pointed out in Chapters 1 and 2, the pace of business decision-making is accelerating. Companies simply have to respond faster if they want to be competitive and build customer confidence. But that does not suggest that strategic decisions should be made by impulse and gut instinct alone.

In most businesses large and small, strategic decisions that create the most benefit tend to be well-informed ones in which everyone is on the same page. When subjected to adequate rigor and upfront evaluation, much time and effort can be saved during implementation and on-going operation.

It should be mentioned that, while generally a best practice, doing a thorough and complete evaluation of options can also be a slippery slope. Waiting around to make the perfect decision can be just as bad as being too hasty. And, while undoing a wrong decision can be a lot like going in reverse, getting caught up in a lengthy drawn-out decision process is like standing still on the race track while your competition goes flying by. Sometimes going in reverse followed by a doubling of speed can produce a better result than standing still. This just underscores the fact that good judgment and a balanced perspective is very important. Getting it "just right" is a real art form and takes lots of experience. This is just another way of saying mistakes are an inevitable part of the process.

Remember, perfection is the enemy of good enough. When you don't know the difference between the two, it is hard to get it right. Getting to good enough is almost always the best answer. The incremental cost to go from good enough to perfection is usually very high. Of course this is all great theory but very hard to nail down in the heat of battle.

Perfection is the enemy of good enough.
When you don't know the difference between the two,
it is hard to get it right.

This can be further complicated by the way we view problems. Inexperienced owners and managers will often confuse symptoms and problems. The most common example is the business owner who sees his/ her profits falling or cash shrinking and jumps to the conclusion that they need more sales. But it is very possible the bigger problem is not sales but rather a fundamental problem with costs or pricing. If the underlying problem is costs or pricing, treating the symptom can actually make the problem worse. A huge number of companies go out of business every year because of this fatal mistake. Understanding the difference between symptoms and underlying problems can be confusing where there is a lack of experience or a lack of essential information.

Once an underlying problem is understood, it becomes easier to identify and evaluate multiple potential solutions and pick the best course of action. Before deciding on a specific course of action, one more step should be taken: determine the criteria for success. The criteria should help describe what the desired outcomes are and what assumptions and conditions are required to achieve that outcome. Then choosing from multiple alternative solutions becomes a process of comparing how well each alternative lines up with the criteria for success. The more you quantify the criteria, the easier it is to score and compare the alternatives.

This is where metrics come into the picture. Following is a list of potential topics with some kind of dollar value or quantity that should be included in the decision process:

- Financial performance goal – this could be the overall goal the strategic decision is going to support or, even better, the specific performance goal this decision is expected to achieve. This could either be in the form of increased revenues or decreased costs (or both).
- Goal time frame – a specific target date for accomplishing the financial goal should be set
- Resources – this could be in the form of increases to staff work load, staff time to be reduced, orders to be processed per day, new leads to be acquired per week, or many other such potential metrics
- Quality – this could be in the form of customer satisfaction survey scores, customer retention, support calls per customer or time required to get a task done
- Risks – generally this will not be a specific metric, but rather specific conditions that make it clear things are headed in a wrong direction. For example, the risk that customer satisfaction might decrease may be identified as a special area of concern and may require additional monitoring and a plan for a response.

Defining these expectations and measurements up front helps tremendously in selecting from among multiple alternatives and helps keep things on track during implementation. With these thoughts in mind, the following is a general checklist of topics to consider when making a strategic business decision. Not all of these apply to all decisions but when these are skipped, it can reduce the likelihood of a successful outcome.

Strategic Decision Process Checklist

1. Problem description

   This begins with a description of the "apparent" problem—the problem everyone can see—and then digging to find the underlying dilemma. The apparent problem is usually a symptom of something deeper, but the symptom and the underlying problem must be described and quantified. If they can't, they are probably not well understood and it will be difficult to know when the problem is solved. (Chapter 6 has a section entitled "Symptoms versus Problems" that discusses this further.)

2. Opportunity description

The opportunity is the forward-looking view of a strategic decision. It is a combination of vision and quantified benefit. Ideally an opportunity should be described at three levels:

Level One: the easy, high-probability, short-term results that could be achieved; ideally this should also be able to achieve break-even on the initial investment

Level Two: the long-term achievable outcome; this will often require more investment but will provide a bigger payoff and is usually the primary justification for going after the proposed strategy

Level Three: the home run hit; this should not be viewed as a big stretch goal with lower odds of achievement but within the realm of possibility; this outcome should not be the primary reason for making the strategic decision, though it should be a driver

3. Desired outcomes

Once the potential opportunities are understood, the most achievable aspects of the opportunity should be converted to specific measurable outcomes pegged to specific target dates. These should be stated as "milestones" and there should only be a few of them. The intent is to turn these into major markers of success. If these milestones are not achieved they become strong indicators of a major problem that should send the management team back to the drawing board. When a milestone is missed, it is unlikely that other remaining milestones are going to be achieved. Recalibration is probably going to be necessary.

4. Alternative solutions

Prior to making any major strategic decision, there should be an evaluation of alternative solutions. Just going through this process often sheds new light on the problem being addressed and leads to important adjustments to the desired outcome. There are almost always at least three potential alternatives and one of those is usually to do very little or nothing at all. Some alternatives may have "sub alternatives" that might be thought of as minor variations on a broad theme. However, it is just as bad to have too many alternatives as it is to have too few. There are usually only a few choices that adequately represent the major possibilities and that is generally the right starting point for an evaluation of alternatives.

5. Costs, benefits, and ROI for each alternative solution
Each alternative should have a high-level understanding of costs, benefits, time frames, resources, etc. This should not be an exhaustive analysis, but deep enough to give a high degree of certainty that costs and ROI (return on investment) for each alternative are adequately understood.

6. Risk assessment
The risks for each alternative should be identified to the extent possible. It is easier to see the potential beneficial of alternative solutions and often difficult to see the risks. When risks are contemplated before selecting an alternative, it is easier to find mitigating solutions that can minimize or eliminate the risks. This is another example of an action that costs a small amount of time and effort up front but which is very expensive if done after the fact. It is common for entrepreneurs to skip the risk assessment and pay dearly later on.

7. Internal validation
Once an overall concept is developed and alternative solutions assessed, it is extremely important to get feedback from the internal team. This feedback should be requested before a final decision is made so there is real meaning to the idea of team participation. Team feedback can bring to light topics that might have been missed and builds team commitment to the final decision.

8. External validation
Getting external input on basic concepts and direction can add a lot. External input can be pivotal and may send management back to the drawing board. You would not want to share all the details with an

external audience but certainly enough for them to get a meaning-ful understanding. It is amazingly easy for a management team to think they have the best idea in the universe only to discover that a few well-placed questions to customers, prospects, and advisors can show fatal flaws that are obvious when given a fresh outside look.

9. Solution ownership and sponsorship

   In very early stage companies it is normal for the strategic decision maker to also have responsibility for planning, implementing, moni-toring, and making any necessary adjustments. As a company grows, the process of developing new strategic solutions becomes a shared team process. The person creating the idea is usually not the person overseeing implementation and a totally separate person is usually overseeing business impact and benefit. Having an executive level sponsor in a mid-sized company is considered a best practice by the Project Management Institute (http://www.pmi.org/).

10. Implementation plan

    The implementation plan should be at least sketched out during the evaluation of each alternative. Each alternative should have a plan showing how it would be implemented and rough estimates of time and resources required. Sometimes a higher cost plan delivered in a shorter time frame with higher quality results can produce a much better ROI than a plan that takes longer but costs less. Understand-ing these trade-offs is easier when a basic implementation plan is part of the evaluation of alternatives. Then of course the implemen-tation plan for the selected alternative will need to be more fully developed as part of the final decision process.

11. Promotional campaign

    All major strategic initiatives should be viewed as a "campaign" to win the hearts and minds of internal staff as well as external players. An investment in a strategic direction should be "sold" to all parties, internal and external. The campaign should begin before the strate-gic plan is launched and should continue during implementation and then on in to the future as the strategy becomes fully operational. Ultimately everything a company does should have a cheerleader. Whether this is the CEO, an industry leader, an investor, or an internal marketing team; this is the ingredient required to build energy, buzz, and momentum, and it helps bridge the troubled moments that inevitably are part of every new undertaking.

12. Pilot test

Amazingly, many new products and services hit the market as if they were ready for prime time only to discover there are serious problems now on display for the world to see. These problems could have been discovered early and corrected before full rollout, far less expensively and with far less damage to market perceptions. Pilot testing with the help of selected "friendly" customers is a great way to do initial refinements. Friendly pilot customers enjoy feeling like they are part of the team and part of your success.

13. Implementation monitoring process

Monitoring and management should take place at two levels. The first should be the management of daily/weekly/monthly performance with oversight to ensure everyone involved in implementation and rollout knows his or her place and is delivering according to plan. The second level is for overall review at defined strategic checkpoints or milestones. The latter is intended to ensure the implementation is sufficiently on track to warrant a continuation of the project. If actual results are significantly different than expected, the milestone review process should be where potential go/no-go decisions are made.

14. Post implementation review

This step is rarely implemented but is considered a best practice by the Project Management Institute (http://www.pmi.org/). A post implementation review can often see patterns across multiple strategic initiatives and see which processes need to be improved to get better results.

Ultimately the success of any plan is all about execution. Great execution can compensate for bad decisions and bad plans up to a point.

Thanks to the information age, there is no lack of input on how to be successful, beat your competitors, grab every share of the market, hire the best staff, and build a better mouse trap. But how many of these "instant success" solutions have you acted on? What people and companies need is someone to help them master two key disciplines that are so often underdeveloped or missing from the management skill set: execution and discipline.

Manuel Palachuk, Palachuk International
Read more: Appendix Contribution #135

Strategic Decision Considerations

In Chapter 10 we described the kinds of strategic decisions, or strategic pivots, that a business will typically make over the course of its life cycle from start-up to sell-off or other end game. In this chapter we have outlined the process of strategic decision-making and now we will touch on some of the optional ingredients you might want to build into your strategic plan.

- Investors
  Generally companies are in business to serve the interests of their investors. Of course that means the company must have happy customers, partners, and employees or its investors' interests will not be served. Normally investors do not get involved in the operating decisions of the companies in which they invest, but there are many ways in which they can contribute to the success of these companies. They should be invited to help when that makes sense. They can help make important connections with industry specialists, prospective customers, bankers, and other potential investors.

- Partners
  Partners can include suppliers, channel resellers, trainers, installers, consultants, advertisers, and industry specialists. These players can

all be parties to business strategies that drive a company forward. Relationships with them are key to building market awareness of your products and services and are also the conduits to selling and delivering the products and services that you sell. They generally have some economic stake in the transactions they enable; often the compensation plans provide incentives to motivate partners to achieve specific results that deliver business results for the company.

Quantifying partner performance is an important aspect of maintaining a healthy relationship. Frequent reporting on volumes, trends, and the overall economic benefit of a partnership can play a big role in maintaining a positive relationship. Reporting with trend analytics should also make it possible for both parties to recognize potential problems early and take corrective action long before the relationship goes negative.

Partners tend to cut their losses quickly if they find quantifiable business value equations that make the cost/benefit equation more attractive elsewhere. The partner who continually provides quantitative data reflecting value with hard-core numbers is more readily kept on as a partner. You want to be able to say, "We can make you more profitable and here's the proof." That is the key. Otherwise, it's merely left to perception or guesswork.

Marek Omilian, Managing Director, Value Prism Consulting, LLC
Read more: Appendix Contribution #113

- Strategic customers
  These are customers that have a special relationship with your company because they do a large volume of business or because they have unique or complex needs or because they provide some kind of business benefit that is of value to your company. The unique value could be that they agree to do pilot testing on new products or help validate the design of new products and services. Strategic partners need to be wisely chosen because they take a lot of time and attention. A neglected strategic customer can be more of a detriment than an asset. Good relationships can provide many benefits beyond those to which all parties formally agree.

- Business ecosystem

  This is a concept that recognizes the interdependence of partners, customers, industry experts, professional associations, publishers, vendors, and other players in every industry. The more a company can be a player in its industry's ecosystem, the easier it is for various other players to get to know it and do business with it. At their best, ecosystem relationships can be a much more effective way to build a market presence than can conventional advertising. One of the game changing forces at work in business ecosystems is the Internet and the various methods of social networking and ecommerce. Business plans and market strategies should have a clear understanding of the players in their ecosystem and should have plans to leverage the various relationships.

  One can judge the connectedness of the ecosystem players by how much information they share. In any given situation this may be for mutual benefit or individual player benefit, but there must be long-term and sustained benefits to all players or the ecosystem will devolve. The cooperation between ecosystem players can be measured by the flow of information.

  -Doug Hall, CEO Focus Seattle
  Read more: Appendix Contribution #136

- Governance

  As companies grow and relationships with the business ecosystem become more complex, governance methods can be used to extend the normal operating hierarchy and drive strategic initiatives. Companies can use advisors, industry experts, consultants, project managers, steering committees, and project teams to drive and manage new strategic initiatives. Using these resources will allow the organization to function more like a matrix than a top-down hierarchy and will help make it much more responsive and agile. All major strategic initiatives should include a plan for governance and monitoring performance. Key to making governance work is (a) a method for providing feedback to all participants so that they can track planned and actual performance, and (b) a tight connection to the operating organization so day-to-day business operations and strategic initiatives do not work at cross-purposes.

- Letter of intent / term sheet
Strategic relationships generally have some form of an operating agreement that defines obligations and major management processes. Prior to creation of the operating agreement, the parties should create a simple outline of the working relationship and get consensus on these principles before moving into the creation of the formal contract. These outlines can be in the form of a LOI (letter of intent), term sheet (an outline of basic deal terms), or MOU (memo of understanding). These are generally non-binding, but sometimes there will be a non-refundable earnest money provision. This step allows the parties to express their desired outcomes and key economic considerations before they formally lock in. Only after agreement is reached on the basic concepts should work begin on the formal contact.

- Contract
The contract could be a reseller agreement, license agreement, joint operating agreement, or other such agreement. This is the formal document describing the relationship between the parties, how value is exchanged, and how conflict is resolved should it arise. The goal of a contract is not to create an instrument both parties can use to control each other. Rather, it defines the relationship and the consequences of not performing as agreed such that both parties have incentive to establish a mutually supportive and advantageous relationship. A contract that clearly defines performance criteria and mutual roles and responsibilities is less likely to have conflict or misunderstanding.

- Scalability
All strategic relationships should be designed to scale up or scale down the volume commitments. In some cases going above or

below a certain volume could simply require that a new formula be devised prior to going further. Leaving limits undefined creates exposures for all parties. Another approach is to define caps or limits to the amount of compensation paid. In other cases, it might be appropriate to define increasing compensation rates at the high end of performance so there is greater incentive to get to top performance. But even when the compensation increases to create incentive, there are probably other changes in roles and responsibilities that should be redefined at the extremes. If there are no mechanisms for making adjustments at either the high end or the low end, there will be a risk that the extremes will break the relationship.

- Exclusivity
  Exclusivity is usually easy to grant in the early stages of a company's growth but often becomes a harmful limitation that puts a drag on business. For example, let's say a company grants some form of exclusive arrangement to a channel partner. As the company grows it learns there are more productive channel arrangements available; however, the early partner has locked them into a low performing arrangement with no exit provision. To prevent such relationships from becoming dead weights, it is important to build in mechanisms that allow for renegotiation of terms or outright termination under certain conditions. One way to do this is to have triggers that require renegotiation of terms and rates. Example triggers could be revenue milestones, elapsed time, or resource utilization targets. Another way to trigger renegotiation is to tie initial agreement terms to an existing release of a product with a provision that rates can be renegotiated when a new version of the product is introduced. This requires careful consideration by an attorney to ensure government regulations are not violated and provisions are enforceable.

- Accountability
  All corporate initiatives should have a specific person assigned the responsibility for ensuring that contractual terms are adhered to and

all contractual obligations are delivered as specified. This person, or perhaps another person, should be assigned to managing operating activities to ensure planned results are being achieved. If there is no individual with clear accountability, it is unlikely that the new strategy will succeed. The accountable person should have specific reporting responsibilities to players in the governance structure.

- Metrics
  All corporate strategies should have an operating model showing the forecasted volumes of units produced, sales, support resources, promotional spending and costs, and revenues associated with the strategy. These metrics should be used to evaluate alternatives, select a chosen alternative, provide investment, set up budgets, and track ongoing production and spending. Metrics should define the relationship of prices and costs as volumes increase. New costs and new potential revenue opportunities are usually discovered as roll-out occurs and need a provision for adjustments to the agreement. Defining and tracking metrics will catch surprises early and are key to a successful partnership.

Much more could be said about each of these points, but the intent here is to provide broad view of the topics to be considered as a company plans and executes its way to success.

As your company evolves, these topics will become intrinsic to routine processes, as well as more comprehensive. To that point, it is important to mention that "complexity and completeness" are the enemy of "adequate" in the same way that perfection is the enemy of good enough. In fact, excess complexity can kill deals and undermine routine business processes. Ironically, it is easier to create high-bulk, complex processes than it is to create simple sufficient processes. Genius is all about making the complex simple.

CHAPTER ELEVEN CHECK-UP

1. What are the keys to making a good strategic decision?
2. Why is post implementation important?
3. What is the purpose of a term sheet? How does it affect the contract?
4. Should all decisions be subjected to the same rigor? Why or why not?
5. When a strategic decision needs to be made, how does the issue of scalability enter into consideration?

Making a Move

CHAPTER TWELVE

Staying the Course

Whatever course you decide upon, there is always someone to tell you that you are wrong. There are always difficulties arising which tempt you to believe that your critics are right. To map out a course of action and follow it to an end requires courage.

- Ralph Waldo Emerson

What do you think marks the biggest difference between successful and failed companies? You might think that it is money, luck, the team, smarts, the market, and other such possibilities. These can all play a role but none are nearly as pivotal as *persistence*. This is the ability to weather the storms, take unexpected hits, talk to unhappy customers, keep doing the many routine daily tasks—it's the persistence that keeps a business alive.

One could argue that no business should ever fail. If a business has the ability to adapt to changing conditions, it should be able to respond to any tough situation with some form of change that will enable it to go to the next step. This means that failed businesses only fail when the owner doesn't want to go through another learning and adaptation effort. This might be insulting to an owner who lost his or her business as it suggests a careful examination will show that, if the owner had a bit more information and had been willing to make the necessary changes and endure some additional pain, there probably would have been a way to keep the business alive.

One of the many hopes for this book is that business owners and entrepreneurs will use **predictive analytics** as a tool to see the road ahead more clearly and make adjustments earlier rather than waiting until they hit the brick wall. It is devastatingly painful to hit the wall, and most people have a limit to the number of collisions they can endure. Owners will get to the place where they simply can't take it anymore. But if they could see ahead and steer around the big barriers rather than hit them, it would be much easier to keep going and build adaptive strategies, one of which would be persistence.

In rally racing, a popular mantra is, "You go where you look." Most people don't look far enough ahead. They focus on the taillights in front of them, not on what's happening down the road. Learning how to avoid tunnel vision so you can see the bigger picture of what's coming at you is a major part of the learning to drive fast.

DirtFish Rally School Sr. Instructor, Nate Tennis
Published in Alaska Airlines Magazine, Aug. 2013, by Jeff Layton

Of course, just doing the analytics and understanding what lies ahead for your company is not enough. It is, however, a big and important starting point. Once a barrier becomes visible, there are evasive actions you can take that can lead to an uninterrupted journey. Bear in mind that companies are encountering barriers all the time. In fact, you can argue that there is no barrier that can't be overcome; it just takes the right moves. The only insurmountable barrier is the one where the decision-maker stops moving. Even though there may be good reasons for stopping, there are, at the same time, many examples of business leaders who went around similar barriers and went on to achieve success.

Staying the Course

Twenty Common Mistakes

In the spirit of looking ahead and taking corrective action before hitting a barrier, let's take a look at 20 common (and avoidable) mistakes business leaders make that can grind their businesses to a halt:

1. Irregular performance reviews – This is like not looking at the road when you are driving. Without a regular and methodical review process it should not be a surprise when you run into a problem that should or could have been avoided. Business owners should spend some amount of time every month with their trusted advisor(s) to review status and then have a review with the whole management team. Weekly would be better, but a monthly review of prior month financial performance should be a must.

2. Lack of a process – Most business owners know that in order to grow a business, you must have standardized processes so team members know how to do their jobs. Without defined processes you don't have a playbook or a team that can make the plays. Along with processes for doing the work of the business, there should be formalized processes for monitoring business performance, prioritizing, exploring solutions, assigning responsibilities, and then cycling back to monitoring. If processes are unstructured and ad hoc, individuals may do fine but the team as a whole will be ineffective.

3. Numbers without connections – most numbers studied in isolation tell a very different story than when combined with other numbers. A single pixel can't give you the whole picture. Numbers from multiple metrics and multiple points in time are the key to the big picture. Knowing you made a profit last month might seem like good news until you look at the rest of the story and see a trend indicating you are shortly going to run out of cash and have used up your credit line. When you link these pieces of information together you might discover you are growing too fast and draining the company's cash. If you see it early enough, you can put on the brakes, conserve cash, and then figure out what needs to be corrected so that growth stops draining cash. Many possible scenarios like this than can be brought to light early and corrected long before things get desperate.

4. Overly broad analysis – Almost as bad as not putting the details together to see the big picture is keeping analysis so broad that problems stay hidden until something breaks. A common example is the company that does not do performance analysis by line of business. This is a level of drill down they have not figured out how to do correctly. Revenues, COGS, and gross profit of an LOB start to create an impression but it is not the whole picture. The next step is to fully allocate overheads to each LOB so you can see how each is pulling its share. If you see that one LOB is covering its own direct costs but is not able to carry its share of the overheads, you can know the others are carrying the extra burden. In some cases that's fine because one LOB is a loss leader that brings in business for another LOB. But even a loss leader LOB can be adjusted to make a contribution and take the pressure off of the other LOBs. The worst scenario is when one LOB is producing all the profits and the others are draining profits. Then when the one star player gets injured, the rest of the team becomes dead weight and the business collapses. This "house of cards" scenario can be very fragile.

5. Stuck in detail – It's easy for small companies to latch onto specific metrics that are crucial to operating a business. These are the numbers owners and managers use daily or weekly to see how the business is operating. For example, an IT services company might count customer help requests and track average time to closure. When the numbers get better it says the company is doing a better job. Closing more requests with fewer labor hours is good. The problem is that many small businesses build a collection of these metrics for day-to-day management and then use them as the basis for overall business planning. It's very possible that a "good job improving an operating metric" is actually working against overall profitability. If you have a fixed fee contract for monthly IT services, the goal should be *eliminating* customer service requests. This will sound counter intuitive to IT service companies that grew up in the time-and-materials world where payment was largely based on hours worked, but a more top-down financial analysis will help make this clearer. Doing analysis and planning at a granular level can feel like great precision, but, in the end, it can mask the big picture.

6. Eroding financial strength – Many very small companies judge their success by the amount of cash left in the cigar box at the end of the month. As they grow and become more sophisticated, they apply this same kind of thinking, except now they use automated systems to generate reports and simulate the cigar box. They usually focus on P&L performance and skip the balance sheet, not seeing it as important to understanding business performance. Of course, when a company gets a substantial line of credit from a bank this perspective will change because the bank really cares about the balance sheet and ratios. The big problem is that banks don't look at the borrower's financial data often enough to spot problems before they occur; when a company runs into financial problems it is often too late for a minor adjustment. Many companies wait until year-end to see if there are balance sheet problems and then it's too late. The bank gets spooked and suddenly the owner has a new loan officer from the "troubled loans" department. Having a strong balance sheet with positive **trend lines** is the ultimate test of a company's strength and value in the market and the key to a great relationship with the bank.

7. Draining cash – It's not that using cash is a problem; it's the bigger issue of how you replenish it and what may be leading to falling cash balances in the company. Looking at cash one month at a time will not tell the story; cash flow tends to jump and fall in erratic ways, making it difficult to see any regular pattern. There are some excellent tools for cash flow analysis and forecasting, but one simple way to monitor it is to look at a 24-month **trend line** of end-of-month cash balances. The peaks and valleys will cancel out with trend analysis and you can see a pretty clear picture of where your cash flow is headed.

8. Runaway peaks and valleys – When revenue is way up one day and way down the next, there is a high probability the company is at risk of not reaching the next peak in time. It can be difficult to fine-tune a company dealing with this problem. Trend data is the only way to unmask the real business picture. If peaks and valleys are just the result of the billing methodology, this should be fixed. If it is because workload is actually coming in big peaks and valleys, that's another issue. Extreme variations in workload can be extremely damaging to

a company, especially if the company is paying for staff needed to support the peaks that are then idle during the valleys. This calls for adding revenue sources that can fill in the gaps or provide a bigger base of recurring revenue. If the peaks and valleys are because of seasonality patterns, that is a completely different matter and can be managed effectively. Seasonal patterns are predictable, so it is possible to manage costs in anticipation of expected revenue patterns. Seasonally adjusted trends are a special science of their own, but they do require extra analysis to know if your overall trends are heading in the right direction.

9. Not ready for the end game – Most business owners do not have a plan for building their company's market value and are not prepared to sell the business if something happens. When a health problem arises or a major family crisis forces the owner to sell on short notice, the end result is usually very disappointing, especially when one knows that, with a little advance preparation, the company's value could have been twice or even five times greater. This happens every day. It could be a divorce, a lawsuit, or any other unexpected event. The real solution is to build your company as if you were planning to sell in the next few months. This can result in seeing your business in a new and more profitable way. Many business advisors specialize in preparing companies for sale and spend two to four years getting their clients to a position of high value. Even if an owner has no intention of selling, this process can be worth much more than it costs.

10. Management team not good at problem solving – We covered this topic in Chapter 8, but from a slightly different perspective. Many business owners view themselves as the direction setter, the problem solver, and, often, the doer. The owner needs to step back from all of these roles as the company grows or this will be the reason the company doesn't grow. One of the last things the owner wants to release is the role of being the person with the answers. Unfortunately, this can be like parenting—never allowing your children to learn to take responsibility for their decisions and actions. Then when the parent is not around, the child is going to make some big mistakes. In a business setting, if the owner is always the one who

identifies the problem and provides the solution, there is nothing left for the employee to do but take the action described by the owner. This makes the employee more dependent on the owner and less able to think through problems and create solutions. More importantly, the owner becomes the one responsible for the outcome. Alternatively, if the employee comes up with the solution and is then given the okay to execute the idea he or she came up with, everything changes. The employee will become more responsible, learn about solutions that work and those that don't, and develop a much greater sense of pride and accomplishment. In the end, this is the only sustainable way to build an effective team. It all starts with the owner being willing to identify broad goals while leaving the solution identification and execution to the team members.

11. Owners being the expert – This is the classic story of business founders that are the experts and want to be seen as the knowledge center and decision center of the company. Generally this becomes a limitation on business growth. Unless knowledge and decision making are pushed out into the management team, the company will get stuck on a plateau that reflects the owner's reach. In the very early stages of company development this is totally appropriate. However, the owner needs to switch gears once the business is sustainable and begin pushing responsibilities for problem solving and decision-making out to the management team. These transitions may happen multiple times in a company's life. They are often tough and may require changes in the team.

12. No advisor – As mentioned earlier, no professional athlete would ever think of going it alone! Even the most experienced business person should involve an advisor or coach to help ensure the business is being observed from as many angles as possible. A savvy advisor can also take on some responsibilities that make it possible to hire a less expensive person in one or more leadership areas. This can be especially true if you need a higher level of experience on the team during a transition and can subsequently pull back to a less expensive manager to execute the newly defined process.

13. No board - Not building an advisory board or external board of directors can be a huge mistake. Ultimately bankers and investors will insist on having a board with outside players as a business grows. A board of advisors and a board of directors can provide perspective along with great business connections. Business owners tend to wait until they are pressured before adding these boards and miss out on a valuable form of assistance. It's easier and less complicated to start with a board of advisors that has less fiduciary obligation and is more focused on markets and customers. As a business grows, building the board of directors becomes an important part of building a company with market credibility. Board members can be compensated with stock or stock options in the early stages and then paid with cash as the company becomes profitable. The benefit of having board members can be immense. The more diversity in views and perspective, the more benefit the board will be to the company. Investors, bankers and potential strategic partners are going to look at board members and draw conclusions about the kind of company they are dealing with. This can be a deciding factor in a variety of business opportunities.

14. Advice from bookkeepers – Confusion about the difference between bookkeeping expertise and financial management expertise can lead to problems. This is an amazingly common problem. Controllers and bookkeepers are experts at getting the records right. Financial managers, CFOs, and business analysts are experts at evaluating financial performance and planning for what lies ahead. An inexperienced business owner will ask his or her bookkeeper for financial advice and not recognize that the answers are not appropriate for planning and management. The worst part is that many bookkeepers don't realize they are giving tactical advice when strategic advice is what is really needed. A financial expert will take the owner's question to another level by providing the questions that need to be asked so a more strategic answer can be proposed.

15. Stuck on a plateau – Most companies will hit a plateau and stay there for a while; getting comfortable and trying to stay on a plateau is often the first step to going backwards. Usually this is an indication that

the company's management processes and organization capacities have hit their limit and attempts to get past those limits are not working. It's difficult for a business owner to recognize that everything about growth is a direct consequence of the dynamics he or she has set in motion. Sometimes a company will hit a plateau with which the owner is comfortable. This will become the "new normal" and there may be no particular urgency to get past it. But it can also be a ticking time bomb if the new normal has underlying unhealthy financial trends and is not sustainable. Most often getting past the plateau will require some kind wakeup call (hopefully not a disaster!) and often some outside influence to help get back on a forward moving track.

16. Repeating the past - The assumption that what made you successful in the past will make you successful in the future is a sand trap. Using the phase, "this is the way we have always done it," is the first clue that a company is stuck in its own folklore. It may seem illogical to let go of something that has worked well in the past and it's admittedly uncomfortable to change processes and disciplines. Everybody tends to resist change, but there is no way to move forward without taking new steps. Moving away from the comfortable and into the uncomfortable is, well, uncomfortable. But that is the only way companies grow.

17. Not listening to the market – Deciding what the customer wants without validating assumptions is dangerous but common. Steve Jobs' ability to determine what the market would buy before it knew what it wanted is a freak of nature. It is highly unusual to guess correctly, especially if you don't have a spare billion dollars to build market awareness. The better and more certain way to provide what the market is looking for is start with customer feedback and then pilot test on a small scale. Then only after demonstrating that the new idea works should it be promoted and delivered on a larger scale. This incremental approach, with validation each step of the way, can eliminate many mistakes, avoid runaway costs, and improve the likelihood of long-term success.

18. Betting big on one idea ("all eggs in one basket") – This is like the singer that produces one hit record and then is never heard from

again. There is no problem if the hit song is big enough and makes enough money. Since that is rare, it is better to assume it is going to take multiple business offerings to build a successful and sustainable business. You can think of this like building a portfolio. A successful portfolio has diversity. It contains multiple complementary assets, some more mature elements, some newer and unproven elements, and some high risk and low risk elements with most in between the extremes.

19. Not achieving balance – An evolving portfolio of business offerings requires constant tuning and adjustment. Some parts will prove to be low performers and others will be winners. When you monitor and track performance of each part of the portfolio, you can spot trends and make early adjustments rather than waiting until it's too late. Monitoring early signs of problems and opportunities allows you to make individual adjustments. In some cases, you may need to dump an investment before damage is done. In other cases, you may want to double up on the investment that is showing signs of becoming a winner. Investments should be made in anticipation of where the investment is headed, not after it gets to its destination. Of course, that is what inexperienced investors do. When they finally know the outcome it's too late to invest. That's where monitoring, trends, and forecasts come in. Make the investments and portfolio tuning decisions before the final outcome has been reached. That is where value can be created.

20. Seeing problems too late – This can aptly be named as the biggest reason for company failures. If you had only recognized the problem early enough, it could have been fixed at a low cost with less effort and far less disruption. If you ask owners of businesses that failed what could have been done to avoid the shutdown, they almost always tell you what could have been done differently to keep the business going. If you ask why they didn't take the alternative course, they usually say they didn't think the course they were on was going to run into a problem. Sometimes you will hear them say they couldn't afford to take the course that would have led to a better outcome. However, a further probe will usually reveal they could

have solved the money problem if they had known about it earlier. We always hear, " Hindsight is 20/20," and, "If I just knew then what I know now." Here is where it is important to point out that **predictive analytics** can come pretty close to showing the picture that hindsight will reveal in the future. **Predictive analytics** can help you change the future!

Successful business owners, entrepreneurs and executives can usually point to a number of failures that came before their big success. Though this isn't always true, failures can provide more valuable lessons than do big wins. In fact, some really sad stories come from people that experienced early success followed by a long string of failures. Very often plain old luck is a big part of the success story and that is a poor teacher. The person with an early win might not know the difference between the part that was luck and the part driven by their actions. This can be very confusing and may require some "un-learning."

There are always important lessons to be learned no matter how many successes and failures people may have under their belt. It is also true that many lessons are unnecessary. Many lessons are simply errors that happen when you don't have the right information. It would have been easy to make the right decision if the right information had been available. This simply says that you can eliminate the need for lots of "learning" by just getting access to the right data.

Paradox

Building a business is much like any other life process. Rarely is there one simple answer to any question. Usually the answer is some form of "yes and no" and other combinations of answers that you would think are mutually exclusive. Here are just a few examples:

- More can be learned from failures than from successes.
- Having successful competitors is good for your business.
- The market can teach you how to be successful, more so than you can teach the market what it needs to do to make you successful.
- Helping your clients' customers achieve success will do more to build your success.

- Giving your team answers to the problems they need to solve is less motivating than letting them come up with the solutions they will be responsible to implement.
- Finding the perfect solution is less economical than finding the satisfactory solution.
- Getting unanimous agreement from everyone on the team is probably a bad sign.
- The things that made you successful in the past often become your barriers in the future.
- Build bank relationships when you need them the least; set up lines of credit when you have the most cash.

There are many more paradoxes where these came from! The point is that often the quick and easy answer is probably not the right or complete answer. The best answers are generally not the obvious ones; usually there is more than one answer that will work.

Even when you look at business performance numbers there are often counter intuitive explanations. It's easy to form the wrong impression when taking the numbers at face value. For example, rising revenues are a bad sign for some companies and falling revenues might actually be a good sign. There are many cases where rising revenues are accompanied by an even faster rise in expenses and falling profits. In other cases, falling revenues might occur when a company is eliminating a line of business that is putting a drain on the company or when it is eliminating a large customer that is a drain on the company. There are also times when expenses will run high while a company is investing in a new offering. All of these situations should be made much clearer when multiple pieces of information are brought together to create a more complete picture.

In essence, this is what vital signs can reveal. No one piece of information tells a whole story; linking together multiple pieces of information will make things much more clear. Accordingly, a vital sign is the combination of two or more pieces of information that tell a story. It's applying the theory of relativity to business: *you can only understand motion by understanding how one part is moving in relation to another part.* By seeing how one metric relates to another, you can identify where things are working well and where the problems are. Bringing a collection of parts together and understanding their combined relationships can reveal a much more complete picture and show exactly where the big problems and opportunities lie—and, therefore, where the highest management priorities should lie.

Conclusion

Many of the topics in this book circle back to the need for information and the importance of seeing that information from the perspective of trends and combinations of trends. It is a combination of trends that provides a complete picture. No matter what information you are looking at, it can be shown in a **trend line** that puts information in context and explains where things are headed. Even when the data has errors or is incomplete, connecting multiple dots can produce a usable picture of what lies ahead and what needs to be fixed.

Management decisions are made every day, some good and some bad. But very few are made on the basis of 100 percent of the needed information or 100 percent certainty. If business owners waited until they had all the possible information to support their decisions, they would never move forward. However, there is a downside to making decisions without essential information and just relying on instinct. Gut feel decisions lead to errors; even worse, there is no way to transfer gut feel knowledge to the rest of the team. Without some form of information driven process, the team cannot function as a team or support the leader, and certainly can't grow. Additionally, from the perspective of team members, gut feel decisions appear random and nobody can learn from that. It takes logic and understandable explanations to make sense such that team members can begin to emulate the leader and produce the results the leader is looking for. Here again, **trend lines** and **predictive analytics** can be a solid way to build understanding and improve team processes.

It's also important to point out that most business results have very little to do with the initial decision. Most of the time it is not the decision that determines the outcome—it's what happens after the decision is made. A great decision can be wrecked by poor execution just like a bad decision can look brilliant when there is great execution. Good monitoring of vital signs can show where adjustments need to be made and help steer decisions and actions to great outcomes. Combining good monitoring with agile and smart execution is the ultimate best practice for reaching high quality outcomes.

As you consider the ideas presented in this book, the best results will happen when you get your whole team on the same page. This has probably been said a dozen times but for good reason. We know that business is a team sport and functions best when there are great game plans.

We're all in this together. Any new insights you would be willing to share would be a fantastic thing for everyone else on this journey. We invite you to check out other resources on our web site and provide your feedback at: http://www.ambientlightpublishing.com.

 **CHAPTER TWELVE CHECK-UP**

1. What is the most important determinant of business success?
2. What is an example of a paradox that could trip up a business owner and damage his or her business?
3. When a company sees flat growth and no real improvement happening, what are the most likely causes?
4. How do financial peaks and valleys impact the value of a company? Why?
5. What is the mistake you think is most common and why?

Appendix

CONTRIBUTORS

#111 – Peer Groups and Metrics – Josh Peterson
CEO, Bering McKinley
www.beringmckinley.com

Peer Groups and Key Performance Metrics in an IT Business
The peer group landscape has changed with the availability of consolidated and real-time financial data. Getting owners to see how they are doing with their peers and seeing what needs to happen to take your business to the next level are things that don't readily occur to business owners. Peers and experts have to come in and ask the tough questions. Together we discover how to achieve measures that are attainable by peers.

Here are just some of the key metrics IT businesses should manage and review monthly. Once you pay attention to them, you can control them:

1. Service Department Gross Profit should be more than 55 percent.

2. Service Salary Expense relative to service revenue. This should be less than 33 percent - plus you should have a bonus program for your engineers and service techs to drive your net promoter score (how willing a customer is to refer you) .

3. Managed Services Agreement Gross Profitability should be greater than 60 percent

$$\frac{\text{Agreement revenue} - (\text{Labor cost} + \text{Licenses cost})}{\text{Agreement Revenue}}$$

4. Effective Hourly Rate (EHR) should be 2X. Either:
   a) For service providers in general:
      total service revenue / total service payroll hours = effective hourly rate on total hours compensated

b) for MSPs:

> total recurring revenue / total service hours against agreements–agreement effective hourly rate (EHR). If your EHR is not greater than your hourly rate, then you have a problem. Top MSPs have effective hourly rates double that of their rack rates.

These are some of the key metrics that peer groups discuss and make it comfortable to work through the issues you face. Knowing them gives you confidence around tough decisions and can really evolve your business quickly.

#112 – Transformative Technology – Len Jessup, Ph.D.
Dean of Eller College of Management, University of Arizona
http://lenjessup.com

Transformative Technology – How Far We've Come
My focus on technology and innovation has a transformational effect on business. The power of large corporate software and ERP tools are now available and represent a change for smaller businesses. Making this technology accessible in the cloud has been a revolution.

You can think of the early days of immigrants to America from bakery to metal shop—Business Management 1.0 where mom and pop businesses did cigar-box or shoebox accounting (where all the cash and receipts were kept for safekeeping).

Then Business Management 2.0 was when the businesses became automated by small computers that were on-premise. Automated accounting was about all a small business could afford.

Now we're seeing a radical change with Business Management 3.0 that takes all the power of the CRM and ERP tools to small business for a fraction of the cost and is accessible and affordable out on the cloud.

What I find interesting is that small business owners can keep track of the same kinds of things the same as the big companies—not just simple P &L but the broader view and trends showing where the company is heading and how they are performing relative to the same sectors. Performance graphics are now accessible by even those without a financial background and can share that with the team. Growth is another area to track to keep everyone connected inside and outside the business—vendors, lenders, and suppliers—to provide the best information and services that you can.

It takes the static-ness out of the picture and borrows best practices out of the big tools used by large corporations and puts them into the hands of the small business owners. **Predictive analytics**, trend analysis, and forecasting with benchmarks on how other businesses are doing provide an amazing new paradigm. I think all businesses, particularly small businesses, need to get on this track to stay agile and financially viable and compete. Being able to take corrective action and do it in real time using the new transformational tools are making possible a new world of business—Business 3.0—and create a new definition of what it takes to run an agile business. It's now inexpensive to put those tools to work in the business to enable it to thrive.

I only wish that these tools had been available for my immigrant-family business owners at the turn of the century. It's amazing to see how far we've come.

#113 – Quantifying the Value of your Relationship – Marek Omilian
By Marek Omilian, Managing Director, Value Prism Consulting, LLC
www.valueprism.com

Every free market economy is built on a small business. Entrepreneurs are constantly starting new ventures to exploit new ideas. In such a fragmented business world no company, large or small, can function without help from other players in its universe, i.e., partners and vendors. For example, our firm's business case consulting practice works with system integrators who pitch their solutions to enterprise customers. We help customers understand the business case, i.e., quantitative costs and benefits behind a particular solution. We also help the SIs close deals with the customers and close them faster. The improved close rate and lower selling costs due to shorter sales cycle can be easily quantified.

One should understand the players in the delivery of products and services to end customers. There needs to be a "what's in it for me" assessment from the point of view of each player. There needs to be clear understanding of the value of each party in the transaction including customer, contributed and received, in the exchange. Once that's done, and the Win-Win-Win scenario is identified, the execution is easy as partnerships or alliances are formed. However, the status quo is constantly challenged. The value equation is tested periodically. Business leaders or owners should follow a portfolio approach to managing partner relationships—investing in new promising alliances, harvesting the existing ones, and exiting those where costs of maintaining them are higher than benefits.

We typically test several new partnerships ideas per year with the expectation that only a handful will generate results. Partners tend to cut their losses quickly if they find quantifiable business value equations that make the cost/benefit equation more attractive elsewhere. The partner who continually provides quantitative data reflecting value with hard-core numbers is more readily kept on as a partner. You want to be able to say, "We can make you more profitable and here's the proof." That is the key. Otherwise, it's merely left to perception or guesswork.

#114 – Spotting Problems Early – Jeff Hilton
CEO, Knowledge Circles
www.knowledgecircles.com

Spotting Problems before Falling Off the Cliff
The real goal of an agile business manager should be to use metrics that inform in a forward-looking manner. For example, you may have noticed that revenues of a certain service line business have decreased. Once you note that, what are you going to do about it? Once you do something about it, you need leading indicators to measure progress about those actions.

A good example comes from the airline industry. One of our clients, a large airline, employed a sophisticated modeling system to predict future capacity utilization and revenues. They analyzed historical data about the number of seats sold and revenues generated on each flight at various points in time prior to and at the end of that flight. Since they now knew how many seats should be sold and how much revenue should be booked at various points in time well in advance of a future flight, they were able to make adjustments to achieve their goals. If, for example, they were below where they should be, they could offer a few seats at a discounted price. Conversely, if they were ahead of their trend goal, they could raise prices slightly to generate additional profits.

Of course, airline prices are highly visible and highly competitive but most IT businesses can leverage this type of analysis in regard to technical and service delivery staff utilization. If you have a model that predicts future revenues translated into service staffing requirements long enough in advance, you can avoid having too much underutilization because you now have time to do something about it.

In my IT training business, we used these airline-type metrics to assess months in advance how publicly scheduled classes were selling. If they were below expectations, we could engage our sales staff to focus their efforts on this class. If they were well above expectations, we could focus them on other classes or add an additional schedule date of the same class. If a class was not selling at all, we could replace it with one that had more demand. The key is to have information well enough in advance that your actions have time to be effective. Depending on our goals, we had a lot of tools at our disposal to optimize business results.

Once you get into the mindset of how to use historical data to look towards the future, you can craft many useful leading indicators to drive your business to success. If you don't have these, you are literally running with a blindfold and can fall off a cliff.

When a well-established IT service company found its finances were deteriorating, the first and most immediate place they looked was at their accounts receivable. They found that their accounts receivables were getting progressively worse and, if they continued, they would fall off the cliff. With several hundred thousand in uncollected invoices, they brought in a person to focus on accounts receivable. What they quickly discovered was that the vast majority of overdue receivables remained unpaid not due to the customers unwillingness to pay but because they had some administrative stall or hiccup that just needed to be cleared. These were things such as incorrect PO numbers, missing or mismatched internal paperwork, or sales taxes being charged when they should have been exempted.

By working with these customers to generate corrected invoices and to resolve the issues, they were able to collect these amounts, which had a huge impact on the business. Rather than having to borrow money to cover cash flow requirements, these collected cash assets were now available for that and other purposes. A relatively small cost and effort yielded a huge return on investment that helped them get them through their bumps and back on a smooth track. Had these issues been identified earlier by spotting the trend around increasingly worsening accounts receivable, they could have recovered even more quickly.

#115 – Getting an SBA Loan – Jennifer Ringenbach
SBA Specialist. KeyBank
www.keybank.com

New Realities in Obtaining Funding: Getting an SBA Loan
A big misconception with the SBA is that anybody can walk in and get an SBA loan and that's not true. You have to demonstrate that you have management expertise in the industry and that you can generate cash on a projected basis. If you don't have a historical cash flow, we have to look at your personal credit scores and make sure you've handled your personal debt well. We're taking a leap that you're going to do with your personal debt the kind of the thing that you're going to do with the business. So we're taking a risk along with you and partnering with you, not being your angel investor. We're going to do this together.

We're not looking for complete ability to repay the loan. What we're looking for is whether they have some liquidity after their equity injection to make sure that if there are some stumbling rocks on the road they can invest some more, or maybe they don't take a salary for a couple of months to get by. We are required to look at personal assets as additional collateral if the business assets won't fully secure the proposed loans.

If you don't have any available assets, then that doesn't mean that you're going to be denied. You just have to be able to demonstrate that you're willing to pledge whatever is available for collateral. This is where banks can differ a little bit. Some of them will have a little bit stricter requirements and may not want full security, especially with the SBA guarantee, but may expect some minimal level of collateral. The bank may not comfortable with just 30 percent collateral coverage instead of 100 percent like a conventional request. With an SBA guarantee, if we're comfortable with your payment ability and management experience, then this program is designed to help mitigate that lack of collateral people can expand and get those proceeds they need.

We do look for a business plan especially when we're talking about new business or expansion. You'll have to explain it and make us comfortable that you know where you're going, what the purposes are for these proceeds. There are free services out there to help you put these business plans and projections together because not everybody can write them and that's not where their expertise is. Your expertise is in running your business, but having good projections and business plans is really critical. I've seen people who aren't putting in time to really work out a business plan and really think about the projections, who struggle later on because they don't have a handle on what's going to happen, what's needed, or what to expect.

There are organizations out there like the Small Business Development Centers and the Service Corps of Retired Executives (SCORE) that are there to assist you with putting those business plans together. I've seen a lot of people utilize their accountants to help them with projections and I favor that approach. I also would suggest that you make sure you can speak to those numbers. I've seen more people bring me projections and when I asked a couple questions about them, they have no clue what I'm talking about because they let their CPA do all the work and didn't even take a look at their numbers. That's not where you should be. You need to understand your numbers. Even if you're not a numbers person, it's something that you need to deal with if you're going to be a business owner and you're going to grow your business. It's worth the effort.

259

#116 – Banking Relationships – Don Brown
Vice President and Senior Relationships Manager at Key Bank
www.keybank.com

New Realities in Obtaining Funding: The Relationship with your Banker
Visibility and honesty are the hallmarks of any great banking relationship from the banker and from the client. Covenants are there to create a discussion. If you're talking with your banker, there's no reason to hide anything. It's going to come out when it's time for review or for renewal in the line of credit, whatever the covenant calls for.

My best clients are the ones that, if there's an issue or a problem they see coming, come to me first saying, "Here's where we're at. Here's what we think the problem is and here's how we're going to solve it. We need your help to work through this problem." That's the perfect client.

#117 – Exit without Capital Gains – Chuck Albers
Founder & General Partner, Dynamic Affluence Group
http://www.linkedin.com/in/chuckalbers

How Do You Sell Your Business without Losing It to Capital Gains Tax?
With more than 90 million Americans over 50, many business owners are looking to pass on their business to their heirs, but they stop short when they find out how much they will owe in taxes and how little would be left over.

Below we are going to address one of the most common problems in tax planning that can be easily solved with a legal, win-win approach that brings philanthropy and tax benefits together.

The Problem
Jack is the Founder & Owner of ABC Inc. worth $20MM. They have another $10MM in various other assets: first home, second home, retirement plans, investments, etc. that take up their combined $10MM of estate exemptions. Jack and his wife have decided to sell the business and "slow" down.

When Jack finds a buyer for the business, he finds himself subject to federal and state capital gains taxes, among other taxes. Depending on his state of residence, the tax bill comes out to approximately 24 percent or $5MM. That leaves them $15MM to re-invest and live off of the income. If he passes away in a few years, the estate owes roughly 40 percent estate tax on the $15 MM (assuming the principle remained constant), another six million dollars. So, the initial $20MM value of Jack's business leaves his heirs only $9MM.

For Jack to be convinced of taking a new approach, three things must happen: Jack needs:

1. Control – this business is "mine"
   What if you didn't OWN but you could CONTROL the business?
2. Income or growth from the asset
   You may not need the $20M, but simply the $1M in cash flow.
3. Access to the principal.
   You may not need the $20M but you'd sleep better knowing you could access it.

This brings us to the "win-win." With some planning and education, a better "scorecard" is readily available and it looks like this:

The Solution: Become the Unwitting Philanthropist

All, or most of, the money due to be lost to taxes is money that could otherwise be directed to philanthropy with some planning and knowledge of the code.

Most people view the "problem" of philanthropy as simply this: every dollar they leave to charity they perceive as a dollar not going to their children and grandchildren. That's not true, but no one tells them this. The mistakes that charities make is: a) they don't help the clients deal with their children and grandchildren first, and b) they don't educate and reorient around the initial incorrect perception. Most think: *I can't donate at the expense of my children.*

But here is Jack's practical outcome:

IRS/Taxes: $0
> (In fact, it could be a negative $6.4MM (approximately) after tax deductions.)

Heirs/Children: $12MM - $20MM
> (or if Jack has no kids, a key employee can act in this nature and may run the business for a salary plus incentive)

Charity/Philanthropy: $10MM to $40MM

Leveraged $10MM – the IRS supplies the leverage. They give you the tools you need; it's money that doesn't go to the IRS.

This is a greatly improved scenario for Jack and his wife, their children, their grandchildren, and charities. Jack and his wife receive more income during their lifetime, they receive a major tax deduction, and they defer and avoid two major layers of taxation. Their children receive more money and, if done correctly, their grandchildren do, too. And, charities end up with millions they otherwise weren't going to receive, not at the expense of Jack's children, but out of the IRS's pocket.

Early on in the discussion, the clients will notice that the numbers in the second scenario add up to more than their initial $20MM. They're correct. They'll ask how that is possible. The answer is a simple one: leverage. It's a concept with which every business person is familiar. The good news is that the tax code provides the leverage necessary.

When clients know that their children and grandchildren are taken care of, and are actually receiving more money, and that the choices are now about who receives the "remainder"–charity or the IRS—the conversation becomes quite simple.

There's More to the Story

There are additional elements to the "win-win" scenario. If Jack sells his business and lives 12 more years, and assuming he can invest money long-term at five percent, he takes in $750,000 annually in income ($15MM x 0.05). On the other hand, if he avoids the capital gains tax on the sale, he now has the full $20MM left to reinvest. Assuming the same five percent investment rate, he takes in $1MM annually in income. That is $250,000 annually in additional income. If he and his wife live 12 more years after the sale, they take in an extra $3MM over their lifetime in additional differential income ($250K x 12 years).

Thus, they take in $3MM more income during their lifetime, and gain an approximately $4MM tax deduction additionally. Their children and grandchildren end up with substantially more assets when they pass on, and the community ends up with millions that were otherwise going out the door in taxes. Also, there is the future growth on money that is saved versus lost to be factored into the equation. Money invested at slightly more than five percent doubles in value every 14 years. In 98 years the money will have double seven times. Thus, $5MM that otherwise would have been lost needlessly to taxes, if preserved, and invested would grow to $10MM in 14 years, $20MM in 28 years, $40MM in 42 years, $80MM in 56 years, $160MM in 70 years, $320MM in 84 years, and $640MM in 98 years.

Lastly, it is not necessary for non-profits to wait until donors pass away for the non-profits to receive the funds. There are multiple ways for the money to be "front-loaded." The tax code turns out to be the best friend non-profits have, and has the power to turn non-givers into major givers; not only it benefits non-profits, but themselves and their heirs, as well.

This scenario is legal and realistic, yet it is not something that everyone knows how to do and is only one idea of twenty tools that experts have at their disposal. Most people don't know how to apply them but when they do, the rewards are life-changing for business owners, family, and community.

#118 – Expecting More from Your Accountant – Edi Osborne
CEO, Mentor Plus, Author, *Firm Forward* available on www.amazon.com
www.mentorplus.com

Expecting More from Your Accountant
Finding the right business advisor requires some sleuthing. It's not as easy as hiring a management consultant or retaining the services of a

good CPA. You need a trusted business advisor who has both a strong financial accounting background AND solid business acumen skills. Although there are a lot of good accountants who can help with tax compliance issues and basic financial reporting, that's old school accounting. Today's business owners need an accountant who understands managerial accounting and how to apply those principles (business acumen) to improve the overall performance of an organization.

The good news is there are accountants all over the world who are working hard to expand their skills and resources to add more value to traditional accounting services. Here are some screening questions to ask your current or prospective accountant:

1. What is your standard advisory services engagement; what's involved and what are the expected outcomes?

2. What can you do to improve the financial fluency and acumen of our team?

3. How do you make sure the financial statements you prepare can be used as a managerial tool?

4. Give me an example of how you helped a client improve their operations, profits, or some other specific benefit.

5. What would you include in a business dashboard for a business like mine?

6. What specific training have you had in the area of performance measurement and management?

7. What percentage of your firm's revenues is derived from advisory versus compliance work?

8. How would you describe an ideal client from your perspective?

If your accountant's responses don't overwhelm you with confidence, it may be time to interview others. Don't give up, it may take some time but the good ones are worth the effort.

#119 – Acquisitions with Metrics – Jamison West
Founder & CEO at Arterian
www.linkedin.com/in/jamisonwest

Using Financial Metrics during Acquisitions: The Good, Bad, and Ugly
Arterian acquired three businesses over the course of three years, each with three different personalities, performance, and outcome. Because valuation is in the eye of the beholder we looked at each company in a different light. The first company was solid in its books. The second company wasn't as easy to predict since it was working on time and materials and simply projecting sales. The third one was a managed service provider with predictable monthly revenues but had financial tracking problems.

The metrics for each business were valued based on customer acquisition, talent, and sales capacity. When evaluating the value of each of the three, key metrics were primarily around percentage of revenue (MRR) and service revenue. So those were the key metrics—along with talent and financial position, profitability, and culture (which became the larger issue as we grew).

We looked at the financials and cash flow analysis. We ran scenarios as to what costs looked like and how it would pencil out; i.e. could we afford it? For each, we identified two elements: 1) Guaranteed compensation, including: a) Equity (investment to mitigate some of the cash), b) Down payment c) Guaranteed payments over time (guaranteed to owner), and d) Earn-out compensation.

Trend analysis was extremely important in our decisions; contractual and non-contractual (longevity of clients) and consistent trending of MRR (monthly recurring revenue) were most critical. The earn-out portion of the acquisition was based on trends.

Part of the due diligence problem with the third acquisition was that some of the financials were not clear enough before a decision was made. They charged for an annual contract but they didn't know how accrual worked. So they were dropping all revenue into the month cash was acquired. The books were not what they appeared to be. It was difficult to figure out how to assess pre-paid liabilities, and the cash basis accounting made it impossible to figure out. On this acquisition, we ended up having to unwind the entire stock–acquisition. Prepaid revenue was a massive liability. They owed tremendous amounts of work that were not on the books.

Our "oh-wow" moment was understanding that cash versus accrual/prepaid was crucial. You need to have a clear understanding of the accrual basis and prepaid liabilities when you look at someone's books. The P&L needs to appropriately reflect an accrual basis.

#120 – The New Era of Information – Harry Bruce, Ph.D.
Dean of the University of Washington Information School
http://faculty.washington.edu/harryb/
www.linkedin.com/pub/harry-bruce/51/208/191

The New Era of Information
In the 1970s numerous books hailed the arrival of the information age and the demise of the industrial age. However, no one had any idea what the global Internet and petabyte explosion would produce—that the "information age" would become a highly democratizing phenomenon, used as much by individual people as by businesses. No one could have imagined that information would become a form of currency and that a new science would be formed around researching and studying information.

The University of Washington Information School is part of an expanding, worldwide coalition of schools that focus upon tackling organizational and societal issues related to the way people create, store, find, manipulate, and share information. We call ourselves iSchools – a term coined on the University of Washington campus. As Dean of the UW iSchool, it is my privilege to work with professors, researchers, students, and business leaders from around the world who are committed to making information work. Our mission at the iSchool is to prepare information leaders, research the problems and opportunities of information, and design solutions to information challenges. Our goal is to support and enhance human engagements with information and technology.

The Corelytics Financial Dashboard is an elegant example of this core value of iSchools. It brings complex business analytics to small business

266

owners who are not mathematicians or financial experts and gives them an easy-to-understand view of what is happening in their business—and they can get this information anytime and anywhere. So, the analytics that once required many experts, and were therefore only found in large enterprises, are now available to even the smallest businesses and are adaptable to fit the needs of the individual user as well.

The University of Washington's iSchool's research, our academic programs are found at http://ischool.uw.edu/. Learn more about the iSchool movement at http://ischools.org/.

#121 – Business Valuation – Norman L. Harshaw

Partner, Murphy Business & Financial Corp
www.NormanHarshaw-Murphy.com

Business Valuation: Determining How Much a Business is Worth

Business Valuation is the process of determining how much a business is worth. It's not as simple a question as it first appears. The basic problem of business valuation is how to set a value on all the assets of a business, including the intangibles. How much, for example, is goodwill, a business logo, a trademark, or a client list worth?

There are several different valuation methods that can be used to tackle the problem and attempt to determine a fair price for the business to be sold. No one method is the solution for any business; if you use (or your professional valuator uses) a variety of business valuation methods, you'll have a more accurate idea of just what your business is worth and a range of prices you can use as parameters for your negotiations.

Following are just a few business valuation approaches; there are many more depending on the size, scope, and industry sector of your business. Except for the Market Evaluation Approach, which uses stock price, all these approaches can be used from small to large businesses and, as stated above, no one approach is best; they should be used in conjunction with each other.

Earning Value Approach

This business valuation method is predicated on the idea that a business's true value lies in its ability to produce wealth in the future. The most common earning value approach is Capitalizing Past Earning.

With this approach, a valuator determines an expected level of cash flow for the company using a company's record of past earnings, normalizes them for unusual revenue or expenses, and multiplies the expected normalized cash flows by a capitalization factor. The capitalization factor is a reflection of what rate of return a reasonable purchaser would expect on the investment as well as a measure of the risk that the expected earnings will not be achieved.

Buyer's Test Approach

Buyers tend to look at a business in a cut-and-dried way. The essential factors that most buyers are interested in are earnings (net income after all expenses, but before capital expenditures or debt payments) and cash flow (the inflow and outflow of cash in the business).

This method is based on the business having enough cash flow to provide a reasonable salary for the owner, a reasonable rate of return on the buyer's investment, annual capital expense, and debt service with a reasonable debt coverage ratio.

Buyers want to know that your business will provide a stream of dollars that's predictable, steady, and high. Some buyers prefer to look specifically at cash-flow statements while others will focus on your income statement to examine earnings before interest and taxes (EBIT). Still others will place the most weight on earnings before interest, taxes, and depreciation (EBITD). The point is your income stream is key. You need to prove the size and regularity of your positive cash flow, preferably with audited financials going back at least three years.

Market Valuation Approach

This is the simplest way to value a publicly traded firm and the value is easy to calculate. Find the price of a single company share on the stock exchange, multiply it by the number of shares outstanding, and you have the equity market value of the company. Once you determine the market value of a firm, you need to figure out either the discount or premium for which it would sell if the company were put on the market. Whether a company sells at a premium or discount depends on those supply and demand forces in the market place.

Comparable Transactions Approach

To use this approach, you need to look at the "comparable" transactions that have taken place in the industry and accompanying relevant metrics such as multiples or ratios. When using this method you are looking for a key valuation parameter. Were the companies in those transactions valued as a multiple of EBITDA, EBIT, revenue, seller's discretionary earnings, or other parameters? Once you figure out what the key valuation parameter is, you can examine at what multiples of those parameters the comparable companies were valued.

#122 – Lessons from a Race Car Driver – Nate Tennis
Sr. Instructor, DirtFish Rally School
Published in *Alaska Airlines Magazine* Aug 2013, by Jeff Layton

Lessons from a Race Car Driver

One of the most important lessons we teach is how to see the road. Most people don't look far enough ahead. They focus on the taillights in front of them, not what's happening down the road. Learning how to avoid such tunnel vision so you can see the bigger picture of what's coming at you is a major part of learning to drive fast.

In rally racing, a popular mantra is, "You go where you look," so by looking out the side window while spinning sideways on the track, you're actually looking down the track instead of out the windshield, which is pointing toward trouble. A tendency to drive where you look is the reason drivers sometimes drift off the road and cross the right-side fog line.

(Like sales) brakes can be used for more than just slowing down. In driving theory, brakes are also used to shift the weight of your car forward to give the front wheels the traction they need to guide you through a turn. Accelerating shifts the weight back so you can use it to gain traction as you exit the turn (a lot like gaining traction in your business before you accelerate sales).

- Eyes where you want to drive (not necessarily ahead)
- Anticipate the turn and how to minimize distance around a corner
- Recall your last lap and how to adjust this (trends and seasonality)
- Gauges check out, all systems go
- Racer assessment (who's ahead, who's behind?)
- Pit crew (advisors)
- Raving fans! (customers)

#123 – Common Sense Cash Management – Ed Patton

Principal, Patton and Associates

http://www.corelytics.net/pattonassociates

Common Sense Cash Management

Working capital is a key measure of your financial strength. It is simply short-term assets minus short-term liabilities. Creation or consumption of working capital should be tracked and understood just as you do with sales, expenses, and net earnings.

Working capital components turn relatively quickly. Therefore, the working capital you create today will soon turn into the cash you have to run your business. Also, remember that a standard working capital line of credit can monetize your current assets when cash is needed prior to accounts receivable being collected and/or inventories being sold. When working capital runs low, an unexpected bump in the road can be disastrous. Building a durable company requires working capital to be maintained at strong levels so you can absorb bumps.

A lot has to go right to increase cash. But any one thing can go wrong and your cash supply will dwindle. Sales have to be made, cash must be collected, spending must be controlled, and with a little luck you will have an increase in cash. And if that's not enough, you can borrow money or sell assets to generate needed cash.

There are many ways to make it all work, but any one of these parts can also trip you up. Making the right choices, turning the right dials, and keeping everything in balance is a basic requirement of business management.

An ideal working capital position for most companies is when current assets are equal to one and one-half to two times short-term liabilities. That means short-term assets need to be **1.5 to 2 times the total of short-term liabilities**.

The next question is where is the working capital **trend line** heading? If capital is heading down while revenues are increasing, there is a danger that the company has fundamental problems where growth is damaging to the company. If working capital is growing as revenue increases, there is a high probability that the company is healthy and will strengthen with growth.

Generally, an increase in working capital equates to building financial strength. But even a financially strong company can have liquidity problems. A well-managed line of credit can make all the difference as it will allow you to monetize your uncollected receivables and inventories on the shelf. This type of borrowing can be a solution to a cash shortage and it can be a way to help a company absorb bumps in the road. But when short-term debt exceeds short-term assets or when it is heading in that direction, it's time for alarm bells. Once you get on this slippery slope it can become impossible to dig out.

A working capital target needs to be set for a company and then actual working capital should be monitored against the target every month. A good standard for most companies is a working capital target equal to one and one-half to twice the company's short-term debt. From here you can create two trend lines: one for the target working capital and one for actual working capital. The target trend line will go up as short-term debt increases and down as it decreases. Then the goal is to make sure that the working capital trend line is above the target trend line and there should be a growing spread between the two trend lines as a company grows and builds financial strength. If the two trend lines are coming together or if the working capital trend line is below the target trend line, the business needs a careful examination. Something is keeping the business from building financial strength.

#124 – Valuation Methods – Bob Dale

Partner, Austin Dale

www.austindalegroup.com

Methods for Determining Company Valuations

There are different purposes and results depending on the purpose of valuation; we will focus on valuing a company for purpose of selling it to a third party. Three basic approaches to computing the value of a business:

Asset approach

A company in financial distress may utilize the asset value, essentially selling for the market value of the underlying fixed (tangible?) assets.

Income Approach

There are two commonly used income approaches: Capitalization of Earnings method where we determine the average earnings, usually on the cash basis, of the business over the past three to five years. Earnings must be solely from the stream of income produced by the underlying business, and income streams are adjusted for non-business items and non-cash expenses. The appropriate multiples can be difficult to ascertain as they vary by industry and must correspond to the cash flow stream being used. In general, the larger the income stream the larger the multiple. The owner typically prepares a pro-forma cash flow statement for the business for the next five years to compute the terminal value, or residual value, which is usually the final year's earnings projected for growth into perpetuity. Then we compute the present value of the income stream to a current value using an appropriate discount rate and ad d the resulting values into a single discounted earnings figure. We determine an appropriate capitalization rate taking into account size, industry risk, cost of capital, and specific company risk and compute the value of the company by dividing the discounted earnings by the capitalization rate

Market Approach

Here we determine the price of a company by using comparative data from sales of comparable businesses. This requires that there is a population of completed sales of comparable companies available for analysis. The advantage is that this is an easily understood way of establishing value and it uses actual data from closed sales. The disadvantage is that it involves a considerable amount of work to locate comparable sales and then to create comparable metrics. The metrics developed are usually stated as ratios. Some commonly known ratios are: Price/Earnings per Share, Price/Revenue, Price/Seller's Discretionary Earnings, and Price/EBITDA. The basic formula is stated as: Value = (Comparable Company Price / Metric) X (Metric of Subject Company)

Example:

We analyze the population of comparable companies and determine that Selling Price / EBITDA is the most closely correlated ratio among the sample sales. Specifically, we determine that a Price/EBITDA ratio of 5:1 is representative of the sample population. We determine Subject Company Metric. Analyze the subject company's financial statements to determine EBITDA (Earnings before Interest, Taxes, Depreciation and Amortization). For the example, we will use an EBITDA of $1,000,000. Using the Price/EBITDA ratio of 5:1 we determine that our subject company has a probable sales value of $5,000,000.

Determining the approach and method to use in determining sales price value for a particular company is usually a matter of experience and judgment. In general, small companies with sales under $1,000,000 are generally valued using a combination of the Income Approach – Capitalization of Earnings method and the Market Value method – SDE ratio. For most companies under $10,000,000 in sales, Income Approach and Market Approach yield the most reliable estimates of sales value. In small to mid-size companies, sales between $10,000,000 and $20,000,000, are valued using the Income Approach - Capitalization of Earnings method, Income Approach - Discounted Cash Flow Method when reliable cash flow streams can be projected, and the Market Value Method. The valuation analyst then uses judgment and experience to determine the final value.

It's important to improve the financial and non-financial factors that will make businesses more valuable and attractive before a sale, based on what we've learned is important to buyers. Austin Dale Group uses our understanding of valuation coupled with our real-world experience of building and selling successful companies to help maximize the value of a company for a sale. Some clients may not even plan to sell their businesses, but they realize owning a sellable business increases its value—often their largest asset—and gives them more freedom to scale it, sell it, or pass it to their heirs.

#125 – Value Propositions – Gareth Wade
Principal, OneAccord Partners
www.linkedin.com/in/garethwade

The Value in Value Propositions
We had a very interesting meeting a couple months ago where we surveyed 25 CEOs and business owners in the room and asked them to write down what their top three differentiators were that made their company stand out. Out of those 25 CEOs in the room, 20 of them wrote down that their biggest asset was their people because, when we drilled down, there really was no clear differentiator.

We have to be careful to ensure that everybody understands exactly what value your company has provided. You really have to consider the quality of your message in the brand qualities and the overall value proposition in terms of going back. Does everybody understand what you do? You've got to ask yourself, "How clear is that value proposition? Does everybody know it? Does it even represent actual value?" But more importantly, "Do your own customers agree with it?"

If your customers, your staff, and members of your relationship ecosystem don't understand what you do or what you're trying to do, then, ultimately, it's going to flat line or go nowhere. I would say the majority of the time it's easy to get lulled into a sense of false security—thinking you're in a better position than you actually are.

CEOs should be running companies and keeping track of the changing forces. They're in charge of strategy and ultimately execution. Again, leverage your ecosystem or leverage your components, and develop members of that ecosystem whether it's your bankers, advisers, consultants, whoever is in there. Leverage the expertise to do that for you.

The ability to recognize that change is happening and being able to adapt to that potential change is very important. The way we've always done things is the comfort zone. How do you cope with that massive change? How does it affect what you do, and what do you need to do to keep with the change? Do we need to keep the change? These are the questions that have to be asked as part of that overall strategic view as we go to 2015 and beyond: "Is my company going to be relevant to my customers?"

It's so important having a different set of eyes looking at what you're doing—a reality check. It's very easy to get caught in the proverbial weeds when you want to be swift at assuming that's all.

With American football, you see the coach is on the sideline with a massive binder, which is a foot thick with all the different types of plays. The quarterback, on the other hand, has a simple flip-up wristband from which he can call plays. At its very simplistic level, one or two slides of a playbook for a different type of partner in your ecosystem is sometimes all that is required. On that slide you may look at the financial implications of that relationship, what solutions you may be working on jointly, but, more important, the relationships. Relationship is really the cornerstone of that playbook. What's the whole point of this relationship? Where is it taking us? Where do we want to go with it?

Companies don't change; people do, and the ability to change is always going to be a competitive advantage; it's really a question of how you influence that change within the company. Inevitably, change happens and you have to be able to display that change.

#126 – Professional Associations – David Labuskes

CTS, RCDD, Executive Director and CEO, InfoComm International
www.infocomm.org - InfoComm International® is the trade association representing the commercial audiovisual industry worldwide.

The Value of Participation in a Professional Association

Professional associations play a crucial part in the business ecosystem; they help build and grow the industry workforce, but they also help to keep it accountable through certification, standards, and best practices.

Members share best practices and new insights about the industry, which get channeled back into the vehicles of individual and business growth. It's a lifecycle that keeps perpetuating itself, thanks to the members' dedication.

Industry professionals are passionate about their work and care deeply about the success of, and quality in, their industry. They foster an exchange of business and technology ideas and find a common voice when it comes to ensuring that their market thrives and that the highest standards are upheld. They bring expertise from various branches of the industry to define regional and global benchmarks so that both profits and nonprofits can successfully apply them to their respective operations.

This cannot be possible without a widespread participation among the members. Just being a "mailbox member" is not enough to maintain such a high level of industry impact.

Taking a class, attending workshops at a conference, learning the best practices, and visiting trade shows all lead to building a stronger professional. And, such development never stops as technologies and business practices continue to evolve. When a business decides to support the association membership of its employees and even make a step further to become an association's sponsor or partner, it begins to make a mark on the industry itself. Therefore, to participate in an association means to invest in yourself and the industry.

InfoComm International is a prime example of an association that has made a global impact on the industry it supports. Over the course of 75 years, it has forged relationships among companies from around the world to create standards, certification, training, and expositions and promote global economy in the various areas of the audiovisual industry. Even associations connect to other associations -- InfoComm has reached out to other related associations to make the globe even flatter when it comes to providing education, facilitating networking opportunities, and defining quality standards.

As globalization has pushed many industries around the world to use data analytics to figure out how to compete, nearly every company is, in some way, in the technology business. Associations, however, allow an exchange of ideas about the latest innovations, services, and integrations so businesses can learn directly from others and be inspired to create something new and improved in this era of true convergence across borders and industries.

The key value proposition of playing an active part in an association is the meaningful relationships with the peers and experts in the industry, which build knowledge, define checks and balances, and drive innovation. Nourishing such relationships should be supported and viewed as an asset.

#127 – Your Virtual Team – Martijn van Tilburg
CEO, 10,000ft
www.10000ft.com

Expanding Your Virtual Team through Common Measures
The increasingly mobile and distributed workforce is pressuring traditional organizational structures to evolve and forcing businesses to rethink the way they view their employees. The impact of this evolution is especially prevalent for teams that work on creative or ambiguous projects. With no clear path or obvious solution, organizations must create a culture that empowers the creative worker, one that enables each person to bring individual expertise to solve a unique problem.

People find meaning when they feel their efforts are contributing to something greater than themselves, and when they are a part of a greater whole that shares a common value system, culture, and goals.

Successful distributed organizations will try to build a culture that focuses on shared responsibility, openness, and autonomy. More than anyone else, creative thinkers (those developing original work) need autonomy. Failure to provide them with that undermines their motivation, sense of purpose and mastery. Creative thinkers are confident in their abilities and role in the organization, and demand more say in what type of project they are working on. Technology enables them to work on their terms—from where and when they want. The result is a tendency towards less hierarchical organizations and teams, in which management responsibilities are distributed across the team members.

Although the projects themselves are ambiguous, the financials and resourcing do not have to be. Real-time insight into how much of the project budget has been used and whether the right resources have been allocated is essential when organizing creative thinkers. Time tracking and resource planning software can offer this insight. But this information is not only reserved for management. In order to support autonomy, all team members are given access so everyone understands what impact this work has on the overall project (including budget).

#128 – Predictive Metrics – Gartner

Gartner Press Release, January 16, 2014
http://www.gartner.com/newsroom/id/2650815

Gartner Says Organizations Using Predictive Business Performance Metrics Will Increase Their Profitability 20 Percent by 2017

Organizations that use predictive business performance metrics will increase their profitability by 20 percent by 2017, according to Gartner, Inc. Gartner said organizations should use predictive metrics to alert workers that a business moment (a transient opportunity exploited dynamically that requires unprecedented business velocity and agility) is about to occur and guide them on the best next action to take in the context of a particular customer's expectations.

As we are entering the digital world, businesses will need to digitalize business processes, invent new digital business models, and compete at the speed of business moments. Senior IT managers and business process directors will increasingly be called on to manage an unprecedented degree and pace of business change, and to seize transient business moments by discovering what customers value and by personalizing processes to deliver that value—all in the same instant.

"Using historical measures to gauge business and process performance is a thing of the past," said Samantha Searle, research analyst at Gartner. "To prevail in challenging market conditions, businesses need predictive metrics, also known as "leading indicators," rather than just historical metrics (a.k.a. 'lagging indicators')." Predictive risk metrics are particularly important for mitigating and even preventing the impact of disruptive events on profitability.

Only 31 Percent of Business and IT Leaders Have Metrics that Contribute to Strategic KPIs

A recent Gartner survey, conducted among 498 business and IT leaders in the fourth quarter of 2013, showed that 71 percent of business and IT leaders understood which KPIs are critical to supporting the business strategy. But only 48 percent said they can access metrics that help them understand how their work contributes to strategic KPIs, and 31 percent agreed they had a dashboard to provide visibility of these metrics. "However, visible metrics won't help drive strategic business outcomes, such as increasing profitability, if business and IT leaders don't have the right metrics in place," said Ms. Searle.

Conversations Gartner analysts had with business and IT leaders revealed that they often misinterpret the term "KPI" (which is a measure that should indicate what you need to do to significantly improve performance, and is therefore predictive) and don't actually have predictive measures in place. "They persist in using historical measures and consequently miss the opportunity to either capture a business moment that would increase profit or intervene to prevent an unforeseen event, resulting in a decrease in profit," added Ms. Searle.

Businesses that struggle to cope with today's accelerated business cycles, which require business and IT leaders to track work in progress, are seeing an increasingly vital need to make optimization adjustments in real time, and increase organizational responsiveness to market dynamics and evolving event patterns.

Today, organizations are adopting intelligent business process management suites (iBPMSs) and operational intelligence platforms to dramatically increase their successful and proactive response to unexpected business disruptions. Such technologies leverage **predictive analytics** and provide information that makes it easier to identify relevant predictive metrics. Gartner estimates that the BPMS market will reach $2.8 billion in 2014, an 8.8 percent growth from 2013.

"Business process directors who don't apply predictive metrics to cross-boundary business processes will leave their organizations vulnerable to the risk of failing to execute their business strategies," said Ms. Searle. This is because they are unable to anticipate how well critical processes are driving strategic business outcomes, and therefore are unable to make well-informed decisions and intervene when process performance has plummeted below acceptable levels. "Business process directors should identify the business processes that are critical to driving strategic business outcomes and strategy execution and determine how best to measure business outcomes in a way that triggers human or automated actions before an undesired outcome occurs. This ability will be crucial in determining the organizations who survive the shift towards a digital world and those who will be left behind," said Ms. Searle.

#129 – Keeping your Strategic Alliances – Terry Wyman
CEO Northwest Strategic Ventures
www.NWSVI.com

Keeping your Strategic Alliances

The emergence of strategic alliances as alternatives to going it alone is apparent everywhere; equally apparent is the failure of most to make these alliances work. In fact, an ongoing strategic alliance requires *both partners maintain control and be unafraid to risk* or they will fail. There are three factors to blame for this failure:

1. Lack of frequent reporting
2. Limited financial visibility
3. Inadequate metrics & trending

As an example, an alliance partner provides critical components to a commercial airplane manufacturer on a just in time basis. In support of the alliance, the partner provides the manufacturer with its YTD financial report without a balance sheet every six months, and predictive trends for the prior six months, their predictive trends for revenues, expenses, cash flow, or A/R. The financials are provided in a form that requires time-consuming interpretation, and doesn't allow the manufacturer enough information to identify or manage issues.

An effective ongoing strategic alliance is only possible when provided current data in the most communicative form in a consistent manner. Graphs, colors, and predictive trend modeling gives you a new and exciting way to separate yourself from the competition and manage today's strategic alliance community. Great alliances must be supported by great information that can warn you and guide you safely through a lot more in today's global marketplace.

#130 – CEO Leadership – Jeff Rogers
CEO, One Accord Partners
www.linkedin.com/in/jeffoneaccord

CEO Evolution Beyond "Answer Dispensary"

A secret to building a management team that is capable of growing a business is to create ownership in problem solving and decision-making throughout the organization to the maximum extent possible. When the CEO or senior executives hold on to decision-making, they stunt the growth of their teams.

CEOs often see their role as being the leader, decision maker, and problem solver for their organization. This works when an organization is small, but soon becomes a limiting factor as it grows. As an organization expands, the CEO needs to shift his or her role to provide vision, set priorities, and facilitate the management process. This transition can be difficult, especially when the CEO may have the answers. Yet, by jumping to the answers, the CEO deprives the management team of going through the learning process. Even worse, the CEO ends up being the "owner" of the imposed solutions, which can lead to lukewarm commitment from the rest of the team.

When the CEO stops short of dispensing answers and, instead, creates alignment and agreement on direction and priorities, a completely different dynamic occurs. When members of the management team are given ownership of problems and issues along with the responsibility for finding solutions, a much different level of commitment follows. As individual managers come up with solutions and have the authority for implementing them, the outcome is much more likely to be positive. Even when the manager's solution is not the best, the outcome is often more effective because there's broader ownership in the decision.

Most CEOs in a growing organization will learn this, one way or another. Often, the lesson is learned the hard way. The big lesson: it isn't who gets credit for coming up with an idea, but rather, who feels a sense of ownership for the solution and outcome. Creating ownership in the organization builds team strength and business scalability.

As decisions are made by the team, those decisions can be formalized and put into process. This is the first step in accountability. Once the decisions have been made and responsibilities defined, there needs to be a tracking and follow-up process. When plans are agreed to but not followed, it becomes time for leadership to hold people accountable. This is the hard part. But, again, if the CEO is giving the team members the latitude to make decisions, it's a much simpler process to work on corrective actions. Accountability becomes much easier to embrace.

Measurements and status tracking are also important to verifying that planned results are actually achieved. Organizations will spin their wheels and not achieve their potential without a clear performance measurement process in place. In organizations where the CEO is not comfortable with playing the role of the facilitator-leader, an option is to bring in an expert to help build and possibly run the needed processes, allowing the CEO to focus on his/her strengths as a leader.

#131 – Beyond CPA – Stacy Kildal
Stacy Kildal, Advanced Certified QuickBooks ProAdvisor
www.stacyk.net

Beyond CPA

The QuickBooks ProAdvisor Program changed my life. That's not an exaggeration. I would be in a different place if I hadn't borrowed the money from my mother to take the critical certification exams.

Now, I leverage technology to help small business work better, faster, smarter, and was named as CPA Practice Advisor's "2013 Accounting's 40 Under 40"and CPA Practice Advisor's "2012 & 2013 Most Powerful Women in Accounting."

There are many different certifications out there that accounting professionals can obtain, whether one is a CPA, or a bookkeeper, like myself. Setting yourself apart and becoming certified lets potential clients know we've gone through training specific to the tools they use to run their business. Certified QuickBooks ProAdvisors are able to provide top level services to clients because we are always up to date on the current software. We also have a large variety of training outside the product: practice management, best practices when working with clients, and even helping accounting professionals to stay ahead of the curve with new technology.

The findaproadvisor.com website is a directory of those who have gone that extra mile.

#132 – Understanding Financial Data – Jeff Levy
Author, *Making the Jump into Small Business Ownership*, 2013 – David Nilssen & Jeff Levy
www.makingthejumpbook.com

Understanding Financial Data
Learning to read and interpret financial data is imperative to understanding a small business—but not just reciting the sums at the bottom of a balance sheet or presuming that the net profit or loss amount at the bottom of a balance sheet is an accurate reflection of the "bottom line." This means fully understanding what these elements actually mean, what they are based on, and what they predict about the future.

If you bring in a professional to manage your accounting, you have to be able to understand if they are doing a good job for you. When you choose an advisor or business coach, choose one who comes with strong references and evidence of objective performance.

#133 – Small Business in China – Yan Ren
Consultant, Sila Solutions Group, Data Management (Certified Data Management Professional)
www.linkedin.com/pub/yan-ren/15/236/995/

Global Perspective on Business Essentials: China
I was born and raised in Taiyuan, the capital of Shanxi province, a second-tier city in China. My parents owned several small businesses at different

times in the past 30 years. At the peak time, one business used to have 20 to 30 employees, and at the downtime, they themselves were the only ones in the company. Their businesses had ups and downs mainly influenced by the industry situations, China's special regulatory conditions, and their own management styles.

As markets mature and standardize in China, more and more small business owners realize the benefits of using information and technology to gain competitive advantage. This situation is especially true in the first-tier cities, such as Beijing and Shanghai. However, with over a 1.3 billion population, it is very hard to make regions develop evenly in China. Small businesses in the second and third-tier cities are still on a different pace in comparison to large cities. But given the speed of change, small business owners are being awakened by the urgency and necessity for information technology.

Section in Chinese

随着经济全球化进程的加快，中国逐步推进与全球会计准则的靠拢。2006 年出台的企业会计准则与国际财务报告准则的一致性已经达到 90-95%。同时，为了规范小企业会计确认、计量和报告行为，财务部于 2013 开始实行《小企业会计准则》，明确了对小企业的会计科目、主要账务处理和财务报表的规范。

虽然会计准则得以广泛实施，还有很多小微企业仍在沿袭传统非规范化的记账方法。而且从历史来看，企业对会计的应用主要在于税收，而非对企业的管理与控制。即使在今天，很多小企业仍视报税为会计的主要目的与手段，很少去解读与应用财务信息，对财务的管理更多是在日常运营管理中实现的。总体来看，中国的小企业仍然缺乏对会计准则的深刻理解与应用。

量变引起质变，当标准的实施达到一定的广度，随之而来的便是深度上地变革。中国在很多发展问题上，最先看到成效的往往是一线城市等发达地区。在北京、上海、广州等资源聚集的地方，即便在小企业间也已经很少看到手工记账，大多有效应用了会计软件，会计软件最明显的好处便是强制了对会计准则的实施，同时也有越来越多的企业主将会计信息作为衡量财务状况的工具，而不仅仅用于报税。引起这些科技信息广泛应用的原因有很多，其中包括同行业间的压力，进入国际市场的需求，和从基于数据决策中获取的竞争优势。

随着企业更有效地利用技术与标准化的财务管理，基于预测分析的新工具也会随之得到推广，更将会为那些善于利用这些新工具的企业带来新的突破。预测分析工具与财务仪表板将财务软件中已有的财务数据进行挖掘，得出有价值的信息并有效展现，帮助小企业掌握财务走向和预测未来的趋势。和很多突破一样，这些技术的应用往往从小开始，并且很多人会认为与我无关，随后在不久的将来人们便开始猜疑，在没有会计技术，信息系统和不可或缺的分析工具的时代，大家都是怎么度过的。

Translation:

With the acceleration of economic globalization, China is promoting compliance to global accounting standards. The Accounting Standards for Enterprises revised in 2006 brought Chinese accounting standards into 90 to 95 percent alignment with the International Financial Reporting Standards (IFRS). In order to regulate small business accounting recognition, measurement, and reporting, in 2013 China customized and implemented small business accounting standards with account titles, processes, and financial statements specified.

Even with extensive adoption of accounting standards, for some small and micro businesses, they still continue to use methods that have been handed down from previous generations. Moreover, historically the usage of accounting for Chinese companies is much more for tax purpose than for management control. For many small businesses, tax is still the main reason of maintaining accounting, and financial management is more informal and blended into day-to-day operations management. Overall there is the lack of deep understanding and utilization of accounting standards in Chinese small businesses.

However, as the breath of the adoption of standards builds, the depth of the adoption starts to become more apparent. As with many new developments in China, it is the first-tier cities that show the depth first. In cities like Beijing, Shanghai, and Guangzhou where resources gather, the majority of small businesses have already implemented accounting software, enforcing the compliance to national accounting standards. Business owners more and more use accounting information as a tool to measure the financial health of their companies, in addition to the tax purpose. The pressure to keep up with peers, the requirement of participating in the global market, and benefits of gaining knowledge from information to support decision-making are the key drivers behind the rapidly increasing utilization of technology and information.

As businesses learn to take advantage of technology and more structured financial management process, new tools based on **predictive analytics** will catch on and be a breakthrough for those who put it to use. **Predictive analytics** and financial dashboards can directly process and analyze the existing accounting data, and present the valuable information in a way that small businesses can easily understand their financial trends and their probable future performance. Like all breakthroughs, this will start small, and many people will think it is not relevant. Then in the near future everyone will wonder how they ever got by without accounting technology, business information systems, and indispensable analytical tools!

#134 – Small Business in India – Anikate Singh

Student, University of Washington, Data Analytics
https://www.linkedin.com/in/aniksing

Global Perspective on Business Essentials: India

I was born and raised in Durgapur, India, a primarily industrial city with steel production as the major economic driver. I was fortunate enough to receive my education from a convent school where the medium of instruction was English. Much of my success at work and in school can be owed to the communication skills I developed during my early education.

Small businesses in India are typically conservative in their adoption of new ideas and their intentions to diversify or expand. Most of them choose to focus on a very narrow demand definition or a customer segment, sometimes even a small region. This is primarily because small businesses are typically managed by families and there is not much infusion of knowledge from outside. As such, they aim to protect what they have rather than grow to build a more formidable presence. Small businesses are under threat from multi-national organizations as India continues to adopt a liberalized and open economy with foreign direct investments in new areas. These large organizations have the benefit of economies of scale as well as marketing budgets that no small business can compete against. The small businesses know their customers' preferences and have existing loyalties. They can compete against larger forces only if they leverage technology to organize the information they have about their customers as well as run a more tight operation fiscally. As the competition heats up, adoption of information technology by small businesses is necessary to retain their customer base from cannibalization.

Section in Hindi

भारत में 28 राज्य हैं,जहाँ अलग अलग भाषायें बोली जाती हैं. यह इस लिए महत्वपूर्ण हैं क्यों की हर राज्य की सीमा वहाँ के रहने वालों लोगों की समानता पर खींची गयी हैं. यहाँ के रहने वालें लोग अपनी भाषा, परम्परा और कौशल एक दूसरे से बाँटते हैं. जैसे गुजरात के निवासी व्यापार की दुनिया में अपने कौशल के लिए प्रसिद्ध हैं, जब की पंजाब के लोग कृषि व्यापार में सबसे आगे हैं. इस ऐतिहासिक रुख को देख कर हम इस निष्कर्ष पर पहुँच सकते हैं कि व्यापार कि दुनिया में कुछ समुदाय के लोग बहुमत में हैं. वह समुदाय अपने हर पीढ़ी को व्यापारिक कौशल विरासत में देते हैं ताकि सामुदायिक ग्यान सुरक्षित रह सके.

सामुदायिक ग्यान पर भरोसा करना काफ़ी लाभदायक हो सकता हैं, परंतु इस आधुनिक युग में सिर्फ़ उस पर निर्भर करना गलत हैं. जब तक बाहर की दुनिया से नये लोग, नई विचार धारायें और ग्यान नही अपनाए जाएँगे, तब तक यह व्यापारी अपने व्यापार को विकसित नही कर पाएँगे. आज कुछ ऐसे व्यापारी हैं जो अपने बच्चों को प्रशिक्षण प्रदान कर रहें हैं ताकि वह बड़े हो कर व्यापार को नई दिशा दे सकें. ऐसे प्रगतिशील व्यापारी नये प्रौद्योगिकी को अपनाने में भी आगे रहते हैं.

हाल ही में किए एक अध्ययन में 100 छोटे व्यापारियों से उनके व्यापार के संचालन पर कुछ सवाल पूछे गये. पता चला की सभी व्यापारी लेखांकन सॉफ्टवेर का प्रयोग कर रहें हैं. 25 प्रतिशत एक्स्सेल (Excel) का प्रयोग कर रहें हैं, 23 प्रतिशत टॅली (Tally) का प्रयोग कर रहें हैं और शेष दूसरी सॉफ्टवेर का प्रयोग कर रहें हैं. इन आँकड़ों से पता चलता है की भारत के छोटे व्यापारी काफी हद तक लेखांकन सॉफ्टवेर का प्रयोग कर रहें हैं. इन सॉफ्टवेर से उनको कितनी मदद मिल रही है, यह इन आँकड़ों से स्पष्ट नही हैं.

भारतीय सरकार की आर्थिक नीतियों के कारण विदेशी व्यापारी भारत में अपनी बुनियाद बना रहें हैं. इस कारण यहाँ के छोटे व्यापारी काफी दबाव में हैं. इस नई चुनौती का सामना करने के लिए व्यापारियों को नई प्रौद्योगिकी का सहारा लेना पड़ेगा. अब तक छोटे व्यापारी लेखांकन सॉफ्टवेर सिर्फ विवरण के लिए प्रयोग करते आएँ है. अब उन्हे ऐसे सॉफ्टवेर की ज़रूरत होगी जो उन्हे निर्णय लेने में मदद करें. कोरेल्यतिक्स (Corelytics) ऐसी एक सॉफ्टवेर हैं जो व्यापारियों को ऐसी अंतर्दृष्टि दे सकती हैं जिससे वे बेहतर निर्णय ले सकें. अब व्यापारी अंतर्जान के जगह तथ्यों के आधार पर अपने कारोबारीक निर्णय ले सकते हैं.

ऐसे नये प्रौद्योगिकी के अंगीकरण में एक ही बाधा हैं. इनके प्रयोग के दौरान व्यापारियों को अपने वितीय जानकारी दूसरे संगठनों के साथ बाटनी पड़ेगी. ऐसी स्थिति में क़ानूनी अर्चन आ सकतें हैं जो व्यापारियों को इन प्रौद्योगिकी को अपनाने से हतोत्साहित कर सकती हैं. इस के बावजूद कोरेल्यतिक्स (Corelytics) जैसे सॉफ्टवेर की स्वीकृति समय के साथ बढ़ती ही जाएगी क्यों की छोटे व्यपीरियों के उतरजीविता का यह एक मात्र उपाए हैं.

References

Relhan, A. (2013). E-Accounting Practices of SMEs in India. *International Journal of Technical Research(IJTR)* .

Translation:

India is a very diverse nation with 29 states, each of which is mostly defined by the vernacular language spoken by the majority of the people in that state. As such, contrary to some other nations, state boundaries are defined around homogeneous communities. These communities share a common language, tradition, as well as skill sets. For example, the state of Gujarat is famous as a state of entrepreneurs and businessmen, while the state of Punjab is famous for agriculturists and farmers. It's this historical trend that results in most business owners originating from the same or similar communities. These communities hand over their business instinct as well as collective knowledge across generations.

While it can be beneficial to rely on tribal knowledge for decision-making, the absence of infusion of knowledge and new ideas can sometimes restrict growth. Some small business owners, especially those that see themselves expanding, educate their children and groom them to take over their business. Such businesses do tend to adopt newer technologies to optimize their operations. A recent study (Relhan, 2013) sampled 100 small and medium enterprises across India and revealed that all of them used some sort of accounting software. While 25 percent used Excel, 23 percent used Tally while the rest used other enterprise accounting systems. This indicates that there is very impressive penetration of accounting software in small businesses, though it is still not clear how effectively they are used for reporting and decision-making within these organizations.

It is encouraging to see such adoption of structured financial management. This is primarily because small businesses are going to be under increased pressure from new competitors. India continues to liberalize its economy and invite foreign direct investment in most sectors. Economic protectionism for local businesses is on the decrease and multi-nationals are making a beeline to set up shop in India. Subsequently, small businesses must leverage and enhance their adoption of technology to better serve their customers as well as closely monitor their business performance. Any technology that allows them to project their growth and perform analysis will help them make decisions and protect their business. Tools like Corelytics that integrate with many financial accounting systems and allow businesses to perform predictive analysis will be crucial in helping them gain an edge and operate based on data rather than intuition. Though adoption of structured financial management is on the rise, it is mostly used for financial reporting and less for decision-making. Decision-making is still to a large extent based on tribal knowledge and intuition. As awareness about new technologies like Corelytics spreads, businesses will realize the value proposition of **predictive analytics** for decision-making. In the absence of insights, businesses in India depend on their leaders to make decisions based on experience. With tools like Corelytics filling those gaps, businesses can rely on facts to secure their future.

The biggest challenge for the adoption of these technologies will be the legal framework in India. The legal system is still playing catch up when it comes to matters related to information technology. With most technologies operating in the cloud, convincing businesses to host their financial data with third party vendors will be difficult since there are no well-defined laws or precedents that deals with such information sharing. Beyond such legal and regulatory issues, the prospect of new technologies like Corelytics revolutionizing small businesses is promising.

Relhan, A. (2013). E-Accounting Practices of SMEs in India. International Journal of Technical Research (IJTR).

#135 – Execution and Discipline – Manual Palachuk
Head Coach and President, Manuel Palachuk International
http://www.manuelpalachuk.com/

Mastering the Disciplines of Business
Thanks to the information age, there is no lack of input on how to be successful, beat your competitors, grab every share of the market, hire the best staff, and build a better mousetrap. It's pressed into your face as soon as you turn on any electronic device, and it's fed into your email folders as you read this. How many of these "instant success" solutions have you acted on?

What people and companies are in need of is someone to help them master two key disciplines that are so often underdeveloped or missing from the management skill set:

1. **Execution**. To avoid procrastination, there needs to be an important emphasis placed on time. It is very possible that you have the sharpest people on your team capable of delivering, but no time to get their key action items started, let alone completed. They need to know how to identify, create, and leverage small increments of time in your systems that will allow your team to continuously and incrementally improve your processes, procedures, and overall business systems.
2. **Discipline** to hold yourself and your people to a plan, process, or procedure that they agree is the right course. Discipline, especially the discipline to execute on a set strategy, is what sets companies apart from their competition. Those who have the discipline to follow the set plan and execute are the leaders!

Just like hiring a personal trainer, you can get a good business coach who can keep you on track with your business goals, execution, and discipline and see to it that you get to the next level. Coaching is an investment in yourself, your team, and your leadership that represents a dedication to continuous improvement in everything you do.

Whether your emphasis is on execution, time management, or simply your service delivery, make it your goal to build a strong, healthy, result-oriented culture in which everyone in your company can thrive, and one that everyone you do business with will respect. You don't have to go it alone.

#136 – Ecosystems – Doug Hall
CEO Focus Seattle
www.ceofocus.com

A business ecosystem is formed in a marketplace that serves a set of customers. Ecosystem players are the goods and services providers in the marketplace. The transaction currency of ecosystem players includes information, not just money. One can judge the connectedness of the ecosystem players by how much information they share. In any given situation this may be for mutual benefit or individual player benefit, but there must be long-term and sustained benefits to all players or the ecosystem will devolve.

Not to devalue the importance of cash because it is the fuel that powers each player organization, but the cooperation between ecosystem players is better measured by the flow of information. Managing the flow of information as a key performance indicator can help each player stay on track to the desired income generation results. A key strategy among ecosystem players is to formalize and manage the flow of relevant information, which gives rise to creating more structured alliances between ecosystem players.

Examples are seen in the ecosystem formed in the B2B computer and peripheral products market. The product manufacturers create their hardware or software products, which are generally sold through distributors to value-added resellers and then to the end-user. The hardware and software manufacturers sell through the same sales channel partners, but do not bundle their products. They create formal and informal alliances and share product, market, and customer information in the pursuit of individual benefit. The information flow benefits each party and actually improves the whole product being sold through the sales channels to the end user. Many of the software and hardware companies don't earn revenue from one another but the flow of information between them is a real form of currency that they can monetize by winning orders from the sales channel partners.

A key role in an ecosystem is the Aggregator. This is an entity in a hierarchical position that allows the collection and review of business or financial results from affiliated entities. In the previous example, the distributors serve as aggregators because they sell many products from many manufacturers to many resellers. The aggregated information can flow both up and down from the aggregator so the ecosystem players gain a broader view of market/ecosystem factors. The aggregator has power to the extent that the other players desire and benefit from the aggregated information. Industry associations can sometimes position as an aggregator; however, their financial benefit is usually limited to continued membership fees through member retention.

RECOMMENDED RESOURCES:

Siegel, Eric and Davenport, Thomas H. 2013. *Predictive Analytics: The Power to Predict Who Will Click, Buy, Lie, or Die.* Wiley Publishing.

Johnson, Spencer and Blanchard, Kenneth. *Who Moved My Cheese? An Amazing Way to Deal with Change in Your Work and in Your Life.* 1998. G. P. Putnam's Sons.

Gerber, Michael E. *The E-Myth: Why Most Small Businesses Don't Work and What to Do About It,* 1990. Harper Collins.

Key, Stephen. *97 Percent of All Patents Never Make Any Money.* AllBusiness.com

Viktor Mayer-Schonberger and Kenneth Cukier. *Big Data: A Revolution That Will Transform How We Live, Work, and Think.* 2013. Houghton Mifflin Harcourt.

Eric Ries. *The Lean Startup: How Today's Entrepreneurs Use Continuous Innovation to Create Radically Successful Businesses.* 2011. Crown Business.

Adizes, Ichak. *Managing Corporate Lifecycles (How Organizations Grow, Age & Die),* 1990. The Adizes Institute.

Davenport, Thomas H. and Harris, Jeanne G. *Competing on Analytics: The New Science of Winning.* 2007. Harvard Business Review Press.

Walther, Larry, Ph.D., CPA, CMA, Head of the School of Accountancy at Utah State University. *Principles of Accounting.* 2014. www.principlesofaccounting.com/

ENDNOTES

1. Ritholtz, Barry "Small Business Success/Failure Rates," *The Big Picture* Blog, 2012. http://www.ritholtz.com/blog/2012/01/small-business-successfailure-rates/

2. "Economic Census, 2013," *The U.S. Census Bureau*, www.census.gov/econ/census/?intcmp=sldr3

3. "Small Business GDP: Update 2002-2010", *Small Business Administration*, January 2012. www.sba.gov/sites/default/files/rs390tot_0.pdf

4. "About Economic Indicators," US Department of Commerce Economics and Statistics Administration, 2010. www.esa.doc.gov/about-economic-indicators

5. "Becoming Number One," *The Economist*, 2014. www.economist.com/node/21528987

6. "Predictive Business Performance Metrics to Boost Profitability 20 Percent by 2017," *Gartner Co.* www.gartner.com/document/2624418. 2013.

7. "Corporations," Wikipedia, Last modified July 2, 2014, http://en.wikipedia.org/wiki/Corporation

8. Jim Horan, *The One Page Business Plan for the Busy Executive,* (The One Page Business Plan Company, Apr 2, 2011).

9. "Small Business Failure Rates by Industry: The Real Numbers," *Small Business Trends,* Posted Sept. 24, 2012. http://smallbiztrends.com/2012/09/failure-rates-by-sector-the-real-numbers.html

Why Corelytics?
Use a dashboard for your own PREDICTIVE BUSINESS INTELLIGENCE

Unlike most other dashboards, Corelytics connects to your own accounting system to show trends and forecasts of future performance (no data entry required).

- Monitor trends for early detection and early correction.
- Forecast futures and best/worst case scenarios with 88% accuracy to see where change is needed.
- View multiple lines of business to see which are profitable and which are draining your resources.

The goal is to understand performance drivers so that you can control your results.

Multiple plans to fit your needs. Starting at just $99/month

Dashboard Subscription

Financial Forecast Report

Dashboard
with Professional Advisory Services

Find out more at www.corelytics.com